Additional praise for *Building a Digital Future*

"Full of case study experience providing a really valuable insight which can be turned into a plan and action for Dynamics 365."
—Phil Scully, Group CIO, Costa Coffee

"Up until now I've not seen a book I would recommend to our customers going on the Dynamics 365 digital transformation journey. Let's be clear, implementing ERP is complex, sometimes traumatic, and filled with challenges – save yourself some time and money and increase your chances of success by absorbing this A–Z guide before you set off on your project – I'm sure it'll help."
—Jonathan Rowley (Jonny), Senior Customer Success Manager for Business Applications, Microsoft UK

"If you want to know the reality of digitally transforming the business and the transition to Microsoft Dynamics 365 for Finance and Operations, read this book. You will see the business transformation like a movie with the advantage of seeing all the phases, actor roles, problems, risk, the fun, the boring, and controls that need to be considered, then present it to the project team to analyze, thus allowing for a more efficient digital transformation."
—Carlos Villasana Gutierrez, Sr., D365 Functional Analyst, Superior Energy Services

"This is the book I wish had existed when we started our Dynamic 365 Commerce project. It examines many issues that we have learned while we faced it, but it would have been helpful if we could have identified them earlier and prepared ourselves."
—Eric Johnson, Director, Consumer Engagement Technology, Ste Michelle Wine Estates

"Successful digital transformation based on Microsoft Dynamics 365 business applications platform doesn't just happen – you need to understand the capabilities of the platform and how other leading organizations are adopting it. This book provides exactly this, with interesting case studies and the right focus on how to adopt the platform, ensuring that it would stay 'evergreen' and would continue generating value for your organization many years in the future. The authors succeeded in working out a surprisingly profound book. Definitely a must-read."

—Linas Sneideris, Associate Partner, EY

"The amount of in-depth knowledge and thought leadership from key stakeholders within the Dynamics 365 community is simply astonishing and has created a must-read book which tackles a complex topic in a very comprehensive and unbiased way."

—Tobias Lång, Chief Technology Officer, Engage Group

"The authors of this book expose the fascinating ways to give the readers guidance on how to be successful in D365 implementation in strategic and yet step-by-step ways. They expressed each chapter in holistic, simple words, and easy to understand ways in overcoming the challenges and groundwork for the success. Everyone who has ERP project management experience can relate to this book although there's so much more in these pages. The authors touch upon the most important part of the implementation, which is the digital transformation. This is valuable, a must-read for project teams and leaders who choose Microsoft Dynamics 365 ERP system."

—Sheila Maria Taestensen, Senior Project Manager

"This book will help anyone looking to transition to Microsoft D365 ERP; it covers many of the major elements enriched by insightful real-life examples."

—Martijn Brons, Global ERP Director

"As a digital transformation expert, the lessons learned from these initiatives are constantly evolving. Don't jump into one of these projects without reading this book. Too many projects fail as a result of missing one or more pieces of the necessary multi-faceted success strategy. This digital transformation bible will be your 'go-to' for implementing Dynamics 365."

—Scott Schultz, Director of Business Applications, PwC

"If you want to understand key trends in modern business you must read this book – it was created in a challenging time by awesome authors. I'm 100% sure that you can find something valuable in *Building a Digital Future.* Enjoy reading!"

—Vadim Korepin, Senior Functional Architect, Microsoft

"Successful implementation of Dynamics 365 helps you achieve a big milestone in your digital transformation. This book covers different aspects of Dynamics 365 and leads you toward successful implementation. A must read for all resources engaged with Dynamics 365."

—Satish Panwar, Senior Program Manager, Microsoft

"This book recommends key salient points to consider for go-live with Dynamics 365, best practices post go-live. Managing backlog post go-live and ensuring a controlled change requests with adequate testing in staging is key before deploying to the live environment. Upgrades to new versions of D365 is one of the most important things to keep your system evergreen. The power of this book is absolutely amazing and doesn't let the reader forget about the plan post go-live and about future phases while the team is busy with the current phase."

—Kim Guldager, Product Owner, Bestseller

"Finally, a book that does justice to the change management side of digital transformation for Dynamics 365 with practical and relevant examples, including how to use new technologies for change activities."

—Lydia Broekhuizen, Senior Change Management Consultant, PowerObjects

"What I see here is excellent research on digital transformation with Microsoft Dynamics 365. *Building a Digital Future* has practical solutions to real world problems many business and IT leaders face. It's a book I wish I had written."

—Arvind Sahu, Head of Information Technology, Kari-Out Company

Building a Digital Future

Building a Digital Future

A Transformational Blueprint for Innovating with Microsoft® Dynamics 365

LIPI SARKAR

VINNIE BANSAL

WILEY

Published by John Wiley & Sons, Inc., Hoboken, New Jersey.
Published simultaneously in Canada.

For general information on our other products and services or for technical support,
please contact our Customer Care Department within the United States at (800) 762-
2974, outside the United States at (317) 572-3993 or fax (317) 572-4002.

Wiley also publishes its books in a variety of electronic formats. Some content that
appears in print may not be available in electronic formats. For more information about
Wiley products, visit our web site at www.wiley.com.

Library of Congress Cataloging-in-Publication Data is Available:

ISBN 9781119747116 (Hardcover)
ISBN 9781119747161 (ePDF)
ISBN 9781119747154 (ePub)

Cover Design: Wiley
Cover Image: © VAlex/Shutterstock

SKY10026211_041421

Contents

Foreword

By reading this foreword, and more importantly this great book, you have made a good choice. It proves that you are interested in growing, developing your experience of digital transformation, and want to add value in your transformation journey. Working remotely in this pandemic situation can be challenging when you need to perform a balancing act between work and personal life while staying at home. If the experience of working remotely is seamless yet efficient, the quality of your personal time is expected to be more relaxed.

As a Commercial Channels Leader at Microsoft, I have witnessed the acceleration in digital transformation and seen two years' worth of digital transformation in two months.

I am incredibly happy and honored to write the foreword of this great book—*Building a Digital Future*. In my Channel Partner Keynote presentation, I said that in today's world, we need bold leaders to take bold action for a bold vision. In times of transition, it takes a leader with a bold vision who is willing to step out and push through the nay-sayers, willing to share his or her vision with everyone, and bring them along in that journey. We are in a huge time of transition and technology has reached the stage where it is in everyone's hand.

What I like about this book is you can tell that the authors have an excellent understanding and have experienced the digital transformation journey themselves. This book is not just about technology; it is a practical guide to planning and implementing a digital transformation strategy using Dynamics 365 and Power Platform. The authors have laid out a roadmap highlighting key areas of concern, planning considerations before beginning the transformation journey, leveraging the capabilities from Dynamics 365 and Power

Platform, and identified business support model considerations post implementation of technology.

In this era of change to digital, organizations must transform their own business to adapt and maybe survive. For leaders who are winners, *Building a Digital Future* is a prerequisite to become and stay successful in this digital world. It helps leaders to identify the right strategy that will outline the scope of their business, find ways to assess the importance of a digital transformation culture, and craft an innovative model to leverage their business using Dynamics 365 in digital transformation.

It is increasingly difficult to engage with various industry leaders and experts when the business is coping and busy with the new "normal," but I am glad to see many experiences and customer stories, views, and quotes throughout this book.

I recommend that you read this practical book, full of sharp insight, thought-provoking ideas, no matter where you are in your Dynamics 365 transformation and at whatever stage of your digital maturity.

Gavriella Schuster,
Corporate Vice President, Microsoft

Preface

Life's most persistent and urgent question is, 'what are you doing for others?'

—Martin Luther King Jr.

The sun has enough energy to continue for another 5 billion years. After that, it will swell to a red giant. We know these facts, when we refer to 5 billion years it seems limitless, but it is not. Everything we feel we have in abundance today may not last forever. Energy resources are either renewable or non-renewable. Mankind was always concerned about the future of humanity and there are various threats to life on the planet, such as global warming, nuclear war, and now the COVID-19 pandemic.

From the days of gazing into the sky, learning about our universe and life-form on Earth, we always wondered how we could contribute to mankind such that someone somewhere would benefit from that contribution, irrespective of how insignificant it may seem. With that desire and dream in mind, we as authors of *Building a Digital Future* felt it is timely to share our digital transformation experiences, combining them with the experiences from various industry experts and senior business stakeholders. We have lived many end-to-end digital transformation journeys across various sectors and have been involved in pre-sales, RFP, and sales processes.

Digital Transformation is not a buzzword and it is not just about technology. When digital transformation is planned carefully considering all factors, it delivers quick-win, competitive advantage to a business. It also helps acceptance across stakeholders, makes collaboration effective and efficient, and the pace of transformation can be accelerated by leveraging the right governance framework and the right technology.

Building a Digital Future provides frameworks and models across all chapters, offers guidance, and leads you to think in the right strategic direction. The frameworks, approaches, and models are applicable for all sectors and flexible to expand for your own organization, enabling you to make your own choice.

During these unprecedented times when businesses are not performing as forecasted a year back, this book helps the reader to identify the key measures that a business needs to consider. Leading a digital transformation by having the right technology of Microsoft Dynamics 365 and Power Platform can make transformation fast-paced, cost-effective, and efficient, with inbuilt industry-led processes and hence takes a lot of challenges out of the way. This book also addresses various roles and responsibilities that are deemed necessary for a digital transformation. While a number of jobs have been furloughed in this phase of the pandemic, the book cites examples of how the Microsoft Dynamics platform helps in empowering employees by providing a choice of self-learning low-code platform, diverting their skillsets, and delivering value to business. The book includes key capabilities of Dynamics 365 on a high level, notes design choices that one needs to consider, makes the reader aware of the Dynamics Roadmap, and releases reference links and Dynamics community and user group links. While this book is not written with the intention to master Dynamics 365 as a product, it is designed to help the reader understand the capabilities that Dynamics 365 can unlock.

The global digital transformation needs to address challenges globally and locally, but some challenges are unforeseen. From our own experience of global digital transformation, the risks specific to organizations, team culture, planning, and change management are highlighted to prepare the readers for any unknown challenges.

Who Will Find This Book Useful and Why?

A primary target for this book is the business executive population, namely C-suite stakeholders, senior management, program directors or managers, implementation consultants, and business managers. In other words, whoever is considering digital transformation to improve and increase efficiencies, optimization, sales revenue across the business of finance and operation, supply chain, retail and customer relationship management—sales, marketing, or services. The book recommends framework, a capability model across the business, powerful tools to automate time-consuming tasks, and approaches to drive innovation and improvements through an evergreen system post implementation. The concepts of digital transformation are laid out and take you through a step-by-step transformation journey, highlighting many of the pitfalls that you may need to be aware of. This book covers digital transformation with the powerful technology platform Microsoft Dynamics 365 and Power Platform.

The aspiration, though, is to reach much further than the current population of business executives. This book is meant to be useful and relevant for business school or management students who are thinking to start their career paths in digital transformation and are not certain where to start from or do not have any preference of the technology roadmap. It is hoped that this book will help to build an understanding about the concept of digital transformation, planning, and change to consider from an organization perspective, working with an implementation partner, the capabilities of Microsoft Dynamics 365, and, finally, driving the innovation and continuous improvements through a workable support model and ongoing improvement framework.

Scope and Structure of the Book

The book is organized into three parts.

Part I, Digital Transformation with Microsoft Dynamics 365, explores the business case for change, identifying capabilities of the organization and why Dynamics 365 is the right solution to transform your business and how Power Platform can empower your employees and deliver business efficiencies.

Part II, Blueprint for Executing a Successful Dynamics 365 Project, expands on the three core areas of leading a successful transformation program with readiness and a planning roadmap, including change management depending on the maturity of the organization and the fundamentals of governance principles that need to be established from the beginning.

Part III, Driving Innovation and Continuous Improvements with Dynamic 365, sets a clear roadmap by engaging the stakeholders at the right time, clarifying various roles and responsibilities of teams across the program, defining the support model and process that is deemed necessary post go-live, and finally how to keep the continuous improvements evolving by measuring user adoption and letting the product and services be evergreen without any shelf life.

Appendices include high-level information of a few tools and key information about Lifecycle Services and Azure DevOps that are key enablers to make your Dynamics 365 program a success. It also includes a section on Microsoft FastTrack for Dynamics 365 and how you can accelerate your implementation program.

Each chapter includes quotes from industry leaders and experts across the globe, including the world's most admired companies with their experiences making the read more interesting and relatable. Each section includes real-life customer stories across various sectors from different countries discussing business challenges, experience of the implementation and key decisions taken, and finally with an outcome on the benefits it has delivered.

Figure 1 is a high-level overview of each part and their respective chapters. It is also presented as an indicative timeline of leading an end-to-end digital transformation program. You can read this book in a linear fashion by reading one chapter after another and you may also deep-dive into one section that you may need in order to understand the concept in more detail if you are already familiar with one section.

We would like to stay engaged with our readers and you can reach out to us for sharing your customer story or if you need to discuss any area of the book in more detail. Here is the book website link: http://buildingadigitalfuture.com/.

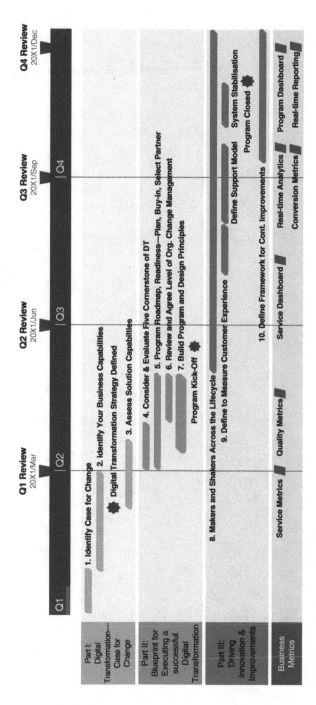

FIGURE 1 Digital Transformation Timeline

Acknowledgments

Watching an award-winning movie in a cinema hall or the luxury of watching from home in recent times, in the end the audience is left with a lasting impression by the actors. Usually, the actors and directors are awarded but there is much more to it than meets the eye. There is a huge team of people that supports and contributes to making a movie award-winning and a success. Until we wrote this book, we didn't realize the amount of effort that goes into the making of a book. We are profoundly grateful for our incredibly supportive, respected, and diligent advisory team who made this dream possible. This book is theirs as much as ours.

The initial drafts of the book have passed multiple hands and undergone several revisions. Each revision provided us with invaluable feedback from the following collaborators. They have been relentless in their contributions, which enabled us to include additional concepts, refine ideas, increase our focus, add clarity, and continuously evolve.

We owe immense gratitude to all our reviewers, who are industry experts and leaders in their own profession and gave their time by providing great inputs, offering insights, and challenging the draft chapters constructively by providing valuable suggestions throughout the production of the book. Without their support our work would not have evolved into the book that you are reading now.

Several Dynamics 365 and Power Platform customers have been kind enough to allow us to mention their work in case studies, and we are grateful for their contribution in sharing their journey.

We are forever indebted to all of them.

Collaborators: Antti Pajunen, Microsoft Business Applications MVP, Power Platform Advisor; Ajay Singh, Senior Executive at DXC

Technology; Ashish Rana, Microsoft MVP, Dynamics 365/CRM Solution Architect & Consultant, Power Platform; Arvind Sahu, Global CIO, Digital Transformation Leader; Ashu Bhatia, Sr. VP - Digital Strategy & Transformation; Carlos R Villasana Gutierrez, Sr. ERP Functional Lead(D365FO) T&L, Manufacture; Carsten Olholm, Head of global IT; Craig Fleming, Senior Manager; Ejaz Ahmed, Microsoft Dynamics 365 Finance Consultant; Eric Johnson, Director, Consumer Engagement Technology; Graham Scanlon, Dynamics 365 Technical Architect; Imen Ben Zakour, Microsoft Dynamics 365 Consultant; Jason Earnshaw, Lead Architect (Business Applications); Jason Gumpert, Editor, MSDynamicsWorld.com; Joseph Colvile, Partner Business Analyst, Supply Chain; Jeff Suellentrop, Vice President, Enterprise Architecture, Digital (DTC) and Programs; Jason Abed, Management Consulting Director, Digital Finance and Operations; Kajsa Hofvendahl, Transformation Leader; Kari Amundson, Business Program Manager; Kim Guldager, Product Owner; Laco Vosika, Trusted Advisor, Dynamics 365, Power Platform; Linas Sneideris, Associate Partner; Lisa Hammond-Marsden, Microsoft Dynamics AX/D365 Principal Consultant; Lydia Broekhuizen, Digital Transformation Manager combining change and project management, specialized in Microsoft D365; Marc Lebeau, Digital Transformation Leader; Martijn Brons, Global ERP Director; Matt Shearsby, Principal Consultant; Maggie Charman, Programme Director; Magdalena Schindler Ademovic, Managing Consultant D365 CE & Power Platform; Nitin Malhotra, Senior Director, Head of Enterprise PMO; Pablo Villa Pascual, Lead Architect; Patrick Mouwen, Solution Architect, Microsoft Dynamics 365 for Finance and Operations; Peter Prokopecz, AX Technical Lead; Peter Edén, Head of IT; Phil Scully, CIO; Pedro Rodriguez, Senior Microsoft Dynamics Technical Consultant; Ragupathy Nagarajan, Lead Functional Architect; Rajesh Rajan, Director, Consulting, Dynamics F&O Practice Lead; Ronald Haantjes, Business Development Executive; Rejin Surendran, ERP Head; Scott Schultz, Director of Business Applications; Senthil Arumugam, Lead Consultant; Shobhit Sah, Head Global Digital Program, D365 FinOps; Sukrut Parab, Microsoft Business Applications MVP, Solutions Architect; Tobias Lång, CTO; Umesh Pandit, Lead Consultant; Vaibhav Pednekar, Solutions Architect; Sheila Maria Taestensen, Senior Project Manager; Steve Snowden, Dynamics 365 Finance and Operations Functional Lead; Lax Gopisetty, Vice

President at Infosys; Laurent Deramaix, CEO at Business Elements; and Andy Hafer, Founder Dynamic Communities.

From Microsoft: Aline Pereira, Technology Solutions Professional, Dynamics 365; Alok Singh, Senior Program Manager (Business Application Group R&D); April Olson, Principal Group Program Manager, Dynamics 365 Finance; Ayman Husain, Director, Customer Success, Intelligent Cloud & Digital Transformation; Bob Hogan, Microsoft Business Applications, Specialist; Chris Knowles, Senior FastTrack Solution Architect, Dynamics 365 Apps and Common Data Service R&D; David Reid, Solutions Architect, Business Applications Platform; Fawad Khan, Cloud & Digital Transformation Leader; Fredrik Sætre, Senior Technical Specialist (Business Applications); Giovanni Tafi, Global Solution Architect, Dynamics 365; Giri Fox, Director, Customer Success for Dynamics 365 and Power Apps; Guylene Tarrazi-Prault, Cloud Consumption Lead; Hemant Gaur, Principal Program Manager; J. D. Meier, Director of Innovation, Microsoft Digital Advisory Services; Jason Newbatt, Senior Solutions Specialist; Jonathan Rowley (Jonny), Senior Customer Success Manager, Business Applications; Katarina Arbanas, Global BlackBelt Microsoft Business Applications; Maria Leuch, Business Applications specialist; Mohamed Aamer, Sr. R&D Program Manager, Dynamics 365 Finance and Operations; Murray Fife, Dynamics 365 Principal Technical Specialist; Paul Kerrigan, Delivery Director, Business Applications, Dynamics 365; Paul Langowski, Dynamics 365 for Finance and Operations, Global Fast Track Program Lead; Raphael Tagliani, Technology Solutions Professional; Ramshanker Krishnan, General Manager, EMEA Azure Cloud & AI; Renee Dothard, World-Wide Public Sector Government CTO; Rui Santos, Technical Specialist; Satish Panwar, Senior Program Manager; Suzanne Quinn, Dynamics 365 Readiness Lead; Shaun Riordan, Senior Technology Solutions Professional, Dynamics CRM Field Service; Somnath Nandi, Digital Transformation Leader & Strategist; Swamy Narayana, General Manager, Customer Success, Dynamics 365 Operations Applications; Tommy Skaue, Senior R&D Solution Architect; Vadim Korepin, Senior Functional Architect; Janet Robb, Customer Success Manager Business Applications; Cecilia Flombaum, Sr Director Ecosystem Lead for Microsoft Business Applications; Darren Hubert, Director, Customer Success - Worldwide Business Applications.

Finally, we would like to acknowledge the great team at John Wiley & Sons. Thanks to Sheck Cho, our Executive Editor, for his guidance and advice throughout. We are also indebted to Susan Cerra, Managing Editor, and Samantha Enders, Editorial Assistant, and many others who edited, produced, and marketed our work. We are also indebted to Dean Carlton and Paul McPherson for their hard work in shaping up the format and outline of this book.

About the Contributors

At the time of the writing this book, we are at a very difficult period with the Covid-19 pandemic. This pandemic has accelerated digital transformation and led to a "structural change" with many customers seeing a shift to digital operations as essential to increasing their business resilience and adjusting to new ways of doing business.

It is a significant decision for an organization to invest and embark on a digital transformation journey with Microsoft Dynamics 365 and the Power Platform and realize the benefit over a period. Every journey has its own unique experience to learn from and hence we have reached out to a few people to contribute to this book. We want to thank them all for sharing their expertise and input, which has helped us to shape the book with their interesting experiences.

Maria Kartousova
Technology Consultant and Serial Intrapreneur. Maria specializes in consulting and driving digital transformation while translating complex ideas into practical strategies and generating solutions for complex issues. She has vast experience driving organizations toward their growth and digital maturity and in her career has worked with various organizations in the United Kingdom and Greece.

Sabine Margolis
Experienced collaborator and innovative thinker with 20 plus years in diverse business-to-information technology environments. Sabine is proficient in developing, communicating, and implementing technology roadmaps to meet business strategy needs with strong visual, verbal, and written communication skills across ERP ecosystems, business intelligence, and analytics.

Ritesh Jain

Cofounder at Infynit—Humanizing Credit and Credit Cards. Ritesh is a former COO Digital at HSBC. He is an entrepreneurial technology leader and board advisor with global experience across various sectors including payments and banking, and led digital transformation at global organizations like HSBC, VISA, and Maersk. He led the future of payments at VISA, introduced Apple Pay, and built a wealth management company as a founder CTO. Presently, he is a member of a G20 Initiative for financial inclusion.

Simon Shaw

Business-focused IT and ERP Consultant. Simon has held positions as diverse as a sales and marketing manager for an international imports company and the ERP design authority for a defense organization. He holds qualifications in business management as well as computing and has managed infrastructure and applications IT teams. His main focus is improving the benefits companies get from their digital transformations.

Manali Tiwari

An ardent technical writer, editor, and proofreader, holding credible professional experience in the industry of book editing services. Manali graduated as an engineer with a Bachelor's degree in Information Technology. After gaining three years of experience as a QA professional in the corporate world, she decided to leave her job to pursue technical writing and hone her knowledge of technology.

Pablo Villa

Business Solutions Architect. Pablo works helping companies in their digital transformation journey. He has worked with enterprise customers from different industries, implementing solutions based on Dynamics 365 and Power Platform for the last 14 years. He is highly focused on business objectives, value proposition, quality, strategy, and technology to help customers to sell more, reduce costs, improve efficiency, collect and analyze data, and improve processes.

Digital Transformation with Dynamics 365

Part I explores the organization's need for a digital transformation business case and identifies key drivers of change and why Dynamics 365 is the right solution to transform the business. Real-life customer stories from organizations on their business challenges, solution, and the benefits they have achieved are also provided.

Chapter 1: This chapter defines digital transformations and sets the scene by identifying the key drivers of change for an organization, talks about all phases of digital transformation—the ways to assess the readiness of an organization and create a digital business strategy including emerging business priorities.

Chapter 2: To drive business efficiencies of an organization, a platform like Microsoft Dynamics 365 and Microsoft Power Platform can accelerate digital transformation and manage change effectively with the right measures. The key is to simplify, standardize, and automate the business process that aims to deliver an outcome and realize early benefits.

Chapter 3: This chapter discusses the capabilities of the Microsoft Power Platform that empowers employees to resolve many complex business scenarios with low-code/no-code solutions, creating a data-driven culture with Power BI, which improves customer experience with chatbots, and all of these factors add up for business to make informed decisions.

CHAPTER 1

Digital Transformation and the Case for Change

The advance on technology is based on making it fit in so that you don't really even notice it, so it's part of everyday life.
—Bill Gates, Cofounder at Microsoft

It was a gorgeous sunny day in March 2020. Jack sounded a bit worried in the morning call I had with him. He had a planned series of client workshops to run through requirements for a transformation program that is aiming to automate and centralize sales engagement globally across 15 countries. The overarching outcome of these workshop sessions was to define and design a program that will result in increasing sales, eliminating dependencies on individually maintained Excel and manual notes.

The mode of delivery for these workshops engaging all key client stakeholders from different countries had to be changed suddenly from face-to-face to virtual session. Due to the COVID-19 outbreak, 2020 has driven transformation rapidly up the Board and Executive priority list. Many organizations had started this digital journey but global and national lockdowns and corporate offices moving to a work-from-home mandate have forced businesses to rethink enterprise and customer processes, optimization, and efficiency.

Even a few weeks back, such an important workshop day would normally involve morning travel by taxi and train, arriving at the venue ensuring the logistics were in place before the workshop starts.

Anyway, the meeting started with Jack sharing the objective of the workshop and he addressed the current challenge of a virtual workshop session and the key rules of communications during the session (including timing of breaks, waiting for turns using the icon hands-up, and managing expectation of possible background noise of pets or children). Interestingly, the session went very well with everyone accepting the current challenging situation, focussed on the bigger picture and how to best utilize the time remotely.

After 6 months of working from home during COVID-19, we have accepted the new normal and understand that our calls might have background noise of pets or kids. Life moves on with continuous change and innovation.

In every decade, we witness a big transformation and a shift in our lifestyle and in our businesses, which are enabled by technology that was unthinkable earlier. What is "unthinkable" today is a new normal tomorrow.

"We must dare to think 'unthinkable' thoughts."

—*J.W. Fulbright*

Change, Change, Change

Our book takes the reader step-by-step through digital transformation, key drivers for change, digital maturity of the organization, and how Dynamics 365 can enable digital transformation in the organization.

The Covid-19 global pandemic has highlighted gaps in the so-called digitally transformed businesses and their operating models. Now it is the obligation of businesses to reflect on their enterprise-wide approach to digital transformation. There will be several new definitions coming through for digital transformation after 2020, and these will have different approaches. The goal of this book is to create a deeper understanding of the concept of digital transformation, and the critical elements for consideration, applying them to Microsoft Dynamics 365.

Let us look at what digital transformation means from different businesses.

Kajsa Hofvendahl,
Transformation Leader,
IKEA Group

"A digital transformation is not a project or initiative with a clear start or an end, and it is not about implementing the latest technology. It is about people, bold leadership and how you leverage the data, competence, and the key technology enablers that are unique for the specific company. That is the first thing someone needs to understand when embarking on the transformation journey, or a continuous evolution as I would rather call it, since that's what it really is. Each company has its own journey and what was made a success in one company may not be true for another. Therefore, to secure your success, set a vision and clear objectives but do not plan for the whole journey. Instead, plan for the iteration that is close to you; by doing so you will be less surprised when you are derailing from initial plans and experience road bumps that you most likely didn't predict. Do not strive for perfection; mistakes are part of the evolution and that is how we learn. Therefore, good enough will take you as far as you need to go for now. The most important part, persistence, is a virtue. Transformation takes time and effort so make sure to create a culture where trust, empowerment, and innovation are key so that the business can continue to evolve."

Graeme Hackland,
Group CIO,
Williams Grand Prix
Engineering

"Digital Transformation is a term often followed by 'whatever that means for your organisation' – there are some common objectives in almost all Digital Transformations: modernization, right-sized flexible IT services, and an easily understandable cost model. At my Organisation, enabling Collaboration and Mobility were the other pillars of our Digital Transformation, which has now morphed into our Digital Journey – constantly ensuring we remain at the forefront of digital technology that will give us a competitive advantage."

A path to digital transformation requires a step-by-step approach with a transparent roadmap involving a wide variety of stakeholders, beyond silos and internal/external constraints. This roadmap considers that the ultimate targets will continue to move forward as the digital transition is de facto a continuous process, as well as digital change and creativity.

Digital transformation has already disrupted many industries and is threatening to disrupt others. The stakes are high, but the risks and opportunities are unevenly distributed. Some sectors are more affected than others. However, there are measures that organizations can take to increase their rewards and reduce their risks. This book defines the transformation of digital activities. It describes the path that organizations must take to avoid disruptions, take advantage of the transformation, and take full advantage of digital technologies and business models.

Continuous advancement in technology at a rapid pace and adoption of technology in businesses are often misinterpreted as Digital Transformation. This view overlooks the value of people buy-in, internal or external (employee or customer), and fails to engage vendors and partners.

Digital Transformation: Key Drivers

Today, customers are increasingly time-poor and in our busy day-to-day lives it is all about time efficiency. Customer experience is critical to remain in business and ahead of the competition. A customer expects personalized services and businesses to understand their needs, which can be provided based on a 360-degree view of customer insight through the latest technology.

COVID-19 has forced organizations to adopt technology, rapidly transforming their processes and attracting customers through new channels that do not compromise customer experience. This period has witnessed a huge shift in everyone's work culture. The mindset of senior leadership has had to adapt rapidly, compressing 10 years of change into 10 weeks. Let us look at some quotes from various businesses and their key drivers of digital transformation.

James Staten,
VP Principal Analyst at Forrester Research and previously chief strategist and GM of Microsoft Azure

"You have to be prepared to be disrupted. CIOs can partner with marketing to help reposition IT as a digital transformation engine. You shouldn't be thinking about what applications you can migrate to the cloud. That isn't the path to lower costs and greater flexibility. Instead, you should be thinking about how your company can best leverage cloud platforms to enable new capabilities. Then create those new capabilities as enhancements to your existing applications. You must think differently as you approach cloud development. There's far more power in application design and configuration once you free yourself from assumed reliance on the infrastructure. The result is new degrees of freedom for developers – if you embrace the new model."

Phil Scully,
Group CIO,
Costa Coffee

"It is highly likely that 2020 has pushed Digital Transformation all the way up the company agenda, and is now maybe even critical to business survival. Transformation needs to move beyond a website, mobile app, or technology to all areas and processes of an Enterprise, now delivering against this revised agenda at pace. Understanding these key drivers and setting principles from the outset for any program provides the best chance of transformational success and the step changes in process required. Technology change must move as an enabler in parallel to people and process for Digital Transformation to ultimately achieve a 'digital mindset' cultural change."

All the digital conferences, keynotes, and articles that discuss the digital transformation with the right strategic partners and the critical drivers for the change have one common theme at the heart of their approach, which revolves around the customer. Digital transformation is all about customers, so let's talk about a few key drivers that are interconnected, as suggested by Nigel Fenwick (see Figure 1.1). You need to innovate and transform business models, transform experiences, transform the tech ecosystems, and transform operations.

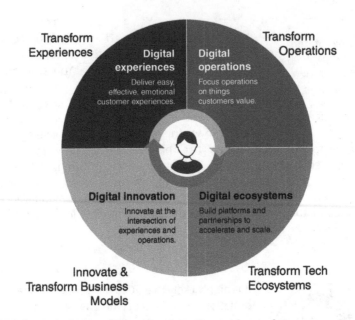

FIGURE 1.1 Digital Transformation into Four Areas of Customer Focus

Source: Used with permission. Nigel Fenwick, VP, Principal Analyst, Forrester (2020) *Accelerate Digital Transformation with the Right Strategic Partner* (forrester.com).

Rising Customer Expectations

Of all customers, 73% pointed out customer experience as an important factor in their purchasing decisions. Yet only 49% of US consumers say companies provide good customer experience today.[1]

A seamless omnichannel experience is critical for customers as ordinary people interact with two to three devices in a day, and the customer loses interest if they don't have a similar experience of customer journey across all channels and devices.

Businesses are serving customers who live in the social age of Uber, Netflix, Apple, and Amazon, which are the epitome of customer experience, and the customer expects a similar experience from other businesses regardless of their sectors (e.g., banking, hospitality, leisure, travel).

This is about looking at the fact that "digital monsters" are transforming the markets around us and using the technological power to raise customer expectations to a new level. It means that digital transformation must be a very high priority and customer centricity should be at the heart for older firms to avoid becoming a "digital victim." In Figure 1.1, this is referenced as transforming digital experiences of the customer and deliver easy, effective, and emotional customer experiences.

Speed Is More Important Than Ever

This is all about timing as speed is the most significant driver in digital transformation. The attention span of a customer is depleted in a few seconds, amidst enormous competition from lean, no baggage start-ups and tech giants alike. It is no longer the case that the big is overcoming the small, but fast is outpacing the slow. Hence, the speed of transformation and organizational agility to adapt to change is paramount. Technology is progressing at a rapid pace and it is not linear. However, businesses still think linearly in many situations, accustomed to being reactive to threat and opportunity. However, the environment has changed its order of magnitude. The biggest challenge for many old brands is to get into the future as quickly as digital disruptors have already marked, and failing to do so will leave them out of competition and ultimately out of business; for example, Thomas Cook collapsed after 178 years in business.

Customer Insight Continues to Be Essential

There is more competition than ever before and the ability to respond quickly to consumer demands starts with a strong emphasis on customer data. Due to advancement in technology, analytics, and machine learning, businesses have access to a significant amount of data, but having data does not mean companies will have an insight! Understanding customer behaviors, their pattern and perception, becomes key to provide an exceptional personalized customer experience. To do so, businesses need to cultivate consumer insight, and gather insights through more profound research, and leverage it to gain a unique advantage over their competition.

AI Is Front and Center

AI is in the front and center of businesses, and using customer insights is the key to the success of companies and the way forward for digital transformation. AI is becoming the fastest emerging priority, inspired by the increasing popularity of "conversational" interfaces like Siri and Alexa. AI strategy is a must for businesses to survive; interpretation of AI was limited to science fiction but now it is at the center of business strategy.

AI Systems consist of five key components.

1. **Detection.** Components receive inputs such as text, voice, image, video, or data triggers from systems.
2. **Understanding.** Components that recognize what the data means (e.g., converting the speech to text and even the underlying semantic meaning).
3. **Analysis.** Components use algorithms (rules) and data sets to get an informative answer or act.
4. **Orientation.** If required, the system checks with people for the certainty of the correct answer.
5. **Action.** Action could be an answer to the user or taking an automatic reaction, sending a message, paying an invoice, or even firing a rocket. To make an action meaningful, the underlying data is important.

Businesses expect the users to interact through websites and apps. However, this behavior is changing now and it will further change significantly in future. User interfaces are becoming AI interfaces where inputs and outputs are in a natural language and systems are making predictive/proactive decisions on behalf of the users, where tolerance of errors is low. For example, in conversational banking, users are even getting used to conversational interfaces to manage their money.

Ramshanker Krishnan, General Manager, EMEA Azure Cloud and AI, Microsoft Consulting Services, Microsoft

"Transformation is about creating a customer-centric culture, an agile technology platform and a data-driven business. The issue most organizations will be facing, with a black swan event like the COVID-19 pandemic, is a loss of signals or need for new ones to be captured. Digitally mature organizations will have a clear advantage, as recalibrating their existing systems to the new signals will be a lot faster than creating an entire system to capture and process signals. Data will continue to be at the center of Digital Transformation and leveraging the innovations around ERP and CRM can help speed up the transformation journey."

Digital Transformation Facts

To better understand the impact of digital transformation on business, here are some key statistics:

- 27% of executives now see digital transformation as a matter of survival.[2]
- A third of the leading marketing leaders in emerging markets believe that their company will become known as a digital company in five years.
- Digital-first companies are 64% more likely to achieve their business goals than their peers.[3]
- 51% of executives believe it is important to implement digital transformation in the next 12 months.
- 71% of digitally mature companies say they can attract new talent based on their use of data, compared to 10% of early-stage digital companies.[4]
- 89% of all companies have already adopted a digital-first business strategy or plan to do so.[5]
- The top industries for digital-first business and strategies are services (95%), financial services (93%), and healthcare (92%).[6]

Nearly half of all companies say improving customer experience and customer satisfaction were the leading influences to start a digital transformation.[7]

Only 5% of companies are doing all it takes to get to payback from digital. To thrive, not just survive, they will need to navigate the maze of economic uncertainty and the breakneck pace of digital.

Digital Transformation: Disrupt or Be Disrupted

In most cases, companies use digital technology to counter the disruption of their businesses by competitors, existing or start-up, or use the same digital technology for the purpose to disrupt or create markets they are not operating in. Through the development of new business models, while utilizing digital technology, they gain a bigger market share, reduce costs, simplify the way of doing business, and most of all improve customer satisfaction and engagement. This sounds simple, and it is something every business owner is striving for.

Digital transformation, however, according to Harvard Business School Professor Clayton Christensen,[8] is "widely misunderstood" and commonly applied to businesses that are not "genuinely disruptive."

Just look at the Fortune 500 list, where at least half of the companies have been replaced by new digital business model organizations since 2000. This does not mean they folded up shop. It just shows that they were bypassed by those organizations that were able to adapt and/or create a completely new business model in addition to their existing core business.

We are in the fourth industrial revolution, and it is not limited to just industries. It is a service revolution across all the sectors, and it is evident with plenty of casualties in the business world, filing of bankruptcies by iconic brands like BHS, Poundworld, Toys R Us, Thomas Cook, Roberto Cavalli, and the list is endless.

There is a growing list of start-ups with unicorn status (start-ups valued at over a billion dollars or more), and these businesses build by disrupting traditional businesses through technology (e.g., WeWork, Airbnb, WeChat). As referred to in Figure 1.1, businesses need to innovate and transform business models and also transform the technology ecosystems.

Phases of Digital Transformation

It is clear that businesses should either disrupt or be disrupted, and there is no single solution that fits all for the successful digital transformation; the best results are achieved through a gradual strategic and holistic progression across the business. In order to disrupt or avoid being disrupted, it is essential to understand three maturity model and stages of digital transformation (Figure 1.2):

Stage 1: Digital Assets/Optimize existing IT. Move the existing infrastructure to the cloud and experiment with new non-core applications in the cloud to save IT operating costs.

Stage 2: Digital Experience—Optimize the current business model. Move your core business data and processes into a cloud-based business application to achieve operational excellence.

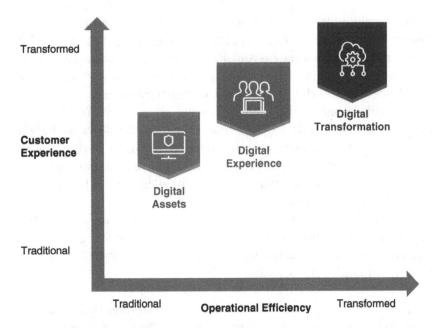

FIGURE 1.2 Three Stages of Digital Journey

Source: Kevin Saunders, Three phases of Digital Journey, www.strategymeetsaction.com/digital-insurer/

Stage 3: Digital Transformation—Create new business models. Use the knowledge of your cloud-based infrastructure, processes, and data to create new offers and sales models.

Are You Digitally Ready?

Digital technology connects people and machines to provide an experience that no one envisaged a decade back, like watching a movie at home, buying a car online, banking services without visiting a bank, to name a few. This is all possible due to advancement in technology and quest to provide a better customer experience by businesses—by continuously finding the right solution and investing in technology, which is a continuous journey!

The COVID-19 pandemic has challenged the human race and businesses like never before; there is competition for survival, whether it is for people or businesses, as the pandemic has tested companies in 2020 for their existence irrespective of their size and sector.

Countries went into lockdown for the first time in modern history. All non-essential businesses were shut. This has put IT/Digital in the spotlight like never before. Some businesses could not operate due to lockdown, for example, airlines, travel, and hospitality, while others thrived, like Amazon and PayPal. However, other retail companies without digital DNA found it challenging to survive as they could not function due to their lack of digital presence.

Primark is one of the biggest upscale apparel chains in Europe, but during the COVID-19 pandemic it was in the news and social media for its $650 million monthly revenue down to $0 due to lockdowns across the world. As Primark did not have an online store, the impact has been harder than for other retailers and it had to close down 375 stores within 12 days.

Like Primark, many other businesses will be adapting to shifts in customer behavior, and consumption patterns will guide many aspects of how business models get transformed post-COVID-19. It is time to realign business models!

Besides the impact of the pandemic accelerating digitization for some industries, some other trends will continue to play out:

- Rapid introduction of digital operating models.
- Digitizing value chains.
- Ever-increasing power of social media.
- Connected customer experience.
- Application of artificial intelligence and machine learning.
- Rise of privacy and regulations.
- Cybersecurity and threat intelligence, which is fuelling business performance.

Digital Transformation with Dynamics 365

Digital transformation does not come in a box or a cloud. We are in the fourth industrial revolution and it is an exciting time. We are experiencing mass adoption of digital technologies and it is evolving faster than ever before, which is becoming challenging for businesses to keep up with the pace while dealing with scarcity of skilled resources.

While the digital transformation of industries will be profound, we must keep in mind that it will have a wider economic and social impact, too, as we have seen with previous revolutions driven by steam and coal and electricity and computers.

It is time to reassess your organization's ways of working by reviewing internal capability, resource utilization, cost efficiency, and collaborative platform that can be used to drive the operational efficiencies, reduce costs, and eventually help you to transform your operation.

We will cover the capabilities of transforming your business in Chapter 2 and discuss the power of the Microsoft platform in Chapter 3. Digital transformation cannot happen overnight. We need to transform the mindset of how we are currently doing business, people who are key to the business, and how we can prepare the program for digital transformation. We will cover this in Chapters 4 and 5. We will dive deeply into organizational change management for Microsoft Dynamics 365 and DX in Chapter 6.

Digital transformation involves using digital technologies to shape the process and to become more efficient and/or effective, and to transform the services into something significantly better. We will emphasize the fundamentals of executing a successful Dynamics 365 project in Chapter 7.

Some of the challenges will require a revolution in skills, and while your business is not running at full capacity (due to the lockdown), you have the opportunity to redeploy some of your team members. This does not need to be deeply technical (you can hire the technical power) but think about those who can work across different departments or business units. You have probably already witnessed this over the past few months where some of your talents stepped up and made things happen under the new circumstances. Giving them an opportunity to be a part of a new direction for your organization will make a world of difference for most millennials and will help you to attract and retain staff. In your new digital culture, roles will become more flexible. Some of the roles will be more permanent in order to provide structure and technical guidance, but your new digital culture with a continuous flow of initiatives will create new roles that evolve with its needs and pace. We will focus on key roles of people in the digital transformation and how we can empower them in Chapter 8.

The Microsoft Dynamics 365 platform offers powerful tools like Workflow, Power Platform, Cloud and Cloud automation tools, all of which help to automate time-consuming tasks. The team can also utilize robust Internet of Things (IoT), artificial intelligence (AI), and machine learning functionality best on internal teams' capability and a vision for expansion on team capability by including some specific skills such as:

- Software engineers, cloud computing specialists, and product managers remain key roles for companies seeking to roll out new products and services. DevOps leaders galvanize software development by merging development with operations, enabling companies to continuously iterate software to speed delivery.
- Data scientists and data architects are also in high demand, as companies seek to glean insights out of vast troves of data, and transformations lean increasingly on machine learning and artificial intelligence.
- In addition, IT departments supporting business-wide transformations also require UX designers, digital trainers, writers, conversational brand strategists, forensic analysts, ethics compliance managers, and digital and workplace technology managers.

It is evident that businesses and leaders need to accelerate digital transformation to survive and thrive in the current economic situations. The key questions that keep the leaders and businesses thinking are where to start, who are the key stakeholders, and how to get their buy-in for the necessary support and budgets?

Writing a business case for digital transformation is an exciting and challenging task; specifically, if it is your first one, it is an opportunity and will enlighten you with the great depth at the start, which helps in planning and success of the transformation.

The critical question you need to ask is: What business outcomes do you want for your customers?

As customer expectations continue to shift, it is important to have the C-suite aligned and CXOs sponsor and champion the digital transformation innovation. To make the sponsorship work, CXOs need to have a strategy, focus, planning, tangible commitments, and a communications strategy to drive impact within the organization. Some companies like Honeywell[9] have taken it a step further and now call their employees Future Shapers. "Future Shapers are dreamers and doers." As Ken Stacherski, Honeywell's VP Enterprise Transformation, shared, the company's internal motto is "The future is what we make it." With those words in mind, Future Shapers are transforming Honeywell inside and outside for their customers. The business case will help drive the benefits and outcomes from the D365 implementation and shape the conversation on what post going live looks like. We will bring your attention to this in Chapter 9. Digital transformation by implementing Dynamics 365 is not a one-off project; it needs to be continuously nurtured and improved as the organization reaches new maturity. This will be covered in Chapter 10. We have included two appendix chapters that cover FastTrack with Dynamics 365 and key tools that are being used with Dynamics 365 to ensure a successful implementation for an organization.

We will also look at the case study of various businesses in three different sections and will bring you their experiences on leading their digital transformation with Dynamics 365, key decisions made during the journey, and their key achievements and outcomes from their digital transformation implementation.

Microsoft Dynamics 365 brings data together in the business, from different landscapes and ecosystems of the business. This is where insights surface from that data, and it is the vehicle used to translate that insight into action.

Summing Up

In this chapter, we have introduced the concept of Digital Transformation and how every digital transformation revolves around the customer, who is at the heart of the transformation. COVID-19 has accelerated the digital transformation in many organizations and reprioritized the case for change. Microsoft Dynamics 365 technology is instrumental in the digital transformation of many organizations and aided the acceleration that we will look at closely in the later chapters and in our case study sections.

Digital Future Checklist:

✓ Transformation is not a project. It is a quest for continuous improvement to survive and thrive.
✓ Think customer as the center of digital transformation.
✓ Plan for your digital transformation in all areas—business model, customer experience, tech ecosystem, and the operations.
✓ Build a problem-solving culture and experimentation should be at the core of it.
✓ People build the culture, and for successful transformation, culture transformation is the key.
✓ Key components for a business case are Scope, Decision Framework, Roadmap, Milestones, and Benefits.
✓ Internal and external customers are equally critical for the transformation.

"Once something is a passion, the motivation is there."
—*Michael Schumacher*

Notes

1. PWC, Experience Is Everything. Get It Right. www.pwc.com/us/en/services/consulting/library/consumer-intelligence-series/future-of-customer-experience.html.
2. 100 Stats on Digital Transformation and Customer Experience (2020). www.blakemichellemorgan.com/blog/100-stats-digital-transformation-customer-experience/.
3. Blake Morgan (2019). www.forbes.com/sites/blakemorgan/2019/12/16/100-stats-on-digital-transformation-and-customer-experience/#64cf2a123bf3.
4. Ibid.

5. Blake Morgan (2019)., www.forbes.com/sites/blakemorgan/2019/12/16/100-stats-on-digital-transformation-and-customer-experience/#64cf2a123bf3.

6. Ibid.

7. 100 Stats on Digital Transformation and Customer Experience (2020). www.blakemichellemorgan.com/blog/100-stats-digital-transformation-customer-experience/.

8. Clayton M. Christensen (2015), What Is Disruptive Innovation? www.hbr.org/2015/12/what-is-disruptive-innovation.

9. Blake Morgan (2019), We Are Future Shapers: Enterprise Transformation at Honeywell. www.forbes.com/sites/blakemorgan/2019/09/05/we-are-future-shapers-enterprise-transformation-at-honeywell/?sh=223c76303592.

CHAPTER 2

Capabilities for Transforming Your Business with Dynamics 365

The greatest danger in times of turbulence is not the turbulence—it is to act with yesterday's logic.

—Peter Drucker

Closely observing the technological evolution, along with the business activities, offerings, and public announcements coming from FTSE companies, the term "digital transformation" seems to be used in each and every public corporate statement and highlighted as a core goal in corporate strategies. But what is this hype and why such a fuzz and why now?

Digital transformation was born as a result of the rapid evolution of the global economy, the imperative demand of consumers to receive better-quality services, the large and ever-increasing competition, and the evolution of buyers/consumers into "smart users" across all channels. Now, it's easy to put that into perspective since both you as a reader and I as a writer have played an ultimate role in the birth of digital transformation, which was shaped by our daily activities and interactions with businesses, for whom we set higher and higher expectations and standards. The reality is that organizations have not taken long to understand the urgent need for change and to become digitalized, but the big question that has been nagging CEOs and managing directors across the globe is "Where do we start?" on top of "Where should we focus first?" During these brainstorming sessions, their worries have been reinforced by examples of failed digital transformation projects.

A digital transformation is dual; on the one hand, it refers to how you offer your services or products on the market and, on the other hand, how you strengthen the internal processes of the company, which has a direct impact on the organizational structure. People, process, technology, and consumers are driving a cultural shift and a digital-first mindset. There are a number of cases where digital transformation projects have not had the expected results and, in fact, evidence from surveys shows that an extremely high percentage fail, ranging from 66% to 84% of digital transformation projects.[1] This makes the situation even more complicated, as in cases of failed projects, both senior executives and lower levels in the hierarchy tend to oppose further investment in their time and efforts into similar projects and falsely reinforce the fear of change. However, if inspirational leaders and digital change advocates learned something from such failed projects, it is that putting things into action without creating a robust background in both corporate cultures and the operating models will always lead to exactly the same result.

From my experience as a digital management consultant, organizations need to start by creating a digital strategy and a roadmap to start small, focusing primarily on the efficacy of productivity on their existing business model and operation and then finally moving on to innovation as a model for continuous improvement. We also need to look carefully into some of the core barriers that can become fatal to a digital transformation strategy if not resolved before starting any initiative.

- **Consumer engagement.** While consumer or clients sit at the heart of digital transformation, it is the utmost priority to engage with consumers first to understand areas that can accelerate or improve the consumer experience
- **Cost efficiencies.** We have all heard the phrase, "This software costs a fortune; we cannot afford it." Indeed, the cost of implementation, maintenance, and licensing may become a big investment and the real ROI will most likely show up after user

adoption. Hence there is a greater need to identify the business areas that can be made efficient that will eventually drive the growth of business, ensuring a cost-efficient investment.

- **Resistance to change.** Humans by nature subconsciously resist change, especially when changes are initiated or forced by the external environment. Therefore, before initiating any transformation strategies or plans, business leaders should proactively draft initial risk assessments, regularly measure and track engagement and commitment from the very early stages of any project, communicate their expectations openly and honestly, but, most importantly, identify opportunities to motivate employees to become part of the planning process.

- **Old practices in a new environment.** It is understandable that a digital transformation strategy is not solely the implementation of new systems but also the change in internal processes due to the ability to automate long and exhausting manual processes. Introducing the latest and most sophisticated technology without evaluating the old and setting new processes will certainly limit the potential of the whole endeavor.

- **The right product or the vendor.** For this subject, there should be an option to make a choice. There are many examples where organizations chose the vendor over the product due to strategic relationships or hidden agendas, which unsurprisingly led to failed projects and broken relationships. Choosing the right product that suits the business and users should be a careful and transparent process, where possible guided by almost agnostic professionals who don't affiliate with vendors but lead the selection process through their experience and base their conclusions on results. In terms of the vendor, the main aim is to choose the right technology partner rather than the implementer who will engage and eavesdrop on the needs of the organization and encourage them to achieve more.

A Platform for Change and Transformation

As discussed throughout this book, it is already well known that we live in the digital age, and we are going through the digital transformation in our lives, politically, socially, and economically. This digital transformation is capable of changing our business models, ways of working and operating, all of which are supported by a technology ecosystem. The technological advancement in the last 20 years has been incredible, accelerating the growth of data and of connected people and devices, and, in the same way, it is expected to continue increasing many times in the short and medium term. Among the technologies that stand out the most in these advances are those related to the cloud, the Internet of Things, artificial intelligence, mobility, business applications, data analysis, and security, among others.

For an organization undergoing a digital transformation, selecting an implementation partner is a key decision. Usually, the selection of a partner is based on a tendering process fulfilling all key selection criteria. A good amount of time and due diligence needs to be factored in the selection process to identify the key strengths and weaknesses of the organization itself, which will contribute to selecting the right partner. However, after the partner is selected, many other factors need to be considered, both in terms of choosing the infrastructure and the technology. Having so many options in technologies and software available at the tip of your fingers, choosing the right solution for consumers who are not experienced and qualified can become the biggest nightmare of executives.

Most vendors will present you with their product's unique selling points and will certainly promise you that their software not only "can do the job" but eventually will offer you functionalities that will transform your business operations holistically. Without a doubt this could potentially add more value to a business that suffers from bureaucracy or poor business flows, but more functionalities should not be considered a primary selection criterion when these functionalities add nothing but cost to the project budget. Microsoft is one of the technological leaders in this field and is clearly one of the market makers, continuously developing new capabilities to enable digital transformation across an organization's key business process. The public product roadmap provides information about what will be made available in the next wave of product updates.

At the end of 2016 the new Microsoft Dynamics 365 applications— a range of flexible applications adaptable to meet the needs of all types of industries, offering tools to transform their finance and operations, supply chain management, sales, customer service, commerce and marketing, and communication processes—was introduced. Microsoft also provides a low-code, non-code application development platform through the Microsoft Power Platform, including the market-leading tools for data analysis using Power BI, as well as a very extensive set of security, integration, artificial intelligence, data storage, processing services, and process orchestration, built on the Microsoft Azure platform. In particular, Microsoft releases two new functionality releases per year to Microsoft Dynamics 365 and the Microsoft Power Platform. Each release includes hundreds of new features, and this information is published in advance so that customers can properly prepare to adopt them.

We can highlight many great strengths within the Microsoft platform, like integrating with Cloud, integration with data, Power Apps, Power BI reporting, Finance & Operation, Supply Chain Management sized for large organizations, and Business Central for medium organizations, which make it an extremely attractive platform to support the digital transformation. The first is related to the completeness and integration of services and products. Virtually any requirement or problem that needs to be solved is already available within the stack of Microsoft products and services. A relevant aspect to adopting technology is that the products are natively integrated. A clear example of this is the integration between business applications and artificial intelligence. Microsoft has developed a series of services and functionalities using artificial intelligence technologies embedded within business applications, for example, within the sales application, so that users proactively know what the next best action is to consider, thus winning the business engagement since the sales engagement process is embedded within the functionalities. The second has to do with the evolution of the platform. Microsoft's investment in innovation and development allows customers to trust that the roadmap of Microsoft products and services will be able to meet business requirements and needs that are not yet known or clear today. Technology changes so fast that a system that was implemented two years ago, perhaps even today, is beginning to become obsolete. Microsoft services are constantly evolving and updating. For instance, all business applications undergo two annual updates, adding an average of 400 new functionalities each time, and each update can be silently adopted without disrupting the day-to-day usage.

These two characteristics of the Microsoft platform make it much simpler for a company to be able to adopt technology and transform its business model, optimize its processes, or create new products or services. From experience, a successful digital transformation strategy must include the adoption of products and services versus the adaptation of them. In addition to taking advantage of the good practices that are already included in the product, adopting further technologies allows a faster implementation, and cost-effective, efficient future maintenance of the solution. However, there are scenarios in which customizing the functionalities and services provided by Microsoft have competitive advantages by differentiating the product from other competitors. Any variation or customization of the product needs to be ring-fenced, closely measured with impact assessment, and monitored by solution design and architecture authority.

The Microsoft platform also allows adapting and personalizing the services and functionalities to be able to adapt them according to the needs of the client. These adaptations allow custom developments, integrations with other platforms, and customizations of products and services. The Microsoft platform adopts technology and security standards and compliance with market regulations, which facilitates such integrations and customizations.

April Dunnam,
Partner Technical
Architect, Microsoft

"The need for digital transformation has never been more crucial than it is today. We are living in an unprecedented time as we frantically try to adapt to 'the new normal.' Businesses are faced with new and emerging financial challenges, coupled with significant software developer talent shortages. This makes it more important than ever to have agile business processes that support fast deployment and delivery of solutions.

The Power Platform can bridge this gap by providing a comprehensive low-code platform that empowers business users and professional developers alike to get more solutions into production faster. The rich analytics and reporting of Power BI, the workflow automation of Power Automate, the rapid application development of Power Apps, and the low-code chatbot capability of Power Virtual Agents provide a powerful and complete toolset that enables organizations to transform their business processes."

Martin Draper, CIO
& Change Director,
Liberty London

"Digital Transformation is NEVER simply about introducing new technology without the culture transformation. Culture is necessary to ultimately deliver a new product, business model, or operating model. Simply 'IT initiative' thinking is doomed to fail if the culture initiatives are not working in parallel.

Since culture 'transformations' do not happen overnight, it is important to get the culture piece correct in the first instance. This is not a project, with a traditional delivery methodology or playbook, like waterfall. It is more about new ways of working, using new organizational structures, processes, technology, and data in innovative ways, to deliver business change in a more adaptive, flexible, and faster way.

The ability to design and deploy initiatives quickly, established from sound analysis of data, and to be able to fail or succeed fast is the ultimate goal. Organizations that embed this thinking into their culture (and investment strategy) are those that are taking digital transformation seriously. Today there are more technology options than ever to accelerate the journey, but unfortunately many organizations are still relying on a proliferation of IT projects to define a digital transformation strategy and avoiding solving the more complex and more important piece of the puzzle."

Chai Ming Kong,
Head, Technology and
Digital Transformation,
KFC & Pizza Hut

"Digital disruption is a question of when and not if. In many organizations, COVID-19 has acted as a catalyst to accelerate their digital transformation and rethink their strategic priorities, investments, and a new market and growth potential. With Cloud as a means of the beginning—the connected value across the ecosystem now is more powerful than ever before with the strong integration that exists across the value chain. Embrace the opportunity."

How to Drive Business Efficiencies

Engaging your customers is more important than ever before. To engage with customers in the way they need means empowering organizations to act on insights across the entire journey, build life-long relationships, and create trustworthy selling and service experiences that are consistent, personalized, and always on.

Microsoft business applications are a complete set of intelligent modules that support the business processes of an organization. Microsoft Dynamics 365 is built on the Microsoft Power Platform, which is constantly evolving. A great example of a successful project implemented using the power of Dynamics 365 applications and Power Platform is shown here:

Michel (Miki) Tabakovic, Country Sales Manager, IKEA Sweden

"D365 and Power Platform gave us a platform for a better experience both for customers and co-workers at IKEA Sweden, giving us the possibility to be part of the total customer journey. We have reduced manual work with the use of the Power Platform. With D365 MVP up and running, we manage to capture a lot of customer insight on behavior and user journey. Now we can ensure that customers feel that IKEA Sweden sees me and for the co-workers that we see the customer. That is a prerequisite to secure a long-term partnership between IKEA and the customer. It allows us to adapt between digital and physical meeting when all depended on the needs of the customer."

Microsoft Dynamics 365 offers analysis through built-in dashboards, reports, and views, and also allows the extension through Power BI and other reporting tools. You can tailor the platform to your company needs as Power Platform allows users to extend Microsoft Dynamics 365 and Azure. You can build your applications and share your data across modules easily, and at the same time take advantage of artificial intelligence and advanced analytics built-in features.

Microsoft Dynamics 365 business applications provide value and impact to organizations through:

- Engage customers: improve customer engagement, collect valuable information, personalize your customer journey and experience
- Improve business processes for sales, marketing, customer service, inventory management, supply chain management, purchases, manufacturing, retail, and more
- Optimize operations, reduce costs, and increment your efficiency
- Data integration for all modules
- Channel integration
- Smart actions through built-in Artificial Intelligence scenarios
- Flexible, easy to scale, and adapts to changes
- Easy to adopt, supports innovation, and accelerates digital transformation
- Empower employees: engage and attract the best talent and provide your people with modern tools
- Transform products and services: support innovation, providing data to detect new market opportunities

Integrating your business data from Microsoft Dynamics 365 with Power BI, you can have a profound analysis of trends, strengths, and weaknesses of your business. This enables you to produce products, predict an efficient pipeline conversion rate, set personalized offers and sales promotions, and enable a better decision-making process for your sales, business, and operation. We know the importance of data and in today's conditions we are leveraging the intelligence of data to make informed business decisions.

Data Platform: The Secret Sauce

Within the digital transformation strategy, the data is an illustrious citizen. We live in the data age, generating about 2.5 quintillion bytes of data per day. Data is the center of the business and powers the insights that can drive the actions of tomorrow.

To compete and be successful in today's market, it is not enough to simply sell products to our clients. Personalization is a key factor for consumers. Examples of this can be recognized at companies like YouTube or Netflix, which offer content to consumers based on their preferences, or e-commerce sites like Amazon, which make offers to customers based on past behavior. Finally, these are data collection platforms that will be used in the future to improve your value propositions or the customer experience, or perhaps to generate new products and services.

Therefore, data management is vital for organizations and there is a recognition that data is an asset and hence it should be managed in the same manner as financial assets; that is, for financial asset management we have accounting policies and accounting systems, so we should also have policies (data governance and appropriate tools, such as DWH/Data lake), proper management of metadata, and ensure data lineage. Businesses need to capture, analyze, predict, present, and report data. To be effective and efficient, data management must be part of the core strategy of the solution that we implement for users and clients.

The data originates from different applications, devices, channels, and services. The volume of data grows day by day. Normally the data is stored in different providers, technologies, and systems, in such a way that it is extremely difficult to integrate them and to have a consolidated database, which is very costly in time and resources.

Microsoft Dataverse was created that delivers a built-in low-code data platform and provides relational data storage, rich data types, enterprise grade governance, and a one-click solution deployment. Microsoft Project Oakdale is a data service in SaaS mode, which is easy to use, easy to manage, complies with legal regulations, is secure, and is globally scalable. As part of the Microsoft Power Platform (Figure 2.1), it requires no or little code to be written, so it can easily be used by everyone from knowledge workers to professional developers through Microsoft Teams. The new functionality empowers citizen developers and responds to business needs in a rapid and cost-effective way. During the COVID-19 pandemic, where certain areas of businesses needed to transform rapidly, Microsoft Project Oakdale through Microsoft Teams was a quick and rapid solution.

The Microsoft Power Platform

The low-code platform that spans Office 365, Azure, Dynamics 365, and standalone applications.

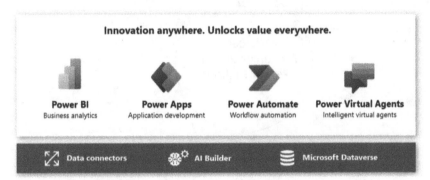

FIGURE 2.1 Microsoft Power Platform
Source: © Microsoft. Used with permission from Microsoft Corporation.

At the time of writing this book, Microsoft has announced that Common Data Service, the sophisticated and secure backbone that powers Dynamics 365 and Power Platform, has been renamed as Microsoft Dataverse. Another key part of that strategy is Microsoft Dataverse for Teams—the essential subset of Dataverse capabilities included as a powerful, built-in data platform for millions of Teams users at no additional cost.[2]

The combination of Microsoft's Dataverse, Power Platform, and Teams enables businesses to address complex and real problems with a low-code platform (Figure 2.2).

Business Process: Simplification, Standardization, and Automation

Digital transformation is about how you reinvent and innovate your products, services, optimize your processes, and empower your people to create value for your customers and maintain a competitive advantage in a digital-first world. Normally in companies, there are dozens or hundreds of business processes. Many of these business processes present opportunities for improvement, either because they are slow or obsolete or because they do not collect

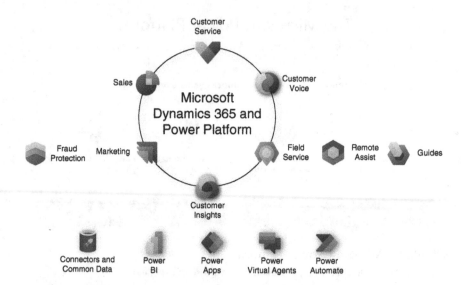

FIGURE 2.2 Combination of Dynamics 365 Power Platform with other components

Source: Used with permission. Created from a presentation that was given at Microsoft Ignite.

all the data currently required, they do not involve all stakeholders, or the software that supports them is obsolete and the data is stored in information silos. There are business processes that do not respond to current reality and others that are more complex than necessary.

The negative impact of these business processes includes wasteful time management due to manual processes, manual or lack of integration between two systems, and in some cases systems prone to human error, which overall leads to a negative customer experience or demotivated system users. Efforts to improve business processes are costly in time and resources, especially if we think of business processes that involve various channels, systems, and areas of the company. It is also costly in time and resources to keep these processes up to date, to be prepared for constant changes, new products and services, new channels, technologies, sales methods, and market conditions.

Part of the digital transformation refers to the improvement of business processes, to improve the value proposition toward the client, improve the experience of the client, and also of the users, so that it is transformed into a better service. In other words, within the digital transformation strategy of a company, it must be considered a high priority to make key processes more efficient for customers and employees of the organization. Customers and employees expect fast, modern applications that can be used on mobile devices, and that are safe and easy to use.

Automation is not a choice any more but is a compulsion in today's digital age. Customers are not willing to listen to the justification of a business working in silos that are not integrated. Businesses cannot justify lost opportunity due to lack of a holistic view of the customer and their preferences when other businesses are disrupting the market and predicting real-time opportunities and increase of sales efficiently and repeatedly with the knowledge of data.

The Microsoft platform allows you to design and implement business processes that involve different technologies, integrations, channels, and types of applications, without the need to develop code. Microsoft Dynamics 365 and Microsoft Power Platform help to improve and make more efficient business processes in different ways:

- It natively contains a series of processes already included in the different products, whether for sales, marketing, customer service, logistics, purchasing, manufacturing, among others. These processes can be modified, without the need to develop code, to adjust to the particular needs of each company.
- The platform allows new data models and business processes to be designed from scratch, in such a way that we can digitize processes quickly and easily.
- It allows us to automate processes, through workflow engines and integration mechanisms. The Microsoft Power Platform's workflow capabilities allow integration of more than 400+ services, such as DropBox, Salesforce, SAP, Azure, Office, among others.[3] These automation capabilities allow us to integrate diverse channels, systems, and applications quickly and easily.
- The Microsoft Power Platform on which the business processes are built allows maintaining and modifying them in a simple way, and thus the business can update them as necessary.

- The Microsoft Platform allows you to create different types of applications to model business processes, oriented to the channel and the needs of each company. For example, a business process that is initiated by a client through the web channel can then be worked on by a customer service agent through a browser or a mobile device, which allows sending a response to the client through an SMS message or involving a chatbot from the web channel to solve a customer problem.

Is There a Choice: Cloud or On-Premise?

Traditionally companies use systems implemented in On-Premise mode. In particular, legacy systems are implemented on-premise. The term on-premise refers to the type of installation of a software solution and, in this case, the software is installed on the client's servers or on a third party contracted by the client. The client is responsible for the administration, updating, security, backups, and maintenance of the software.

In a Cloud implementation, in particular, in a SaaS service (Software as a Service), the company consumes software and can always stay current with the upgrades and maintenance releases per year by Microsoft.

There are many variables to consider in order to decide on the best suitable option for a particular company, which includes the following factors but is not limited to:

- Costs
- Compliance
- Scalability
- Features
- Update frequency
- Security
- Performance
- Data integration with other systems
- Resources and skillset
- Change capabilities

If there are no legal or technical restrictions, do not hesitate to go for the Cloud-based online option as this will be the most viable, maintainable, and scalable option.

I will argue about this recommendation with some relevant aspects:

- **Features.** Microsoft Dynamics 365 offers a series of functionalities that can only be implemented on the On-Line option. These features are proactively announced in Microsoft's portal and public announcements; therefore, the client can plan well ahead of any changes in the utilization of these features to improve their day-to-day activities. The On-Line option will always have a competitive advantage due to richer and technologically advanced functionality. With On-Premise, customers have to wait much longer before being able to take advantage of them.
- **Update frequency.** As mentioned in this book, the Microsoft update rate of On-Line applications is every six months, while updates of On-Premise versions are once a year. In the real experience, customers don't update their software every year as there is no direct push from the vendor. Therefore, On-Premise clients frequently have very old installed versions, which are obsolete as they have not taken advantage of many of the new features.
- **Resources and skillset.** To keep the software updated in the On-Premise mode, it is necessary to have access to specialist resources that have these skills. This means that either you should hire full-time staff or contractors or be dependent on hiring an external resource/vendor to complete the software update on your behalf. In the On-Line mode, Microsoft's dedicated team of engineers take care to run all relevant updates.
- **Infrastructure.** On-Premise solution implementations essentially require the purchase and installation of a series of servers. In addition, if the solution needs to be made redundant, a full lifecycle of duplication should be made that adds a stream of requirement time, resources, cost, and risk. In the On-Line mode, creating new environments and redundant environments, increasing storage capacity, and making backups are very simple, along with quick administration and configuration tasks.

Alistair Wallace,
Senior Director of
Technology Solution
Delivery, Coca-Cola
Consolidated, Inc.

"Cloud computing and Software as a Service (SaaS) has drastically changed the way companies look at utilizing software. Everyone today is accustomed to downloading an app on their phone to meet every need; many now have the same level of expectation in the workplace. Today, throughout the corporate world, individuals are deciding to head in this direction alone, rather than seeking any technical expertise or guidance. The significant benefit is that any company, large or small, can now utilize enterprise-grade solutions. The big downfall is that many of these SaaS solutions/platforms are designed to meet a specific niche need. The technical knowledge and foundational data integration requirements and the cost associated with keeping everything connected present a much more significant hurdle over time as more and more of these solutions are stitched together. It is the local IT department's responsibility to provide mechanisms to help with how the decisions are being made to onboard these solutions and assist as early as possible to enable success. It is impossible to stop or even slow the movement to the Cloud, but there are ways in which we, as technologists, can make it much less painful."

Summing Up

Microsoft Dynamics 365 comprises a complete set of modules that accelerates and enables the digital transformation of companies that is flexible, scalable, and maintainable. The common data foundation layer is a key component, allowing the implementation of artificial intelligence, analysis of tools, simplifying the data integration with systems, and hence allowing the decision makers to maintain their key focus on the strategy of improving their core business.

The implementation in the SaaS modality has a series of determining benefits for the success of a project and its subsequent evolution. The amount of functionality available is much greater than that of an On-Premise deployment, and the ease and speed of implementation, administration, and maintenance allow the client to be able to make changes in an agile and efficient way.

The On-Line version also has all the innovation related to artificial intelligence and data insights, within a strong roadmap from Microsoft for machine learning and service improvements.

Digital Future Checklist:

Capabilities for Transforming Your Business with Dynamics 365
✓ Evaluate your capabilities in-house.
✓ Identify key factors to drive your business efficiencies.
✓ Key strengths of the Microsoft Platform that you can leverage.
✓ Relevance of the data within the digital transformation.
✓ Key advantages of the online platform.

"Over the next 10 years, we will reach a point where nearly everything has become digitized."
—*Satya Nadella, CEO, Microsoft*

Notes

1. Barry Libert, Megan Beck, and Yoram (Jerry) Wind, 7 Questions to Ask Before Your Next Digital Transformation, *Harvard Business Review*, July 24, 2016. https://hbr.org/2016/07/7-questions-to-ask-before-your-next-digital-transformation.
2. Cunningham, R. (2020), Reshape the Future of Work with Microsoft Dataverse for Teams, Reshape the Future of Work with Microsoft Dataverse for Teams—Now Generally Available | Microsoft Power Apps.
3. Microsoft Connectors. https://flow.microsoft.com/en-us/connectors/.

CHAPTER 3

The Power of the Microsoft Platform

Great power involves great responsibility.
—Franklin D. Roosevelt

Putting in your experience of digital transformation, can you visualize the process and the outcome of your business transformation? We will focus on this a bit more closely. Depending on the level of engagement, you are bound to be part of many decisions taken during your digital transformation journey, starting with identifying the processes that can be made more efficiently. Is this efficiency in process going to deliver an improved customer journey or will it improve the business growth by entering a new market? The outcome of your digital transformation needs to be clearly linked to your business vision and strategy, which will help to lay out a strong foundation for a digital roadmap. The roadmap of the digital transformation needs to take into consideration various aspects—to validate the scope of transformation by identifying the business processes to transform minimizing the urge of replicating the existing process, to identify and confirm availability of key stakeholders as the subject matter for experts in the workshops, and to communicate the benefits and vision of the program throughout with an engagement plan.

Based on my experience as a management consultant and program director, I have lived through many of these journeys. You need to have the sponsorship of the leadership team before embarking on the journey of business transformation as this will need engagement across all levels of the business and will have an impact on employees and the processes. In this chapter, we will explore the capabilities of the Power Platform, but my recommendation would be to introduce these capabilities at different stages of the program as your organization gains maturity in using the Power Platform and familiarization with Dynamics 365.

Once you and your organization have made a decision and identified the technology that will work for your business, you also need to find the right solution integration partner who will lead and guide you through the journey. In this book, we will refer to digital transformation using Microsoft Dynamics 365 technology. As part of your evaluation process, you need to set up key criteria for selection and whether it is the solution partner and the technology as part of your request for proposal (RFP).

Digital transformation is about people, process, adopting new technologies, and change culture for the betterment of the current and future business processes. The solution needs to be designed that meets the current business requirement and is future-proof with new evolving technologies and changing business needs. During the unprecedented times of crisis like COVID-19, it has proved even more worthwhile for businesses to be agile, flexible, and scalable, enabling the remote working and meetings the business needs.

For instance, we talk about the future of retail business; the adoption of new cutting-edge technologies can take it to the next level. For example, Lowebot is a robot that can keep track of real-time inventory and inform the respective person about it, improve the use of storage space, guide customers toward their products, and retrieve products for them.

COVID-19 has forced many companies to rethink their strategic priorities, future investments, ways of working, and facing the new reality. In some organizations, digital transformation has been accelerated, whereas in other cases employees are empowered to innovate and deliver value.

"Because of new and changing occasions during the pandemic, keeping in touch with customers and consumers gained so much importance. By promoting the new Coca-Cola digital platform with under-the-cap promotion usage, we enabled our consumers and customers to stay digital. New online digital, differentiated, and flexible consumer promotions created awesome feedbacks & results in terms of financials and customer satisfaction."

Hakan Elbasi, Group Technology Solutions Executive, Coca-Cola

Rise of the Citizen Developer: Improving Productivity with the Power Platform

To understand the need of the Citizen Developer, first let me take you years back to those days where a client's need was to automate the manual processes in the ERP solution, which resulted in too many customizations into the product. The business processes across different countries were not unified or centralized and hence led to unique customizations per country and obviously these were not cost-effective or manageable after a few years. This resulted in siloed businesses, lack of seamless integration, and an unmanageable and very costly upgrade.

In the last few years, we have seen a paradigm shift among the clients with the recognition of unmanageable expensive enterprise-level customizations and willingness to change business processes aligning with the core out of the box—a "vanilla" ERP solution. Many organizations are still running on a legacy, with ERP platforms that still need to transform with pace and be flexible. As the core solution would not meet all complex business needs, Microsoft introduced a feature of Power Apps that will allow the business user community to create solutions with a low-code platform. This is the beginning and rise of the citizen developer. Every organization has individuals who have brilliant skillsets using Microsoft Excel and PowerPoint, who can be empowered to solve business problems by leveraging their skillsets leveraging low-code platform.

Digital transformation is not a one-time project as it needs continuous improvement. With the Microsoft Power Platform, Power Apps is an integral part of the Microsoft Dynamics value proposition with its cost-effective low-code/no-code solutions. Power Apps is an amazing tool that improves user productivity dramatically, enabling citizen developers to turn on the insight deriving from data into action without compromising the IT governance of the organization. Citizen developers feel empowered to solve business problems, creating unique experiences. For many citizen developers, these capabilities created new opportunities in their personal career growth path. It is a true win-win for the individual and the organization. We will look into real-world examples in our Case Study section.

Finally, empowering these solutions without moving the data out of the secure, trusted, IT-governed cloud—in other words, keeping it in the Dataverse—allows agility in unleashing the citizen developer without surrendering IT governance. This is a key difference between the solutions of power users built in Excel in the last decades and the modern Power Apps story.

We have seen the increase in usage of Microsoft Power Apps during this crisis time of COVID-19. While it is unfortunate to see many organizations are putting employees in furlough during this period, we have also seen employees creating new opportunities for themselves by utilizing the furloughed time to learn and leverage Power Apps capabilities. In the next section, we will take a deep dive into Power Platform components.

Building Custom Apps with Power Apps

We will start with the Power Platform components, that is, Power Apps. Power Apps is a platform as a service that enables you to create modern apps that can run on Android, iOS, and all mobile browsers. It can be done using Power Apps studio with a drag-and-drop user interface and a low-code solution. This means that you do not have to write the code; you can drag and drop the functionality that you need in your app.

Along with applications, it can also create business-to-business (B2B) and business-to-consumer (B2C) portals, which leads to an optimized user interface for multiple device types. Power Apps can be accessed using different authenticated accounts such as Microsoft, Facebook, Google, LinkedIn, and anonymously.

The Power Apps also use the Dataverse, such as the Power Platform. Through the Dataverse—now with Dynamics 365 Finance, Supply Chain, and Commerce data accessible via either Dual Write or Virtual Entity technology—it is easier to build these great experiences around Dynamics rapidly rather than other business applications. Apps built using Power Apps provide rich business logic and workflow capabilities to transform your manual business processes to digital, automated processes. Power Apps have a responsive design and can run seamlessly in browser or on mobile devices (phone or tablet). Using Power Apps allows you to create three types of apps: canvas, model-driven, and portal.

We will start with Canvas Applications. Creating Canvas Applications is similar to creating a painting; all you need to do is drag and drop elements on the canvas. You first need to design a user-friendly interface of your app and then you can connect it to any data source or connectors available.

Then there are model-driven applications where the application layout is predetermined for you, and is primarily designated by the components you add to the app. An excellent example of model-driven applications is the Microsoft Dynamics 365 platform, which is integrated into the Microsoft Dataverse, enabling you to create entities and a data structure for your apps while building them.

Finally, the Power Apps portal, which is a WYSIWYG (what you see is what you get) tool, adds and configures webpages, components, forms, and lists.

Microsoft has introduced some techniques that can help to swiftly incline users with different levels of experiences to keep up with various Power Platform components. To get your firm up to speed with Power Apps and Power Platform tools, check this link, http://aka.ms/PowerAppsResources; it can guide you all through the beginner level and then take you to the required level of proficiency.

Resources and Community Groups

Microsoft has a vast collection of education resources for users. Please refer to https://docs.microsoft.com/en-us/power-platform. Here is a brief outline of the contents that you can find.

- The product for educational assets, for example, "Power Apps."
- **Documentation.** This is the official text-based documentation from Microsoft for the user's products. It covers all the high level and the most technical details of the products. Advanced users can use it to expand their knowledge. Some users might be frightened by it and may take time to get up to speed on the product. However, it comprises some tutorials and examples found within this method.
- **Learn [*product*] (e.g., Learn Power Apps).** This is the official "Guided Learning" documentation from Microsoft. Data is organized into Learning paths and topic "modules," which can be filtered as needed; for example, you can set the filter for a specific product or experience levels or user roles. Modules are assessed by the user's level of proficiency, and also involve time that a user might need to learn and understand.
- **Microsoft Community—forums.** This is a wonderful source of information where a user can access a large bank of individuals, from consulting partners to end users who are pleased to share their experiences and knowledge.
- **Videos.** This is the official Microsoft YouTube channel for the Microsoft product. The content is continuously updated with the newest videos, making it easy to absorb. Subscribe to the pages for the updates and stay in touch with the latest information.
- **Microsoft Solution templates.** These are located within the development studio and act as examples and starting places for new solutions.

As a business leader, you want to react quickly to business needs and there is no time to wait for development of software solutions. Keeping that in mind, some organizations are establishing CoEs for intelligent automation using the Power Platform. Workshops like "App in a day" are remotely conducted in-person by experienced individuals. They provide a guided end-to-end support while building your first app in one day.

- **Microsoft Business Applications Communities.** This is the Power Platform community hosted by Microsoft for brainstorming ideas and questions in open forums.
- **Dynamic Communities User Groups.** This is the Dynamics and Power Platform communities hosted by Dynamic Communities especially for end users. These great conferences and online communities aid with active involvement from other companies and implementation partners.

Andy Hafer,
Founder of Dynamic Communities

"A key to bringing a community together is figuring out the specific values each of the members or constituent groups bring to each other. Once specific values are identified, the community leaders can set up communications, collaborative tools, events, and platforms to make sure all those value-laced interactions happen often and happen purposely.

Except perhaps for the vows expressed at my wedding or the first words uttered by my children, some of the most endearing words spoken come from exclamations of satisfaction from community members. I have heard it thousands of times and it never gets old. It goes something like this:

An implementation team member from a company working diligently to go-live on Dynamics 365 is stuck on some obscure process in their organization. That person finds another member of the user community in a similar industry and strikes up a conversation about their dilemma. The community members share information with each other until the second one says to the first, 'Oh. We had that issue. ... Here's how we solved it.' Then it happens. The reply back is the sweetest words spoken in a community: 'Wow!' 'Thank you!' 'That's exactly what I was searching for! 'You have saved us!'

That scenario happens between customer companies. It happens between partners and customers. It happens when a customer is seeking an ISV solution. And it happens when Microsoft is seeking feedback and direction from customers for future versions of their products. It all happens when the community is dynamic enough that each member sees value in each other. I've often said, 'There is no power in the universe greater than people coming together in Community!'"

Using Power BI to Create a Data-Driven Culture

The data in companies is ever growing, but what is its use if we cannot use it to gain insight? If we don't constructively use this data, then it just becomes reports that someone might end up using only 5% of the time. To create a data-driven culture, it is essential to gaining a user's confidence in reporting and understanding why we should use historical data to gain insights.

When you use data to make future decisions, it is called data-driven insight.

1. The culture of a group is a significant factor that determines those who interact with the culture. It can be described as "fun," "innovative," "toxic," "competitive," "empowering," "defeating," "informed," "engaging," and so on. Creating a word cloud from the feedback of all firm employees can be a useful tool to assess a culture instead of asking the employees about the company. Therefore, the question now is, while creating a data-driven culture, what would someone expect from the company that is successfully establishing the concept to drive growth?
2. Culture can be defined by a branch or division, a project implementation team, a management team, a geographical office location, or even an individual. The unifying factor of a group is that they all understand and believe in the power of data that can be used to make an informed decision, and that, if not used correctly, can cause more harm than good.
3. The organizations should make data-driven decisions based on insights obtained from multiple data sources and then have a manual observation on them. Data insights drive business decisions, followed-up action, and the rationale of a decision that is transparent as it is based on evidence.

Some people will always hinder the process followed in data-driven culture by saying that a computer can never help in the decision-making process. However, they might not understand the concept behind it; the computer will only give you the possible decisions that can be made observing the patterns or based on a certain event. All you need to do is investigate these decisions, communicate, and empower your teams to make more informed decisions based on the underlying factors responsible for the decisions.

Let us understand it with an example. There are many e-commerce websites that use data-driven culture to boost sales and enhance profits. We all, at least once in our lives, have shopped from the e-commerce giant Amazon. While shopping, you must have observed a product recommendation section, similar product section, and products bought together section. These are all examples of data-driven business culture.

Amazon created its own recommendation algorithm to scale tens of millions of products and customers. It currently focuses on *the item-to-item collaborative filtering* algorithm that scales massive datasets and provides high-quality recommendations in real time. This type of filtering concentrates on customer's purchases in the past, similar products that have been rated after purchase, a list of products in their virtual cart, and the products that were only in the viewing list. All this data is combined together and processed using key engagement metrics such as opt-out rates, click-through rates, and open rates to recommend the product to Amazon users.

This algorithm proved to be an effective way to integrate recommendations on every process, from browsing to checkout, to drive sales by increasing average order value and the revenue generation from each customer, thus providing a personalized shopping experience for them.

Microsoft invented a platform called Power BI that can help promote and produce a data-driven culture. Power BI is comprised of various software and service offerings that can aid users to visualize and associate with data that is aggregated together by a series of connectors. It focuses mainly on collecting data from multiple sources and translating them into something meaningful.

The data collected from multiple sources can be in any form, such as a historical database, basic text tile, Excel file, doc file, or web service. You can either build your own custom dataset or can use existing connectors from Microsoft to get the work done. If we talk about connectors, there are some specific third-party subsets of built-in connectors, also known as *certified connectors*. These certified connectors enable others in the community to analyze data flowing into Power BI from multiple sources, such as a government web service or a connection to their established software offering. The connector is not created specifically for the organization unless it is created by https://docs.microsoft.com/en-us/power-bi/connect-data/desktop-connector-extensibility.

Solution Components

Power BI possesses three main fundamental components for the solution to promote the creation, distribution, and consumption of the reports:

1. **Power BI desktop**
   a. It basically helps designers/power users.
   b. It must be an installed application on a PC and should not be accessible from a web browser.
   c. It can help experts and citizen developers to build reports and dashboards.
   d. The resultant content is then shared with the Power BI service.
2. **Power BI service**
   a. This service is meant for everyone.
   b. It is browser-based (Software as a Service).
   c. It is used to inspect reports and dashboards as an end user.
   d. All the content that is created in Power BI desktop is published here for others to access.
3. **Power BI apps**
   a. It is meant for everyone.
   b. It is a cross-platform Device Applications (Windows, Android, iOS).
   c. It consolidates your data and envisions the reports and dashboards in a mobile-friendly view that is optimized according to the device being used.
   d. It also contains reports and dashboards.

Power BI supports a few key concepts for creating content to review at a high level: datasets, workspaces, reports, dataflows, apps, and dashboard.

- **Key starting point.** The key starting point is datasets and dataflows, as they are known to be data aspects or building blocks of Power BI. Datasets are views of data that are combined to provide a single pane of glass view of the data. Think of a traditional, non–Power BI business data report. These data reports can pull from a couple of different tables and data collections to provide a single view of data. That is what a dataset is in its essence. They are required for Power BI reports.

- **Dataflows.** Dataflows accumulate data from multiple sources and combine them into one single location known as the Dataverse entities. It takes a data source and brings all the data into a dataset. This process involves scheduling the extraction, transformation (calculations, aggregations, etc.), and loading (ETL) processes from the data sources. These dataflows enhance datasets that can be consumed within Power BI reports (Figure 3.1).

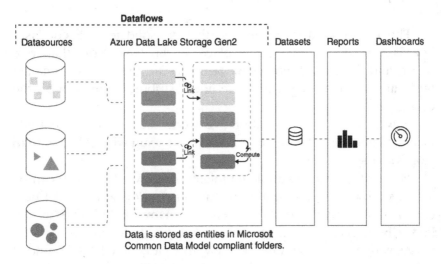

FIGURE 3.1 Dataflows and Self-Service Data Prep

Source: © Microsoft. Used with permission from Microsoft Corporation. Dataflows. https://docs.microsoft.com/en-us/power-bi/transform-model/service-dataflows-overview.

- **Reports.** Reports are a detailed graphical view of the data and represent data in charts, graphs, tables, lists, etc. Reports are used by analysts to determine valuable insights and actions that need to be taken accordingly. They are also used to build dashboards.
- **Dashboard.** Dashboards are created based on the organization's requirements to gain objective, valuable data insights. It is displayed in the form of a summary built from reports, which helps employees understand their specific role based on the reports' data. For example, how many orders are placed within a month, let's say for August? Through dashboards, employees can understand the business's current situation and how this data can help to add value. Dashboards are the single summarized representation of the data gathered from multiple sources that can be used to make future decisions.
- **Workspaces.** When all the data and visualizations are grouped at one place for utilization, it is called a workspace and apps within Power BI can be used.

The Power BI app is the one that consolidates related dashboards and reports, all in one place. It can have more than one report and dashboard. Power BI *designers* are the ones who create these apps so that they can share and distribute them with all the other colleagues.

Power BI apps are collaborative workspaces that are centrally managed and shared with other users of the team who collaborate to work on a specific content.

Microsoft provides sample templates for Power BI, which can be leveraged by your organization to gain inspiration or to model new content accordingly. However, there are many helpful links in any Power BI application that can help you to get up to speed.

As with any data, and especially with a view on GDPR, you need to have a data governance and change controls in place. If data is not governed periodically, then it can compromise on the quality of data and the data-driven culture. With proper measures in place, Power BI can provide a great insight into your business and lead you to put together and attain informed decisions of your business through the use of reports and dashboards.

"Tools like Power BI, Tableau, QlikView, etc. drive value in an organization by making the data accessible to anyone and everyone in the business. Their power lies in the ability to conduct quick fire analysis and provide self-service analytics to business users through interactivity and rich data visualization."

Dan Wakefield,
BI Team Lead,
Domino's Pizza

Accelerating Organizational Capability and Driving Efficiency

Today organizations are going through an unprecedented rate of change due to digital transformations. A complete digital transformation process involves various technologies and in this section we will discuss Azure Machine Learning and Intelligent Automation. At some point, each of us has encountered a machine learning–enabled service, whether we realized it or not. The most common example includes product recommendations while shopping online on e-commerce websites or searching something specific in your phone photos (e.g., search food, drinks), which are mostly based on the concept of machine learning (ML). It accumulates customer's historical data such as previous orders, browsing information, search engines, social media, and user information, and then analyzes it to recommend the most suitable product to improve sales.

As the data is ever growing in organizations, it is hard to explicitly code for all situations, which are continually evolving for so many different behavioral patterns. This is where we can make use of machine learning. We all make mistakes, but we also learn from that, which helps us grow. Similarly, applications or services using machine learning follow the same concept; they find behavioral patterns and learn from the historical data fed, and produce results accordingly.

Microsoft has introduced a machine learning platform called Azure Machine Learning that enables us to build, train, and deploy machine learning models through codes such as Python or R or no-code, drag-and-drop designers. Features like automated machine learning empower organizations to accelerate their model development process by recognizing proper algorithms and machine learning pipelines faster. Organizations can also enhance model accuracy with hyper-parameter tuning. It helps organizations save a lot of development time, thus accelerating the overall delivery time and a faster go-to-market (GTM) strategy.

Usually, an ML application will gather all the necessary dataset(s). This data is then "prepared" or transformed, removing all the data silos and converting unstructured data into structured data before beginning data analysis. The dataset is then "split" into two. The first version of the data is sent for training the model and the other for testing how well the model is performing. Then we use an algorithm to train the model. The Azure Machine Learning Algorithm Cheat Sheet is an excellent tool for selecting an algorithm. We can understand this by selecting the Linear Regression algorithm, but before training the model, we need a training set. The linear regression algorithm is used to predict the value of a constant variable X based on one or more predictor variables Y. It establishes a mathematical formula to discover the objective and effect between those two variables. When we have values for variable Y, the model will try to predict X.

The training process requires only 70% of the dataset and then predicts the other part. Once the scoring is concluded, a model needs to be evaluated to see how well the trained model performed on the test data. This would help us to improve algorithms for any odd or non-desirable predictions. This entire process can be twisted to justify a concept called a "pipeline." Pipeline groups all the concepts in this paragraph into a single manageable entity.

Once you have successfully created an ML model, the company can start leveraging these ML models in all aspects of its organization (Figure 3.2).

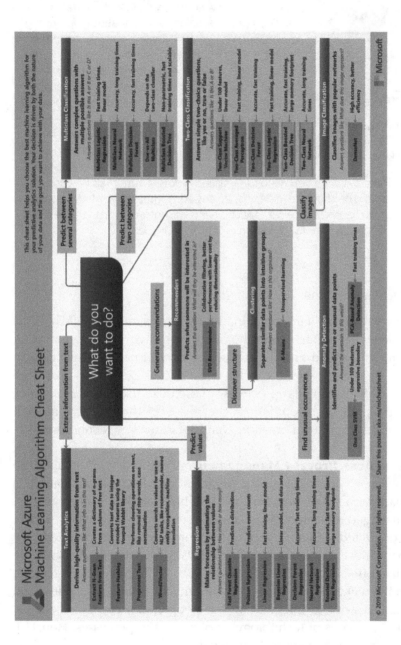

FIGURE 3.2 Choose the Right Algorithm

Source: © Microsoft. Used with permission from Microsoft Corporation. Azure Machine Learning Algorithm.
https://docs.microsoft.com/en-us/azure/machine-learning/algorithm-cheat-sheet.

Ralph Foorthuis,
Global Domain Architect Data, Heineken

"There is a wide variety of ways in which data science can be of practical value to organizations: optimizing logistics, analyzing data quality, seeking opportunities for new sales, understanding and predicting the world, detecting misbehavior, et cetera. However, there is also a wide variety of ways in which analytical applications can be implemented and employed. Therefore, regardless of whether you develop analytical solutions yourself or leverage them in the form of embedded functionality in procured software, it is important to understand their key assumptions and conditions. You need to familiarize yourself with their functionality and the way they have been developed, tested, optimized, and fed with data. This avoids that they remain a 'black box' and will ensure you can truly exploit data science solutions for your own organizational goals."

Intelligent Automation

This involves enabling a machine to perform simple repetitive tasks and teaching the machine to adapt and improve its performance at an incredible speed based on evolving conditions. Intelligent Automation, in simple words, can be described as a solution that digitally transforms business processes to organize users, systems, tasks, and robots (RPA) depending on the needs of the business at each moment. Intelligent Automation comprises four key technologies:

1. **Business Process Management.** A method used to optimize business processes in an organization. Every organization is based on processes, but there is no meaning if they are not managed efficiently. A process is a sequence of activities that are conducted by employees and the systems in an intended way to achieve a specific objective. IBPMS is an intelligent software that offers greater functionality such as content management, human interaction management, analytics, business rules, and connectivity to integrate all the people, devices, IT resources, and all types of technology involved in the processes. Hence, it acts as a base layer for organizations.

2. **Robotic Process Automation.** A technology that objectifies to reduce human intervention in IT applications. It aims to automate all the repetitive tasks, increasing employees' productivity because now they have more time to spend on essential tasks.
3. **Artificial Intelligence.** A technology that enables machines to imitate human intelligence. It comprises concepts like natural language processing, machine learning, and deep learning. In short, it analyzes historical data and deciphers patterns from it to make intelligent decisions, predict the future, and improve user experience.
4. **Integrations.** It is crucial to integrate system applications and products into your business processes to increase your organization's productivity and control. If you opt for custom programming to integrate them, it will become costly for you.

Automation has been with us since the Industrial Revolution; thus, as it has advanced, so has artificial intelligence. If we bring these two technologies together, automation can achieve the advantages supported by intelligence. Intelligent Automation enables us to transform vast amounts of data into insights, suggesting a possible course of action. As it is intelligent, it can track and automate work processes and can make choices and learn as it goes. Intelligent Automation can deliver significant reductions in cost, reducing manual intervention, reducing errors, giving better quality and higher satisfaction rate, which all leads to driving your organization's efficiency.

We are confronting a transformation with unimaginable advancements in AI, robotics, and automation, which is powering another intelligent automation era. Conclusively, intelligent automation has enormous potential for improving the average organization's performance and productivity, while being a game-changer for giant enterprises.

Moving from Reactive to Proactive with IoT Integration

More organizations than ever before are adapting their service business models toward proactive maintenance to reduce expensive on-site engineer visits, dramatically improving customer experience by putting in place controlled and insightful product feedback loops. The journey to predictive maintenance starts by connecting things, people, and information. The Internet of Things (IoT) is a technology that connects everyday objects, devices, and sensors to the Internet and captures huge amounts of telemetry from them. Field Service Operations have been leading this transformation to offer alternative approaches to customers from a perspective of service management. The primary aim is to generate and capture real-time data and develop a level of deep insight on that data that can be analyzed, understood, and used to drive business outcomes. Here is an example to help understand how real-time data analysis can help businesses.

Back in February 2020, Panasonic launched IoT-enabled air conditioners that consist of auto-diagnostic features that gather real-time data through their daily operational cycles. This data is collected and analyzed through real-time insights to identify potential anomalies in the data across a huge amount of data points. If issues are identified, a technician can be scheduled to attend to it before the product goes out of service or the customer becomes aware of the issue. This enables Panasonic to move from a reactive to a proactive service model.

Businesses require critical equipment to be running at peak efficiency and utilization to realize their return on capital investments. These assets could range from air conditioners, as described earlier, to aircraft engines, turbines, elevators, or industrial chillers—that cost millions—down to everyday appliances like photocopiers, coffee machines, or watercoolers.

We will now look at different levels of maintenance that business usually operates on and find what is the next level the business can move to with the use of IoT.

- By default, most businesses rely on *corrective maintenance*, where parts are replaced as and when they fail. Corrective maintenance ensures parts are used completely (therefore not wasting component life), but costs the business in downtime, labor, and unscheduled maintenance requirements (off hours or inconvenient locations).
- At the next level, businesses practice *preventive maintenance*, where they determine the useful lifespan for a part and maintain

or replace it before a failure. Preventive maintenance avoids unscheduled and catastrophic failures, but the high costs of scheduled downtime, underutilization of the component before its full lifetime of use, and labor remain.

- The goal of *predictive maintenance* is to optimize the balance between corrective and preventative maintenance, by enabling *just in time* replacement of components. This approach only replaces those components when they are close to a failure. By extending component lifespans (compared to preventive maintenance) and reducing unscheduled maintenance and labor costs (over corrective maintenance), businesses can gain cost savings and competitive advantages.

Today, more organizations are opting for Microsoft solutions like Dynamics 365 and Power Platform than ever before. This combination across the connected business cloud brings unified data and applied intelligence together in a way that enables customers to take proactive decisions that positively influence their business outcomes. The Internet of Things is an enabling technology that helps drive digital transformation. A primary concern of organizations is how the IoT platform they invest in delivers security, scalability, data connectivity, and data insights across a multitude of end points and a massive amount of data. To address these issues, Microsoft delivers several highly scalable IoT SaaS capabilities, such as IoT Hub and IoT Central. They help organizations to build enterprise-grade IoT applications swiftly, providing high-level security along with local availability and reliability, alongside the global scale of Microsoft Azure. They also deliver IoT best practices, empowering every organization to benefit from transformational IoT.

As IoT evolves, organizations can quickly scale to millions of end points from a start point of a few connected devices. For this purpose, organizations need an enterprise-grade IoT solution setup that can be achieved with prebuilt capabilities that Microsoft Azure IoT delivers. In this way, they can save time, save cost, and find the skills needed to build a powerful IoT solution. It makes it easier for enterprises to plan their IoT investments and achieve their IoT goals. Azure IoT delivers capabilities and functionality across many typical end-to-end scenarios, including telemetry ingestion, device management, command & control, rule-based alerts, and rich visualization.

Let us look into each one of these individually:

- **Telemetry Ingestion.** Every device that has a sensor on it generates telemetry data. Evaluating this data is the essence of driving toward the delivery of a companies' service-aligned business outcomes. For example, in the industrial business, it is essential to compare the temperature of each machine to the average temperature of others; it could help an operator identify the risks of failure and would be able to perform predictive maintenance. However, for this to happen, businesses need telemetry data from hundreds or thousands of connected devices. More importantly, they need to analyze this data to provide valuable insights and visualizations. Hadoop, a "big data" framework, creates a solid data-processing foundation that can scale up alongside the installed base of devices.
- **Device Management.** Azure IoT Central manages devices by monitoring the temperature of all those connected. When a connected device's temperature exceeds a threshold, it sends notifications.
- **Command Control.** Azure IoT Central uses Azure CLI for command control. Azure CLI (Command-Line Interface) delivers a set of rules and commands to create and manage Azure resources. Azure CLI comprises two parts—Azure CLI core and Azure IoT CLI extension. Azure CLI **core** concentrates on configuration and infrastructure management; for example, configuring IoT Hub message routes and IoT Hub CRUD operations. However, Azure IoT CLI **extensions** offer valuable features and functionality to control, manipulate, and interact with the data, objects, and entities on the infrastructure itself.
- **Rule-Based Alerts.** Azure IoT empowers users to create a specific set of rules based on conditions to drive actions. These rules are based on device telemetry or events.
- **Rich Visualization.** To analyze historical data and telemetry data, Azure IoT provides rich analytics capabilities that can help you drive valuable insights. To monitor your IoT device's

performance, you can also use Power BI Solutions for Azure IoT to create a compelling Power BI dashboard. The dashboard can help you analyze data per device, compare data volumes between different streams, filter data sent by specific devices, and view the most recent data.

Azure IoT empowers customers to immediately onboard devices, ingest telemetry, build KPI dashboards, perform remote maintenance, and even integrate with third-party solutions.

Azure IoT is a cloud-hosted service that acts as a message exchange application between IoT devices and Azure to enable bidirectional communication. It is highly secure and offers to connect with any device virtually. Authentication of each device can happen independently at the device management level, allowing for elevated security while still enabling IoT devices to scale.

Azure IoT Edge is another SaaS capability that expands the public cloud capabilities to extend Azure IoT Hub by allowing IoT devices to interact with an "edge node" of a given area. It can run edge-optimized services such as Azure Stream Analytics, Azure Functions, and Azure SQL Edge as modules. By moving certain workloads to the edge of the network, your devices spend less time communicating with the cloud, react more quickly to local changes, and operate reliably, even in extended offline periods.

The applications and opportunity for connected IoT and field service are boundless. Imagine a car's engine management systems sending data back to the manufacturer or a breakdown service to provide them with the capability to deliver a completely new service offering to their customers. Or imagine an offshore oil and gas drilling rig sending data to the service engineer about the fault detected in the shaft or sending data about the engineer finishing the shift and handing over to the next service engineer with details of all faults along with images.

The capabilities of combining all MSFT technologies are limitless using the IoT Hub with Dynamics 365 Finance and Operation or with Dynamics 365 Customer Service, Sales integrating with Power Apps enabling your business to be proactive and optimizing performance and efficiency at every aspect of your business.

Mark Gerban,
Digital Partnerships,
Mercedes-Benz AG

"Over the past decade, IoT as we know it today was a solution looking for a problem, and generally experienced a prolonged infancy stage. As we are now seeing exponential growth in the segment, IoT is playing a bigger role in the advancement of 'smart' devices, such as watches, appliances, automobiles, and various everyday objects. Consumers and businesses are now finding real-world practicality, where IoT actively enables multi-channel health monitoring, automated inventory and resource management, real-time quality-control feedback, and a multitude of other scenarios. We are only beginning to scratch the surface, but it is clear that beneficial change will one day be democratized for everyone."

Improving Experiences with Chatbots and Natural Language Processing

In recent times and more during the pandemic crisis, there has been a proliferation of chatbots on commerce websites. The acceptance of these chatbots by users has been mixed and the reception is largely due to how well the bot programming has been done. The chatbot features have transformed customer experience of web users through personalized greetings and responding to personalized query, thus increasing the web user retention rate.

Another part of the Microsoft powered toolkit is the Power Virtual Agents. Along with aspects of the Microsoft Power Platform, it continues the call to the citizen developer. No longer is the development of chatbots the domain of software developers or data scientists, but now the citizen developer can get into the act. Who better to drive development of chatbots but the key users themselves, be it the customer service team or service managers? The appealing feature of the Power Virtual agents is that it is a low-code solution without the need for programmers or people with artificial intelligence skills. The advantage to this is twofold; first is that deployment of development is quicker and second the rectification of chatbot issues is quicker as well, because essentially these are managed by subject matter experts, reducing the dependencies on IT.

Having the key stakeholders driving the development via Power Virtual agents means that you can have more accurate answers being developed to questions that only come from the key users who possess the specific expertise. For example, follow-up questions can be developed with the appropriate scenarios. Take, for example, a chatbot that is developed within the HR system. An employee goes into the HR system to ask how much vacation leave they have. The chatbot responds with a factual answer but then the very nature of the initial question raised by the employee leads the chatbot to ask a further question as to whether they wish to apply for vacation leave. Another example during the recent pandemic is the use of chatbots by the Airways Authority allowing customers to ask queries related to flight cancellation, and boosting confidence.

Every decade we see a phenomenal change in industry and its revolution. The main objective for decades has been to bridge the gap between humans and computers using natural language processing (NLP). Today, asking questions or commanding home devices to perform a specific action is a widespread phenomenon. NLP's basic concept was to understand different dialectics, languages, accents, new slang terms used commonly, regional idioms, etc. Building a chatbot for business is a very straightforward process. The IA/AI chatbots can record and track the data and questions being asked.

Microsoft currently provides two technologies to develop chatbots: the Microsoft Bot Framework and the Power Platform's Power Virtual Agent. Both chatbot development engines have different purposes and different communication channels, such as Microsoft Teams and Skype. Both are equally important to an organization. If you offer access to a low-code chatbot, you enable companies to focus on their core business.

The introduction prompt to a user while starting a conversation is the same in both technologies. Also, there is a workflow to handle queries, user input, exception handling, and intensification to a human for further assistance.

Microsoft's Power Platform technology classifies them into topics, actions, and details. They can run queries like select/insert/update statements into databases. Eventually, these bots are trying to translate human language into action. Next, we will look at the platform differences. The Bot Framework uses Azure Cognitive Services. It has some AI capabilities that are available when defining actions. The Power Virtual Agent can support the integration of the Dataverse. All the stored entities of Dynamics 365 products can be attainable via a query and parsed into variables for workflow consideration.

Apart from chatbots, NLP can manage IoT workflows using devices such as the Microsoft Kinect. Using Azure Cognitive Services, we can drive contextual knowledge to communications.

Today, the technology capabilities in the form of NLP, ML/AI, and chatbots are available for the business to assess and make an informed decision on what business challenge needs to be resolved.

Summing Up

The capabilities of the Microsoft Power Platform combining with Power BI, AI/IA, IoT, and chatbots empower you to drive your business organization efficiently through continuous innovation, enabling you to take rapid and informed decisions on your strategy, whether it is related to new opportunities for growth or enhancing customer experience in the existing or new target market. You have a single glass pane view of your customer, market, services, supply chain, finance, and operation that allows you to be agile and scalable with any change in the market situation.

We have looked at various capabilities of the Power Platform, but it is not recommended to implement all capabilities at one time. Digital transformation is successful when it is treading with pace, a program roadmap is built with an outcome and benefit at each stage, empowering employees in this journey, and adopting new technologies.

"Creativity is contagious, pass it on."

—Albert Einstein

Digital Future Checklist

✓ Understand the capabilities and key components of the Power Platform.

✓ Key concept of Citizen Developer.

✓ Identify business challenges for quick and rapid solution using the Power Platform.

✓ How Power BI can help leadership and management decisions.

✓ Introducing IoT and AI/IA with examples from business.

✓ How chatbots are helping to drive customer engagement.

Customer Stories

ETIHAD REACHES NEW HEIGHTS WITH MICROSOFT DYNAMICS 365 AND CUSTOMER SERVICE OMNICHANNEL CAPABILITIES

Challenge

Etihad Airways is committed to create seamless customer experiences and put traveller needs at the heart of its innovation strategy. Their key motivation is to be as close to the customer as possible. Etihad developed an omnichannel strategy based on Microsoft Dynamics 365 Customer Service and wanted to offer all information via a single point of contact.

The COVID pandemic situation forced Etihad Airways to promptly rework their original plan. Their call centers were running over capacity, but it was crucial that they were able to communicate to their customers directly.

Solution

Etihad Airways enabled the live chat channel in Dynamics 365 Omnichannel, where customers can ask a question and have agents supporting them in English and Arabic 24/7 across the globe. Customers can go to the website, ask any question, and be sure to get an answer in around 2 minutes. By providing the capability to solve queries in a flash, the airline boosted travelers' confidence throughout the crisis. Etihad Airways was probably the first airline in the Middle East region to use live chat for wellness queries and provide travelers with official, verified answers.

Outcome and Benefits

"We have put traveller needs at the heart of our innovation strategy. To engage with our clients across their preferred channels, we have deployed Microsoft Dynamics 365 with Omnichannel for Customer Service, enabling a live chat service solution for greater customer experience and a swift response time. During COVID-19, it was absolutely crucial to be able to talk to our customers directly using the chat solution that allowed us to gain on the customer experience while also saving money."

Nikhil Rajkumar Gandhi, Customer Relationship Management Product Owner.
Reprinted with permission. Despite all challenges and reworking on the original plan during COVID-19, Etihad Airways have managed to engage with their clients across their preferred channels.

Etihad Airways have achieved:

- Close to 96% satisfied customers
- Thousands of monthly customer engagements
- 2.2 average parallel chat sessions per agent

G&J PEPSI LEVERAGING THE CAPABILITIES OF LOW-CODE POWER APPS DRIVEN BY POWER AUTOMATE INTEGRATING WITH POWER BI SOLVING BUSINESS CHALLENGES

Challenge

G&J Pepsi-Cola Bottlers is the largest family-owned business and operated Pepsi franchise bottler, with more than 1,600 employees at 13 different locations in Ohio and Kentucky, including production facilities in Lexington and Winchester, Kentucky, and in Columbus and Portsmouth, Ohio.

G&J Pepsi-Cola's business cannot have empty shelves and lose to their competition; they wanted to streamline their business and be efficient in their business operation.

In 2019, G&J Pepsi-Cola identified the challenge with their sales budgeting process, which was time-consuming, inaccurate, and not rolling up to the company's financial reporting.

G&J Pepsi-Cola has around 70 to 80 trucks running out of the building and they have 100 different parking spots. With all trucks looking the same, it was difficult for their drivers to deliver their customers within a small window.

G&J Pepsi-Cola also engages in a lot of community work and wants to support those who share the same passion. It is even more pertinent to be able to reach out to the community and to help rapidly during the COVID pandemic situation.

Solution

G&J Pepsi-Cola has leveraged the capabilities of Power Apps, Power Automate, and Power BI. They did not have to rely on external consultants or professional developers. With the low-code platform of PowerApps, their business employees have resolved many business challenges.

Store Audit App was used to identify the trends of strengths and weaknesses about their business, adjusting the strategy where they needed to go to market, identify where the business is executing against the strategy, and need improvement in their execution.

Parking App was a solution created to help warehouse and sales team assign parking spots and drivers to receive the information about the parking spot once they login to their app in the morning.

When Microsoft first launched Power Apps, G&J Pepsi went live with their first application in November 2016.

Integrating Power Apps with Microsoft Teams, G&J Pepsi can respond to community information rapidly whilst transforming and evolving the data in Dynamics 365.

G&J Pepsi-Cola was working on implementing Dynamics 365 (Sales and Field Service) in 2021.

Outcome and Benefits

"We are amazed at how quickly we can put things together with Microsoft Power Platform. And we're in control of our own destiny using a low-code solution to create professional, user-first apps. During the pandemic, we have helped HR to track COVID-related information and reporting through Power BI bridging the gap and giving an insight to the management team."

Dan Foster, Director of Digital Technology. Reprinted with permission

"We always have a host of other initiatives around collaboration, cybersecurity, and networks. We can focus on all those things while also building applications with Power Apps and Power Automate and we do not have to rely on outside consultants or developers."

Eric McKinney, Enterprise Business Systems Manager. Reprinted with permission

G&J Pepsi-Cola has achieved:

- Savings of $500,000 in their first year
- Overall savings of $1.5 million so far and growing
- Tapping the value of integration, continuing to move work loads into the connected platform
- Saved the company an estimated $100,000 in outside development costs
- Increase in employee satisfaction
- Empowered our team hiring internally and increased our team size threefold

HEATHROW AIRPORT INSPIRES EMPLOYEE ENGAGEMENT WITH MICROSOFT POWER APPS

Challenge

Heathrow Airport could almost qualify as a small city. Every day, 76,000 people go to work at one of Europe's busiest airports to facilitate the travel needs of more than 80 million passengers. These passengers could be headed almost anywhere, as Heathrow serves more than 200 destinations in 84 countries. Orchestrating logistics at this magnitude takes a lot of doing, and Heathrow is constantly looking for ways to optimize its operations.

Solution

By exploring many aspects of Microsoft Office 365, Microsoft Power Apps and its capabilities of being a cost-effective solution was discovered by Samit Saini, IT Solution Specialist of Heathrow Airport. This was the beginning of self-empowerment, growth mindset, and motivating factor within the employees of Heathrow Airport innovation, which has led to a business problem-solving culture and building of many apps: Safe Not-Safe App, Security Equipment App, Insurance Claims App, Passenger Service App, End of Shift Report App, Crew Compliance App, Acornymaid (jargon-buster) App, Site Vsit Pre-check App, and Vehicle Search App.

Outcome and Benefits

"Microsoft Power Apps gives everyone the ability to build apps. Completing a project like that gives people a sense of accomplishment. It certainly has for me. With Power apps it doesn't matter what your background is. This will help you open up your mind to new things."

Samit Saini, IT Solution Specialist, Heathrow Airport

With Power Apps, the user community at Heathrow has done the following:

- Developed and released 30 apps with more on the way.
- Eliminated 75,000 pages of paperwork overall and reduced data entry by nearly 1,000 hours.
- Vehicular Security App saves security personnel approximately 8,000 to 10,000 sheets of paper each month.
- Power apps applications currently deployed at Heathrow save their colleagues 950 working hours and 75,000 sheets of paper each year, which equals nine trees.
- Seen a shift in the change of culture and encouraged a culture of creative problem solving among the airport's first-line employees.

- Employees feel self-empowered and have grown personally and professionally.
- Saving of £300,000 in staff costs.

TIVOLI GARDENS USES DYNAMICS 365 CUSTOMER INSIGHTS TO DESIGN VISITOR EXPERIENCES THAT ENCOURAGE LONGER STAYS AND MORE VISITS

Challenge

Tivoli, also known as Tivoli Gardens, is one of the oldest amusement parks in the world, located in Copenhagen, Denmark, and the second most visited park in Europe, after Europa Park. Initially, the park opened its doors on 15 August 1843 and today is hosting more than 4.6 million visitors per year, offering rides, pantomimes, concerts, and other attractions to its young and adult guests. Regardless of their success and global reach, Tivoli's managing directors always had an innovative vision and a proactive approach toward the future of Tivoli Gardens. Based on this foundation, they shaped the new strategy supported by the powerful tools of Dynamics 365 Customer Insights, Dynamics Power BI, and AI functionalities.

In 2019, a period of high performance, customer satisfaction, and financial performance, Tivoli's management team decided to take important strategic decisions regarding how they offer their services to their visitors. Their main aim was to replace the annual pass by offering a new "Tivoli pass" in a subscription-based model, which would automatically be renewed and charged yearly or monthly. The main purpose of shifting toward a subscription-based model is to improve customer loyalty, provide a seamless customer experience, and reduce churn rate. This new service model would holistically offer a new improved digital experience to Tivoli's regular visitors and, most importantly, offer Tivoli a 360-degree view of their customers, their needs, and their preferences.

Solution

Tivoli's management team had a very clear vision of what they wanted to achieve, but one of the most important aspects to consider was ensuring that they could collect as much data as possible from their customer and translate this valuable information into shaping a new future strategy. The realization of their strategy was not a straight line, taking into consideration the situation they faced with their data and existing systems. Tivoli has had a plethora of their client data spread among multiple non-connected applications, meaning that it couldn't be used most optimally. To achieve their goals, I envisioned the capabilities of artificial intelligence with machine learning, both functionalities offered by Dynamics 365 Customer Insights. With the use of Dynamics 365 Sales and Service applications, Tivoli's service desk employees could easily record customer's data into a unified database and monitor customers' interactions on a timeline. By taking advantage of the AI capabilities, they would be able to predict visitor churn, the likelihood of visiting certain attractions, customer engagement, and their demographic segmentation. Based on this powerful knowledge, the Marketing and IT team utilizing the Machine Learning and Dynamics 365 Customer Insights Power BI functionalities would be able to personalize the communication and experience for their guests and optimize guest experience based on data and deep insights.

Outcome and Benefits

"Dynamics 365 Customer Insights brings data to life. We can finally harness the data for insights, without the need for bespoke integration or specialized resources. The packaged solution, with artificial intelligence and machine learning, enables us to quickly and easily unify customer data scattered across multiple systems, unlock insights, and in turn empower each of our 2,500 employees to delight our guests in person and via digital touchpoints."

Bernt Bisgaard Caspersen, Head of Solution Team & Architecture, IT

Tivoli managed to unify its visitors' data, record visitor logs, and feedback into a unified customer data platform (CDP). Consequently, this added extreme value to the efficiency and effectiveness of the marketing activities.

Also, with the use of Power BI reports, all internal stakeholders managed to have a clear vision of their revenue, customer preferences, and needs—all valuable data to allow them to make better and more effective decisions for Tivoli's future operations.

Tivoli Gardens has achieved:

■ Marketers have had fresh and accurate insights to personalize digital communications and actions toward improving customer engagement and loyalty.

- Using Dynamics products and subscription-based model led to aggregated customer data, capable of improving the accuracy of predictions toward returning guests and eliminating manual error.
- Receive a real-time 360-degree view of each Tivoli guest.
- Build a solid foundation to be used for personalized communication at all digital touchpoints aiming to improve engagement and loyalty.
- Using the power of AI to predict and proactively predict and react to the needs of each guest.

Blueprint for Executing a Successful Dynamics 365 Project

Part II provides the blueprint for executing a successful Dynamics 365 program or project. It starts with establishing five cornerstones of digital transformation with some practical examples. This part also defines preparing a program, selecting an implementation partner, and preparing for all shifts in the future state. Another key element of the digital transformation journey is change management; hence this part provides an analytical view on this subject. It discusses the key governance framework that needs to be established from the very beginning. The part ends with real-life customer stories from organizations on their business challenges, solutions, and the benefits they have achieved.

Chapter 4: This chapter defines five cornerstones of digital transformation and how one needs to prepare before starting their digital transformation journey. It helps identify essential areas within the organization that need to be taken care of and provides a governance framework that will enable you to control the entire journey step-by-step.

Chapter 5: This chapter shows that leading a digital transformation program with Microsoft Dynamics 365 and Microsoft Power Platform is no different from leading any other digital program or project. It also describes how communication across the board, having clarity on roles and responsibilities, identifying risk factors, and choosing the right implementation partner for an organization mixed with the right combination of people and process is the key to success of a successful program.

Chapter 6: This chapter shows that the importance and the right balance of organizational change management is quite essential for digital transformation. Irrespective of your having a budget or not for change management, you should read this chapter to understand how to strike a balance. Finally, it provides an option you can consider for measuring user adoption.

Chapter 7: This chapter makes you aware of various ways of designing the solution and highlights the key design principle that needs to be considered. It also analyzes various methodologies and framework approaches and recommends one approach that accelerates the pace of solution build with key governing principles.

CHAPTER 4

Five Cornerstones of Digital Transformation

At any moment, the decision you make can change the course of your life forever.

—Anthony Robbins

In this chapter, we will explore the various shifts that we consider necessary before the transformation journey is fully synced within the organization. Understanding your organization is an integral part of the journey that precedes laying out your transformation roadmap. Gareth Morgan has metaphorically referred to organization in his pathbreaking book *Images of Organisation*[1] through different lenses—organization as machines, organization as organisms, organizations as brains, organization as cultures, organization as political systems, organizations as psychic prisons, organizations as flux and transformation, and organizations as instruments of domination. We will take you through five cornerstones of the transformation program that are linked to understanding your organization.

Strategic Shift

Is your digital transformation part of your strategic plan or is it instead of it? Any business needs to know where it is going and why, and what will be the benefit. This could be using the concepts of organic or acquisitional growth, vertical or horizontal integration, or a more modern approach of innovate and test. Whatever your plan, for most companies a digital transformation is likely to be needed at some point if you are to survive.

However, there has to be a "why?" and if you are to be competitive it must not just be "to keep up with the competition." Most importantly, if you are to succeed in your digital transformation, the reason has to be based on your customer. The digital revolution has shortened the distance between the CEO and the customers and future business. No modern company that has been ultimately successful (e.g., Google, Facebook, Apple, Amazon, Microsoft, Vanguard, Tencent, Alibaba, eBay, PayPal, Uber, AirBnB) has grown by ignoring their customers. Google's strategy and growth have been entirely based around the ease of use and speed of response of the company to the customer's unstated needs. What they do all have in common is the desire to make the customer's interface with the company convenient, faster, and easier. It is this aspect that your digital transformation must aim to achieve.

As a transforming and forward-thinking board of directors, you need to be released from the bonds of old-style business. You need to be encouraging the entire company to consider the easiest, most efficient, and most repeatable ways your customers will be buying from you. This applies to retail, manufacturing, charity, technology, business-to-business, government, and so on. Because that is the way the direction of travel is going. Expending massive effort getting your internal systems to work for you is a waste of your time and resources. For this reason, it is critical that you understand your processes and direction and utilize your effort early in getting the systems to be as transparent and understandable as possible so that your company can concentrate on the customer. Set your vision and work hard in the transformation to release the company from the bonds of your ERP (or any other) system. Get the processes clear, automated, and homogenized as much as possible, apply people to the outliers that cost money, and get on with making your customer have such an easy time dealing with you that they cannot stop ordering.

Once you know what you want to achieve for your customers, work backwards. Explain the vision to the executive team. Get their buy-in and start their thinking on how they will engage the resource in their departments to improve the customer experience. Explain to the people in the organization that this is a journey. Communicate the vision and the reasons for that vision. Ask for their help with ideas and be prepared to nurture people's ideas with time and resources. Explain why the digital transformation is needed and what is intended from it. Communicate the outcome and also reassure people that this is not about cutting costs but about making time for the customers. As the improvements take hold, release people's time to work on customer-focused projects and make this available in every team and department in the company. You will be surprised what comes out of this.

Communication with everyone working in your organization is absolutely key. Keep people informed, show how the small steps forward make a big difference in the long term. Explain compounding (multiple tiny steps forward at the beginning lead to massive improvements later on). Encourage feedback on the process and explain the 80/20 rule so the nitpickers understand why moving forward even when everything is not perfect is still efficient. It is better to try and partially succeed than not to try at all. Remember that customers are people too and that means all the people in your organization are customers; they can help you get better, so involve them, encourage them, inform them, and protect them. It is a well-known fact that it is much cheaper to keep a customer than to get a new one. This also applies to employees. Keeping them in the dark, treating them badly, ignoring them, and generally annoying them will eventually make them leave and your company will fail, customer or employee. Conversely, informing them, encouraging them, engaging them, and keeping them happy will lead to more of them, customer or employee. Align your digital transformation with business strategy as your first cornerstone.

Cultural Shift

"Culture eats strategy on breakfast," a phrase originated by Peter Drucker,[2] is an absolute reality, and a cultural shift is the second cornerstone that we will explore in this section. Company cultures are like family ones; they have a great many influences and a lot of history. Finding the underlying culture of either takes introspection, honesty, and open-mindedness. There are plenty of companies and individuals out there who will come in and help you determine the culture, but are they going to confirm what you already know or tell you something completely different? You should have some idea and it should be based on facts rather than your own observations.

Do you know what the prevailing culture in your company is?

You might think you do, and you may be right, but what tells you? Here are some suggestions on how you could go about looking for the information:

- Look up ex-employee ratings for your company on websites such as Glassdoor, LinkedIn, and greatplacetowork.com.
- Observe (with an open mind). Go to the canteen, coffee machine, or near the watercooler, spend a little while there from time to time, travel on some of the commuter routes into your offices, walk around your office areas and talk to people—especially early morning and late afternoon/evening. A cheery "good morning" or "have a good evening" is worth a lot to people but also gives you the option of asking why they are in so early/late and learning something.
- Be aware of your own style; you will find that this influences others more than you think. Also discuss the culture of the executive team; again, this will be influencing the rest of the organization, particularly the departments people are heading up.
- Survey your employees or set up a cross-departmental group that can feed in information on the current culture. You can also set it tasks on how to change the culture.

Do your managers exhibit the cultures and values you want?

Once you have an idea of what the current culture is, look at your managers. Are they displaying this culture? Do you want this to continue and, if not, how are you going to encourage change? Cultural behaviors or practices are often habitual, so can you identify the triggers for the habits that people display and, if so, how do you influence these?

A key issue for managers is often training. So often they are promoted because they do a good job but then have no training on how to manage. Is this the case in your organization? One key piece of training is to explain that the way they behave influences their team members. You can give them all the theory on management you like but if they feel that bullying or cajoling their staff gets the best out of them, then the culture will be going down the drain.

There are plenty of management training schemes out there—get your HR department to find some that train on how to manage people as well as how to influence culture. Basic is fine—the latest fad is not. Be consistent, with the same training for all; there is nothing worse than a manager who regularly gets trained on the latest idea and comes back to change everything. Use the same training for all managers for five years and then review. Management philosophy and trends do not change that much, and dealing with people is a skill everyone should learn as it is less about management and more about human interaction. Ideally, send everyone on management training and then they all know what to expect.

Have you looked at what other people say about your company?

Customers, suppliers, and consultants all see different sides to your organization, and all have key insights. Ask them what they think. You should be getting your customers to give feedback, but are you asking your suppliers and consultants for theirs also?

Simple questionnaires are one method, but current suppliers and consultants may feel restricted by a desire to stay working with your company. Try instituting exit interviews for anyone leaving you and also make them anonymous as much as possible. The simplest structure would be the three questions as follows:

1. What should we stop doing?
2. What should we start doing?
3. What should we keep doing?

I would add an additional one:

4. If there is one thing about our culture you would change, what would it be?

Culture is not just about an internal culture; it is also about how your culture is viewed externally. There is a view that as individuals we are happiest and most able to deal with the things that life throws at us if the following overlap as much as possible:

- How we see ourselves
- How others see us
- How we think others see us

The same applies to a business with one notable difference—it is about whether the company is perceived as caring for itself and its customers. Therefore, the circles are as follows (see Figure 4.1):

- How the company treats its customers, suppliers, and staff
- How its customers, suppliers, and staff perceive they are treated
- How the company thinks they treat their customers, suppliers, and staff

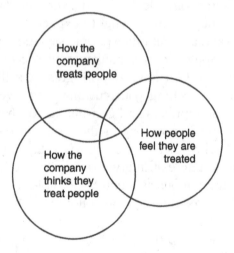

FIGURE 4.1 Identify the Blind Spot

The ideal position is for them all to overlap and this is where your digital transformation needs to be used. There is a difference between how people are treated by a company and how people in the company think people are treated; for example, you may have a focus on treating new customers well but no effort is put into keeping customers in the long term. This will show itself in a disconnect between the company thinking it treats customers well but your staff and customers thinking that they are treated badly over time.

You need to know both how you are perceived by the customer and the reality of how you actually treat the customer so that you can work on getting the greatest overlap possible.

Do you read (or even have) exit Texts?

Exit Texts are an opportunity to find out from people who know your company well and no longer have any reason to be less than honest to tell you what they think of how the company treats all their stakeholders. They can give you key insights into how you really treat your staff, your customers, and your suppliers. You may feel that asking questions of an obviously disillusioned employee is counterproductive, but your biggest critics may have the unvarnished insights into what really happens in your organization.

These are all ways to find out where your culture is now, so you know how far you need to go, who you need to influence, and how you can influence. None of this is of great importance, but if you don't have the capacity and goodwill in your people, you will not be able to start these changes. We will look this at in the next section.

Sebastian Kister,
Platform Owner
Kubernetes & Public
Clouds, Audi AG

"Two things are so important when you want to move forward as a team, no matter how big it is. First of all, you need a team. Second of all you want it to communicate the most transparent way with each other. A team can be small or even an entire enterprise, but what are we seeing in the 'big enterprise world' and even small/medium enterprises—a bunch of silos mostly avoiding accountability and responsibility and thus errors. Only when we started accepting that we all do errors but then we make sure to learn from them, we encourage transparency and avoid going into the wrong directions for too long, making the error exponentially expensive. If your organization thinks in silos like a plan-build-run organization, your digital product won't survive customer contact. Your organization needs to understand they all share the responsibility. Everyone is a part of it. Knowledge-sharing and consulting across the entire lifecycle is the key to change an organization and to really live up to the shared responsibility concept. But how do we get there? Passion is the key to knowledge-sharing. In organizations where most IT knowledge consists of pushing specifications through a more than annoying purchase process it is pure magic to see the sparkling eyes of your team members when they finally contributed something for real to the product that they actually own. When putting processes over people because enterprises in many cases falsely believed standardizing and centralizing helps them to scale, they lost their team members and all of their potential creativity. They generated a generation of purchasers instead of innovators. Now they need to face the past errors and move on. But no transformation happens overnight. In enterprises we now do create germ cells in the organizations and a safe environment in which to grow. We now convince with quality, not decisions, we pitch MVPs and we give full end2end accountability and responsibility to the product teams and give them space to grow. Basically, we create start-ups wherever we find it beneficial for the customers' needs. What happens next? We create a generation of passionate people who love to share what they are doing. They inspire and motivate the projects and people they work with along the line and that is exactly the foundation of change.

The unstoppable upheaval in digital product development is driven very much by one factor in particular: time-to-market. You cannot expect product lifecycles of several years to survive the first customer contact. That is why it is so important to work with the MVP approach, to build, to measure, and to learn from it. Let the early adopters in on the development and get to know the customer better with each iteration. That is what start-ups do in the tech world. Why are enterprises not also able to do so? Because they specialized in creating silos and thus destroyed the ability and agility to move fast due to overhead communication, loss of clear responsibility, and too many hands over milestones where knowledge won't be transferred accordingly. The end2end responsibility of so-called product teams is what gives them a foundation to work like a start-up in that regard. If they fail, they fail fast, learn, and try again. If they succeed, they move fast, iterate, and improve. Give your teams accountability and responsibility and they will own the products."

Shift in People's Mindset

Our interactions with people are affected to a large extent in how we perceive them, how they operate in their role, and how they interact with others. People are an organization's asset and the third cornerstone of a transformation program.

Do you have resources and capability in-house to spend educating the implementation partner? Are you considering back-filling your employees, reducing workloads from their day-to-day job, and making their time available for digital transformation? Or are you running really lean? Check staffing baselines with similar companies. In-flight projects, can they be completed faster, put on hold, or canned completely? Have you assessed your internal resource capabilities and identified strengths that can be utilized for the digital transformation program? Do you have the data of your resource utilization across different business units or departments? How effectively does your organization manage resources?

If you said no to some of the questions above, start with baselining and mapping skillsets. Otherwise, I am assuming you have all the data in hand to move on to the next section of identifying gaps.

Baselining and Mapping Skillset

You might already have a skillset list for your organization. Please review the skillset and map with a standard framework, which are soft skills that may be required for the project. Here is a list of pointers provided to help you map the skillset.

- List the skills you think you need; make them real skills specific to you and your project. Some, such as the Skills Framework for the Information Age (SFIA)[3] for IT, can give you a framework but are meaningless in this context.
- Ask your teams to add any skills they think you have missed.
- Don't forget the soft skills (assertiveness, for example, skills with people).
- Get people to grade themselves.
- Correct their gradings (see below).
- Talent profiles and succession plans.
- Look for the gaps.
- Ask people what they do for hobbies and what they see as their most recent achievement outside of work. You will be surprised what people are doing and often find skills in people you did not know they had.
- Softer skills such as decision making, collaboration, and comfort with change and pace should be mapped.

Gradings

What skill levels do your people have in the areas you need? Ask your staff what they think their skill levels are. Then sense-check and try to correct them if overestimated or underestimated.

Gaps

Look internally before externally as now is the time to keep people if you can; you do not want to be losing experience, knowledge, and history if you can avoid it. There are people who think a cleanout is a good thing, but unless the people going are disruptive or unpleasant to work with, it is better to keep as many of your current team as possible. You want a stable, committed team who can help each other and the partner, to get a good start on the project as soon as they can. Then consider training; are there people who could fill the gaps you have with a little training? However, also be aware that you are going to have to back-fill people as you elevate or redeploy within the organization. These opportunities can often be very powerful motivators for teams, and ambitions can be harnessed to drive adoption.

If you find you cannot fill the gaps, you need to identify the roles that are only going to exist for the project and get the third-party partner or contractors to fill these posts. Think about strategically important future roles, what the differentiators for the future are, where the intellectual property of the business or transformation is, and consider permanent skills and recruitment. Remember, the project will take time and you want to retain as many skilled people as possible. They will help you to resolve any short-term issues after the project goes live and will also be more efficient once you have gone live. The other reason you are best advised keeping, promoting, or offering redeployments is that you are showing your employees that you want them to stay through this change and you value them.

Avoiding Long-Term Overload

It is inevitable that there will be periods when the workload is more than the people available to do it. There are two ways to reduce this; employ more people, lengthen the project timeline, or make efficiencies. When overload areas are recognized, some things need to be decided:

- Is this a long-term (two years or more) increase in workload in this area?
- Can efficiencies be made in the systems to reduce the effort and how quickly?
- Is the time to make efficiencies likely to take more than three months?
- Can temporary staff be brought in to back-fill permanent staff?

If it is a yes to question 1, then employ more people.

If it is a yes to question 3, then it is imperative to find more resources, ideally through contingent resources. If you cannot bring in resources for any reason you will need to support the staff whose workload has significantly increased. This can be done through combinations of recognition, overtime, or extra pay, and by reducing less immediate important tasks.

Setting Expectations

It is important to recognize before you start a program of change that it will throw up challenges. If you can identify these challenges, it is worth making them clear to people before you start. In this way people will have an idea of what to expect. However, just listing them is not enough; you must also say what will be done to mitigate these when they arise. Just saying there will be more work and more stress is too negative; focus on the opportunities and on the benefits to people by all means, but add in practical efforts such as banning any recruitment freezes on temporary staff for any area affected by the change and making overtime a payable rather than time off in lieu. It could also be worth putting in additional staff benefits that will help manage stress, such as exercise classes, mindfulness sessions, and guaranteed lunch breaks to attend these. I have seen bans on meetings between 12:00 and 13:30 to allow staff free time.

Beginning Organizational Change Management

The reason for the failure of organizational change given most often is opposition from within. McKinsey estimates that 70% of change programs fail to achieve their goals, in large part due to employee resistance.[4] Keeping people engaged, consulted, and informed means they are more likely to be promoters of the change rather than resisters. Criticism of change is not resistance; it can be positive and should be such. In fact, you should be more cautious of blind acceptance as this can indicate people are not engaged and are therefore more likely to be passively resisting (a much more divisive and insidious form of resistance).

Change management used to be seen as something you did as a project; it had an idea, followed by a plan, then an implementation phase, and finally an outcome. However, a digital transformation, if done properly, is just the beginning of a journey to bring the organization and the customer closer (and closer) together. To do this there has to be organizational change and this is also going to be a journey. Consequently, the traditional change manager will need to evolve and move from a project style to a collaborative one. The change manager now needs to be finding ways to help people support the continuous changes needed to keep up, both with the customer and the technological and structural evolution we are all living through.

The consequence of the need for a digital transformation, and therefore organizational change management, is a need to engage with people at all levels and accept that the ideas do not only come from the top. There will be organizations that look for staffing efficiencies constantly, but these will be unable to make the changes needed to transform. The company that recognizes the most efficient way to move forward is to do it with their own people, allowing them to change the ways they work together, the levels of their collaboration, and the benefits to all of them of creative thinking is the one that will eventually be able to leverage the flexibility of their staff as and when change is needed. The 80/20 rule will apply, your staff will always be there for the 20% outliers, and your Dynamics 365 system will take care of the 80% of your business that consists of the more standard workload. If you can release your people to follow a directive of "there's a way to do it better, find it" while the Dynamics 365 system manages your enterprise resource planning, you (and more importantly, your customers) will benefit time and time again.

Organizational change management does not wait for the digital transformation but precedes it, often in small ways. A subject matter expert group brought together to cross-functionally discuss how to work better together and make suggestions for business improvements, an employee working group to look at the working environment and asked to make recommendations on collaborative working structures, a customer portal giving access to employees within the organization who can help solve any issues, and a supplier forum facilitated by employees to look at improving the ways of working together are all examples of organizational change initiatives.

John Kotter (1996), in *Leading Change*,[5] shared an eight-step process for powering change within a company. We have taken this model and illustrated the relevance of Kotter's model in today's organizational change management process in the following table and in Figure 4.2.

8 Step Change by Kotter	Relevance of Kotter's Model in Today's Organizational Change Management Process
Create a sense of urgency: Make other people in your company see the need for change as soon as possible.	**Create a sense of need:** Build a need for change in your company as soon as possible by engendering a sense of group purpose.
Build a guiding coalition: Recruit people most motivated by the need to change and delegate different roles to help enact the change.	**Build a guiding coalition:** Gather people most motivated by the need to change from all levels and areas of the organization and create groups to encourage change.
Create a strategic vision and initiatives: Tell your team members about the desired state and how it will benefit them as well as the company.	**Form a strategic vision and initiatives:** Explain to your team members about the desired state and how it will benefit their customers and them as well as the company.
Enlist a volunteer army: To get things moving, you need to mobilize a large number of people who agree with your vision.	**Enlist a volunteer army:** To get things moving, mobilize a large number of people who agree with your vision and empower them to promote change and changed thinking.

(Continued)

(Continued)

8 Step Change by Kotter	Relevance of Kotter's Model in Today's Organizational Change Management Process
Enable actions by removing barriers: Identify all the things that can stop you from realizing your vision, then eradicate them.	**Enable actions by removing barriers:** Encourage a culture of identifying all the things that can stop you from realizing your vision; encourage participation. Participation gives a sense of commitment and helps to eradicate some behaviors.
Create short-term wins: Each step should be a goal in itself. And as they are realized, reward your team for doing a good job.	**Generate short-term wins:** Every improvement should be a goal in itself. And as they are realized, reward your team and encourage the positive change habits.
Build on change: Don't lose steam after the first few successes. Use your team's new-found confidence from short-term wins to take the change to a higher level.	**Sustain acceleration:** Don't lose steam after the first few successes. Use your team's newfound confidence from short-term wins to take change and customer focus to a higher level.
Institute change: Once you have your desired state, make it a part of your organizational culture.	**Institute change:** Your desired state will include enabling and encouraging constant innovation and a relentless focus on the customer; make this a part of your organizational culture.

These are minor changes to Kotter's original but reflect the need for a habit of change in the organization and a relentless focus on the customer. The Dynamics 365 implementation you are planning for is a part of this and will help you to embed and automate those aspects of your business that repeat. The flexibility of Dynamics 365 will also permit you to make the changes that allow for the things that your internal and external customers want, and the continuous focus on giving them what they need.

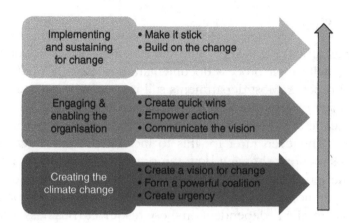

FIGURE 4.2 Eight-Step Change Model by John Kotter

Source: John P. Kotter, 1996, *Leading Change.* Boston: Harvard Business School Press, 1996.

"A great way to start improving your people's readiness is to create a Centre of Excellence. This is a central group (or groups) of people who are already recognized as subject matter experts in their own areas and can learn the cross-functional impacts their area has. These people will be the core to making sure that the digital transformation is supported, promoted, and successful."

**Cheryl
Bevelle-Orange,** IT
Director, FedEx

"A digital transformation will shift the power base of the organization as it empowers and enables the organization, which means that a culture change programme should be a keystone to the initiative. Without the commitment to change the culture of the organization a digital transformation is just another technology project."

Neal Sunners,
Interim CIO, DHL
Parcel

Process Shift

In our experience it is very often the case that organizations do not keep up with their process documentation or have not got a standardized process. Most departments still rely on new people learning how to run or input into the internal systems from another member of the team. It is rare for organizations to have a proper induction program, and even rarer for this to include process diagrams and work instructions showing how the organization wants or needs to have the job done or the team/department run. In some organizations, operation runs like a well-oiled machine by a group of people and you are highly dependent on these resources. Business processes are internal and as this is not billable client work, documenting the processes or even trying to standardize them comes as a low-end priority unless there is a bigger vision and goal to achieve or transform. You have guessed it right: shift in processes is our fifth cornerstone.

This is not to say these companies are not being run well at the moment, but they do not know whether they are or not, and they can not identify where efficiencies could be made unless an individual already doing a job pointed it out to them. This will not bode well for the future of any transformation program. Often it is also the case that team leaders do not know how their teams do the work, let alone department managers. This must not be the case when you are preparing for an ERP migration or upgrade and the consequent digital transformation.

How does this get resolved for 80% of the processes you are running? (Don't try to change, criticize, or improve these at this point. You need to know what you do now, and trying to make changes will stop this process dead in its tracks.) As discussed in Chapter 3, the following activities need to take place in order to get the processes well documented.

1. Get the people who do the work to write down what they do, step by step. This should involve every person, even if they perform the same task. Then a team leader or manager should review that they are all the same. If not, agree on the way everyone should do it and pass this process to step 2.

2. Get someone from another team to try to repeat this. If they can't, get them to sit with one or two people doing the work and rewrite the process so it can be followed.
3. Wherever there is a hand-off to someone else, write that into the document, and that person then also needs to write down their process (follow the same method as steps 1 and 2).
4. Gradually link all these processes together. Get someone in to map these, which is boring, and they don't need to know the process/in fact it is better that they don't), but they need to be accurate.
5. The managers and team leaders of the people doing these tasks then need to check that they are accurate. Where you have more than one person doing a specific task, they should all now be following the same method.
6. Once everyone in every department has completed this, you have nearly all your processes mapped (there may be some infrequent ones you miss).

Once you have these you will know how all the main business processes work. This is your starting point for improvement and for planning the transformation or transition to Dynamics 365.

Now that you know your current state, it is worth reviewing your strategic direction and setting some milestones. These can (and should) range from the specific, measurable, achievable, realistic, and time bound to the more general statements of intent, such as "within three years our Dynamics 365 transition will be complete and we will have started a program of customer engagement at every level of our business." These more general statements will then need to be firmed up as progress is made in the digital transformation process.

While your staff are critical to being able to implement the changed thinking, you will need to embed them as you transform your third-party partners, who will be important for the life of the ERP system. They will not only help you to make the best of the benefits of the system, but should also be part of the change process. Keeping your Dynamics 365 partner informed of the strategic plans and the short-, medium-, and long-term goals will ensure that they are aligned with your own thinking. They should then be helping you plan and con-figure the Dynamics 365 Finance & Operation and Dynamics 365 Customer Engagement systems in a way that fits with these future plans.

A good third-party partner will also be contributing to your flexible planning and staffing, but not spending all their time upselling you to increase their own profitability. Always be mindful of the importance of you controlling them and not the other way around.

One way to ensure that the third party is delivering is to ensure you give clear functional requirements when detailing the needs of the Dynamics 365 implementation or transition. Ensure that you are not trying to give solutions to them, as this is confusing and is often misinterpreted, but a combination of functional requirements in order of importance and expected outcomes (ideally in the form of test scenarios) will keep the various deliverables on track. Keeping your partners informed of the strategic direction and medium- to long-term plans will help to ensure that they call out any functional requirements that may clash with or slow down progress later (for example, a plan to merge companies that might require a different financial structure in Dynamics 365 at the start).

Once you have your current processes and you know where you are going, you will be able to put in place the plans based on the gap between the two. You have the internal resources and a third-party partner, you know what your end game is, and therefore you just need to plan out the gaps. This sounds simple but it often needs to be broken down much further. Often you are in danger of losing the internal support you have if you don't plan your requirements. This is because your people can see all the additional work coming their way or can see all the interesting work going to the third party and no plans to support or include them. With forethought and planning, however, this should not be the case and the risks of alienating your own people can be avoided. There are additional benefits to trying to ensure your staff are kept in the forefront of the planning process. They will be engaged for certain, but as you come toward milestones and deadlines if they can see that the next steps will bring benefits, they will ensure that these targets and the concomitant benefits are achieved.

Governance and Control

It will be impossible to keep on top of all the work that is being done to support a digital transformation. Like the matriarch of a large extended family, the admiral of the fleet, or a multinational CEO, the way to keep in touch with progress is by delegating control, with members empowered to make decisions. Governance and Control is our fifth and final cornerstone that will enable us to progress our digital transformation through various stage gates, steering groups, decision gates, and different forums for consultation and progress update. Anything else ages you and is counterproductive.

Your project or program director and manager will be guided by the governance set from the onset, as they build an iterative approach for everything starting from a review of the business processes, assessing impact, designing the solution and architecture, and building the solution. If this is too hands-off things may come as a surprise; if it is too overbearing it will slow progress and choke creativity in solutions. Largely reporting by exception once the project has begun should be sufficient for between-gate activities. At the gates, however, you will want to make sure everything is on track (there should be no surprises) or that you have all the possible information to hand to make decisions on next steps to correct the projects course.

Good governance will have the following elements:

- Agreement that the project governance is the responsibility of the management board, whether this sits at the executive level or elsewhere.
- Steering meetings are set up with the correct representation from the client organization and implementation partner.
- There are defined approval gates at which progress is reviewed and the project is approved to continue.
- All decisions made at the approval gates are logged and then communicated throughout the stakeholders and made available to the wider business.
- Risks (even if sensitive) are shared, managed, impact discussed, and mitigated across all levels as appropriate (the Architecture board to discuss risks associated with solution design and architecture, the Program board to discuss risks associated with the impact on cost, timeline).
- There are clearly defined roles, responsibilities, and accountabilities for the project governance.
- The business strategy and the project team are aligned through the governance board.

- The business case is supported by information that allows reliable decision making.
- There are processes to enable independent scrutiny of the project by the leadership.
- There is a culture of improvement and disclosure of the project progress.
- The project teams have the capability, resources, and authority to make appropriate decisions.
- Stakeholders are engaged at all levels and in a way that promotes trust and underlines their importance.
- Suitably qualified and experienced people are employed on the project and supported within it.
- The project management team can show they are adding value in all areas of the project and across the organization.

With proper governance in place, it will be much easier to have confidence in the progress of and information coming from the project. The gates are then the opportunity to direct and, if necessary, correct the course of the transformation based upon the strategic direction of the company. It is important to remember that any corrections must in themselves be carefully scrutinized. Changes partway through a project can add significant costs and make it difficult to control the budget properly, and can also have the effect of confusing the people working hard within the project team, which can be a destabilizing factor. Consequently, changes must be for good strategic reasons, not because there is a new manager wanting to make their mark. If there is a good reason for a correction in the course then all the processes mentioned earlier regarding involving people, communicating, and bringing everyone along with you are as important (or even more so) here as they were at the beginning of the transformation.

Targets are important and setting them is critical to ensure things stay on track and the benefits are being realized. Having said this, a business transformation coming from something as crucial as a Dynamics 365 implementation or migration is a journey, and benefits from the process should now be realized in the form of greater collaboration, engagement, and customer focus right from the start. Don't let anyone lose sight of these benefits and celebrate the journey as much as the milestones. Fundamentally, when you have Dynamics 365 in place and working well, this is far from the end. The most important benefit you want to keep is the focus on continuing the journey and improving the customer experience wherever that customer is.

If it is to succeed, a digital transformation needs constant leadership, which also needs to be seen as active, engaged, and available. Transforming your business and your ERP are projects that are exciting to everyone in the organization and this interest must be fed and watered if it is to support all the goals and the strategic direction. If the senior leadership team are not seen to be positively involved and able to articulate the benefits in their own areas, then others will take their cues from this. Be available, be positive, and be clear.

Summing Up

The journey of digital transformation starts with strategic alignment, which is internally focused but leverages on various other factors that the organization may or may not have as internal capabilities. Hence the journey starts with internal assessment of the organization to identify key strengths and areas of improvements. Building a culture of trust by empowering and influencing your people, preparing for change, and taking everyone on the digital journey makes a digital transformation stick together. Being transparent throughout, being collaborative, and governed by gated controls builds confidence and leverages to measure the progress even if the shift is a small step to start with.

Digital Future Checklist

✓ Consider five cornerstones of DT.
✓ Evaluate your internal capabilities.
✓ Empower your team to make decisions.
✓ Create and communicate your strategic vision at regular intervals.
✓ Challenge existing processes.
✓ Identify quick wins.
✓ Build small iterative progress in governance principles.
✓ Effective governance and control to balance all shifts.

> "A simple paradigm shift is all it takes to change the course of your life forever."
>
> *—Jeff Spires*

Notes

1. Gareth Morgan (1986), p. 1, *Images of Organisation*.
2. Peter Drucker, Culture Eats Strategy for Breakfast. http://www.supplychain247.com/article/organizational_culture_eats_strategy_for_breakfast_lunch_and_dinner/legacy_supply_chain_services.
3. SFIA Framework, The Global Skills and Competency Framework for a Digital World. www.sfia-online.org.
4. McKinsey (2015). www.mckinsey.com/featured-insights/leadership/changing-change-management#.
5. John P. Kotter (1996), *Leading Change*. Boston: Harvard Business School Press.

CHAPTER 5

Program Readiness

Before everything else, getting ready is the secret of success.
—Henry Ford

Readiness is defined as "the state of being fully prepared for something"; it is the readiness we want to cover in this chapter. However, it must be remembered that if you wait until you are 100% prepared you may never start. A wise person "never lets perfect get in the way of sufficient" and as you constantly revise your plans you should also regularly update your state of readiness across all aspects of the plan. Combining the traditional waterfall project methodology and an agile methodology helps and is explained later in this chapter.

Being ready (or ready enough) is not sufficient, however, as you also need to be willing to act. All the business leaders and entrepreneurs who have a vision and an outline plan still have to start to "do something!"

When Richard Branson (British business magnate, founder of the Virgin Group, investor, author, and philanthropist) started his first business venture, he admits to not having much of an idea and even less of a plan. What he did have was an initial vision and a readiness to start. As his ambitions grew his planning improved, but he has never lost that readiness. If you are directing a business venture of any size, you will have people you need to enthuse, educate, and encourage to come along with you. You will need to be ready and you will need to plan like Branson, whether it is a small venture or a larger venture. In this chapter, we will help you ensure that your business is ready for your Dynamics 365 transformation to begin.

In this chapter, we will explore all aspects of program planning required before you start:

- What needs to be understood before you start the project.
- How to define the outcomes you want for the customers of this project.
- What needs to be completed before you start the project.
- What needs to be communicated before you start the project.

Plan Before You Leap

The essence of planning is key before you take the leap. If you are planning a digital transformation journey, you need to be ready rather than surprised. Having a roadmap of your digital transformation journey helps you and your business to prepare across all unknown areas that you will tread on your path. It will help you to identify any risks early on, which will help you to plan your journey, assess the impact on time and costs, and assess the time to realize the benefit. Without this planning, the project is at risk of failure before you even start.

Where are your people now? Why not have temperature checks at all levels?

You need to know what the capacity for change in your organization is. If you cannot carry your staff, it will be an uphill battle. Now is the time to check how people are feeling about their organization, as knowing how positive people are about the whole company will indicate the level of goodwill you have for trying something new.

You will already be doing employee engagement surveys. What are these telling you? It is important that these are prepared carefully and all the questions are tested to ensure they are clear and people can answer the question in a way that gives you maximum information. As an example, I recently saw an employee question-naire that asked, "Do your managers exhibit the right behaviors?" This brings the question, which managers? My immediate line man-ager? His manager? The SLT? Directors? How is it possible to get a clear answer to this question if everyone who reads it is likely to interpret it differently?

Before you start the transformation journey, and at least every six months throughout the transformation project, ask all staff this simple question. It will help supplement your staff survey and get a point-in-time check of how people are feeling about the company.

"On a scale of 0 to 10, how likely are you to recommend this company to potential employees?"

This should be anonymous and down to the level of depart-ment, where 0 to 5 are detractors, 6 to 8 are passive, and 9 and 10 are promoters. Averaging this by department will give you an idea of how happy people really are (the Net Promoter Score), while regular checks will give you a trend. Do not publish the results but do take action to improve. If the average is below 60% you should address your staff problems before starting any project. We will expand on this in the People Readiness section, but it is critical to have engaged and positive staff at the outset. The transformation will place them under pressure and you need to know the levels of goodwill that exist now, and, just as importantly, whether it is dramatically declining.

A digital transformation project can only be successful if your leaders believe in the need for change. This change process requires leadership buy-in to make it successful and if you have people who don't believe in the "why," you will not be successful. Ultimately, the strategic direction will drive the need for this level of transforma-tional change. The Digital Leadership section will help you to deter-mine the current situation and get the buy-in needed.

Do not start unless you have an Executive Sponsor who is pas-sionate about the program. Typically, the CFO is a good sponsor to have; they have in-depth knowledge on how to access sufficient budget, and have the ear of the board. You must make sure this is seen as a business-led transformation and not an IT-led one.

Define Program Benefits and Outcomes

Do you have clarity on the goals? Are they focused on cost saving, income generation, improving your controls, helping your staff, supporting your customers, or just improving your technology?

Clarity on these goals is extremely important before you begin your transformation. If you have not nailed down the reasons why, you will not be able to draw together the transformation in technology, people, and processes that you will need to make. These reasons can be many and varied but should be positive, customer focused, and articulated in the language of the end customer. You need to be able to explain your return on investment (ROI) both in the financial effort and the people effort. You will also need to be able to explain the benefits your customers (and stakeholders) will receive during and at the end of this process, and how these will benefit all.

ERP (and CRM) programs can continue for quite some time. People might come and go and suddenly a senior executive might start questioning why this is being done. A "Business Value Assessment" would then be valuable to conduct during the readiness planning stage to create a case for justifying the investment. Depending on circumstances, a Business Value Assessment is something that Microsoft can provide as part of the service offering.

Refer to Chapter 1, Digital Transformation and the Case for Change, to look at the drivers for change. You need to communicate consistently across the whole business the key drivers of change for your organization. The Digital Leadership section will add some suggestions as to how you do this.

Knowing Your Business Processes

This is not a question of how to run the business, but is obviously a known quantity. This is how it is run day to day. Often department heads cannot actually describe to senior leaders how their area of the business is run. They can give you the metrics, they can justify the headcount, but the processes being followed are not documented, and they may not know how they are being achieved.

Williams F1 know to the micron the build of every part of their racing engines. This is not because they are massive geeky petrolheads but because they are constantly striving to improve. If you don't know the detail of the core processes in your business you are going to have to find out, or pay the significant extra costs of not knowing.

Do you currently have your key processes mapped? Do you have off-system processes and applications? Or, more simply, how many spreadsheets are being used to run your business? How many disconnected systems and business methods are you using? Are your teams working in silos or do they work together to achieve objectives? If you are a global business, are your system processes streamlined or do they differ from country to country? Who sees the whole picture or the effect of each individual job on the whole process?

If the answer to these questions is "We don't know," then you should not consider starting the project until you can answer in detail. If you know you are using a lot of spreadsheets and disconnected systems and methods, then the project will take longer and cost more. You will need to account for this in your planning and not take the transformation lightly. More on this is given in the Operational Readiness section.

Have you mapped current processes? Do you completely understand what they are? Changing something that you don't wholly appreciate in detail is likely to lead to confusion and a lack of direction. If you don't know where you have come from, how will you know you are moving forward?

Identify the critical processes to the running of the business and map them—all the way down to the work instructions. If you have this you will know so much more about your business than just these process maps. A good way to start is to create a Business Process Master List (BPML) that includes all the subprocesses, to determine what is in scope. Then map down to level 4.

Is your data trusted? Are you making decisions based on it?

Data is the single, biggest problem for most programs. Start early. It is usually the responsibility of the business to ensure the data is fit for purpose and migrated correctly. Never underestimate this area, and don't think that you can outsource this problem. It is one of the main areas that must be focused on by the people who know the data—this means your people. Fix the data where you already know it is wrong. If part of the reason you are transforming is a lack of clear data or no ability to confirm it, then consider how you can track and validate. It is likely to be a lack of homogeneity that is causing you the most pain. You can start the project without fixing the data, but unless you can improve it throughout the project, you will struggle to show the benefits from the transformation. You also need to consider single versions of the truth once the data is becoming clearer; this will help with trust in the reporting.

Assuming you have the budget for business transformation, identify the risk factors on cost, processes, data, and resources early on. Keep reviewing the risks and mitigate those risks throughout the program lifecycle as standard practice.

Here is an illustration of contingency that you may need to build upon to the project costs based on various risk factors. Review these factors (and costs) at every gate:

- **People.** 1% for every point average below a 90% net promoter score. (Down to 60%, as lower than that should pause your change at the start. Also, once you have started the project this should be monitored regularly and additional costs added without the 60% floor.)
- **Current processes.** 2% for every critical process not documented and understood.
- **Data quality.** 10% if you cannot make quality decisions based on current data.

These should be cumulative, so calculate as follows:

- Initial budget estimate = $1,000,000
- Net promoter score = 82%, so add 8% = $1,080,000
- Critical processes not documented = 3, so add 6% = $1,144,800
- Data quality poor, so add 10% = $1,259,280

Cumulatively these problems will therefore add just under 26% to the cost of the project. You can include them in the overall cost of the program and also need to review the risks periodically with an intention to mitigate and close the risks in order to keep the cost down.

An assessment of these risk factors should be reviewed as you go through each project stage gates.

Pre-Project Communication

Once you have done the groundwork and secured the budget for the program to start, you will need to communicate the strategic initiative across all levels within the organization and cover the following:

- **The vision.** Why are we doing this (what will it mean to our customers)?
- **The goals.** Break down the vision and set goals for each process or user group.
- **The plan including the proposed timeline.** How are we doing this?
- **The people.** Who will need to be involved and to what extent?

Digital Leadership

Leadership actions define the culture of the organization. If the actions do not promote a digital culture (or there are no actions at all) any desire to move toward a digital focus and future, whether it is with Dynamics 365 Finance and Operation or Commerce or Customer Engagement, will be doomed to failure. Digital leaders need to articulate the vision and then role-model the cultural attitudes that are needed to achieve it. Standards need to be promoted and incentivized throughout the organizational structure for change to be achieved, and this has to come from the sponsor and executive leadership team.

Are the Executives Ready for This?

In traditional business structures, the executive would be setting and then supporting the implementation of a strategic direction. During a digital transformation, the executive team will be much more than this. They will be key to driving transformation, but not by dictate; it will be by encouraging entrepreneurship and a level of individual thinking. Collaborative working, respect for individual views, and a sense of community (and ideally family) are all positive values in the new digital organization. There are benefits to being able to agree to a way of working top to bottom and it is this attitude that the executive team will be required to engender.

Are these the type of people you already have in leadership roles? If not, there is some work to do to change the attitudes, habits, and methods of the people at this level before you can be sure of effecting great change. You do not need to change the people, but they may have entrenched behaviors that may need to be influenced toward change.

Personal qualities that need to be shown by individuals on the Executive Team are:

- They listen to both customers and employees.
- Collaborative and open, but can make decisions and take personal responsibility.
- Put the organization's customer at the heart of what they do.
- Data Driven: they use the data rather than a personal view to make decisions.
- Open to change, new ideas, and focusing on flexibility in their department.
- They are committed to cultural change and happy to lead it.
- Relentless focus on evidence-backed results.
- Clear, engaging communicators.

Do They Understand Their Roles and Responsibilities?

The executive team (and the senior leadership team they direct) need to understand and, equally important, make time for the role they will need to fulfil. Additionally, they will need to take responsibility for directing and/or driving the necessary changes, and this will require their time and commitment. You can have all the governance bodies set up by the project team (sponsors, steering boards, etc.) with all the right people invited, but if for any reason they are unable to give the commitment the project will fail.

We have added a list of items to help you identify what makes a digital leader at any level in the organization:

- A digital leader will articulate the vision (whether they set it or not) and set standards of behavior, value, and habit that promote that vision in everything they do.

- They will have a customer focus that applies the vision, and act as a role model for others. The consumer experience is king to these people.
- If they are in a leadership position (as a team leader, manager, or executive), they will mentor others in the habits and values that promote the changes required to the culture in the organization.
- At every level of the organization digital leaders use key performance indicators (KPIs) to progress the changes required and then backed by incentives that encourage the right behaviors.
- Simple things like gratitude and respect are embedded into the culture by leaders as they promote change at every level and in every interaction that people have.

Risk Factors with the Leadership Team

You need to consider the risk factors associated with the leadership and sponsorship team related to change (i.e., loss, resistance, ambition, and decision makers).

- **Loss.** The right people are in the right roles, but can you keep them there and will the change fail if they leave? As part of preparing for change there must be a risk register and one of those risks must be the unavailability of key people. If they really are key people then they will have been encouraging and mentoring others in the skills and attitudes needed to complete the transformation. One of the changes you will be trying to develop within the organization is a supportive and collaborative mindset, and the leaders who encourage and promote this will be the most successful and the least needed in the long term. However, in the short term there must be a succession plan in place in order to avoid the transformation stalling because there is no leadership, guidance, and encouragement.
- **Resistance.** The sum of the leaders is greater than its parts, but, conversely, if you have a member of the executive team actively resisting progress in any way (overtly or covertly) then this undermines the entire project. It is imperative that the individual is brought on board through discussion and an understanding of

the benefits of the changes. If this is not possible, then they have to be removed from the group and moved to a position where they are no longer an influencer on it.

- **Ambition.** The leadership team should consist of people who are ambitious. For the purposes of a digital transformation, this ambition needs to be directed toward the greater good of the organization rather than that of the individual.
- **Decision makers.** You need to consider at the executive level (and in fact at all levels) decision inertia, a state of being scared of making decisions. This is common within an organization that lacks confidence when making decisions. It could be due to an organizational culture where you are afraid of being punished if you make incorrect decisions. Ultimately, having teams that need to wait for management decisions and managers who are afraid of making them affects the project progress significantly.

David Reid,
Architect/Technical
Specialist, Public
Sector and National
Security, Microsoft

"Successful Dynamics 365 implementations are always delivered WITH the business rather than TO the business. This leads to much greater empathy to the needs of customers and users of the system, and those users should always be involved in the process of ideating and creating the solution. A successful implementation engenders greater employee satisfaction, not only as the user experience and tools are easier and more familiar to use but also users will feel more invested in the success of the solution and your organization.

We often hear about business vs. IT, and how a breakdown of trust has become a barrier to success. If this resonates with you, you urgently need to do something about it in order for your business to survive and adapt. Empower your business users to be the change, and work with them by providing the tools, along with effective governance, to ensure solutions you develop and co-create with them are implemented successfully. Every employee and partner must be invested in the success of the organisation, otherwise competition and negativity will erode the effectiveness of your business."

Selecting an Implementation Partner

When you start the selection process, you need to have knowledge of your own business and the resources you have before going out to the wider market or you are in serious danger of paying much more than you need. I have often seen companies paying for consultants to come in and repeat what their own staff have been telling them all along. This is wasteful and demoralizing if you are the staff concerned. Take the opportunity to gather information and suggestions internally to begin with. After this you will have an idea of where the skillset gaps are and you will certainly need help deciding how to run the project. This is the time to get in some independent consultants, who will be able to identify any skillset gaps you may have missed and the type of partner company that will fit for your purpose. You can also ask them to help with preparing the tender documents that will be used during the selection process. It is important to be mindful of any bias in these consultants, however, and make your own decisions.

An implementation partner needs to be a good cultural fit and understand your business and what you need from a Dynamics 365 implementation. An implementation partner should also be able to save you money by running your implementation and all the cloud environments you will need in the most efficient and cost-effective way possible, as well as thinking about the transition to the business-as-usual support post go-live. It is not their job to make money for the service provider; they are there to save money for you.

Partners need to be carefully managed for them to operate as a true trusted advisor. Unfortunately, a naïve client will be at risk of the partner taking advantage of their inexperience. It is in the partner's interest to have a long-term engagement, particularly if the terms are time and materials. More time equals more money! The client can best protect themselves by having an experienced Dynamics 365 specialist program director (or similar) to help negotiate contracts and control and manage the partner.

If you are not clear on the current state of your business, where you want to get to, and what you think you need that you don't currently have, then consider speaking to Microsoft in order to understand Dynamics 365 capabilities, which will help in shaping your business need.

If, however, you have all the current critical processes mapped out and understood, your people believe in the changes that are needed (from the shop floor to executives), and you are confident in your data, then follow the process of creating a request for proposal (RFP) for selecting an implementation partner.

The key here is to find an implementation partner who best fits your organization and with whom you can have a long-term partnership. It is true that people work with people and you have to be able to work at all levels of the organization for a digital transformation. It is important that you can control who in a partner organization you work with and that you keep control over the project and the costs. A partner that is comfortable being challenged and still shows they will put you first is one you want to work with and the relationship with them will only improve over time.

Eric Veldkamp,
Partner at HSO Group

"When you start the selection process you need to have knowledge of your own business and the resources you have before going out to the wider market or you are in serious danger of paying much more than you need to. The road to business application modernization is a journey. Similar to travel, if you want to know what the journey takes and costs, you need to know where you want to go to as well as where you are departing from. We have often seen companies paying for consultants to come in and repeat what their own staff have been telling them all along. This is wasteful and demoralizing for the staff concerned. Take the opportunity to gather information and suggestions internally to begin with.

Engage the right Systems Integrator—All Dynamics 365 Programs are not the same and talent in one platform is not necessarily transferable. Demand Dynamics-specific technical talent & knowledge, as well as integration skills, are key and these should be demonstrated by CV and experience. Also, consider the Microsoft relationship with SI and appropriate thought leadership for your brand and industry. Do not be afraid to change Systems Integrator if you get off to a poor, disjointed start and be afraid of sunk cost. The decision is big and thorny but ultimately can save burning time and money."

Preparation and Readiness Before Program or Project Kick-Off

It is possible to overprepare before kicking off the project, but it is impossible to overestimate the impact of starting with poor knowledge of where you are as a business—particularly knowledge of how the business is running and the quality of your data and processes. All too often your people are covering up the cracks in order to feel they are doing a good job. If you don't know this, you are heading for trouble when you start the project. Readiness planning is making sure you know where you really are as a business and then making sure all the business knows as well. Only then can you really promote the need for change.

This is especially prevalent in organizations that have a good "family" culture with a lot of long-term employees. The employees see it as part of their role to keep the organization going but changes at the middle management level have further hidden this culture from the executive team. The Digital Culture Challenge: Closing the Employee Leadership Gap[1] details questions asked of the employees and of the executive team and reports on the gap between the two. The wider the gap, the greater the costs to the business of the digital transformation and the harder it is to pull together all the elements needed to make the change successful.

A recent attempt to transform a UK charity to bring in a digital focus has so far taken twice as long and three times the original cost because these factors were not understood at the outset. The problems stemmed from believing that a change would solve endemic issues and this led to a focus on the change rather than on the underlying problems. The outcome was a confused and constantly changing project that had a lack of clear direction and a partner who was trying to solve problems using additional systems and other third parties. Costs spiraled and no one was prepared to press the reset button because so much had already been spent. If there had been proper planning at the start, it would have been recognized that the plan being followed had serious flaws. Additionally, managers (particularly senior managers) did not listen to their own staff who had been telling them that there were serious issues that needed focus before starting the project. Eventually it was completed but it took two partners and a great deal of additional cost that should have been avoided. If the costs had been foreseen at the start the project would never have gone ahead. This is not an isolated case; in fact, this seems to be the more prevalent experience.

You should not set the strategic direction of your company or department without information. Without knowing all you can about the current state of the company, the market conditions, and predictions, why would you embark on a digital transformation (or even an ERP migration) without all the facts? It is not as if the facts would be difficult to come by as most of them are internal; they just require some honesty from your teams.

People: Temperature Check

The first step is to get a temperature check of your company. So often you can be sold on the whole detailed employee satisfaction survey but as a baseline this is not necessary and can be counterproductive. Take the following steps to get a baseline for morale (Net Promoter Score, as mentioned at the beginning of this chapter):

1. By department, send out one question to all staff that can be answered completely anonymously.

> The question is "on a scale of 1 to 10 (1 is least likely, 10 is most likely): How likely are you to recommend working here to someone thinking of applying for a role in your department?"

2. Based on the replies score as follows:

> 1–5: Detractors
> 6–8: Passive
> 9–10: Promoters

3. Add all of the response numbers and divide by the number of replies. This will give you the temperature check for the department. Add these and divide by the departments and you have one for the organization.

What this will give you is a real indicator of how people (on average) feel about where they work. More important, it tells you whether you are ready for a digital transformation.

A really low score can suggest you might as well go ahead, for how much worse can it be, but then you are betting the company on it. Not a great situation to be in. In this case you will need to start to listen and act on feedback as to why your employees feel trapped and undervalued. Look first at your senior leadership team and whether they have any idea what their people are doing. Putting a table-tennis table in will not cut it.

If you fall in the neutral area overall, you will need to think carefully about resourcing, planning, and communication. Bringing people with you will be tough and it is likely to require some really excellent consultants and third-party partners. Getting this bit wrong could cost you dearly, both financially and in key staff. Your key partners will be worth their weight in gold, but never forget the staff, and listen to what they are telling you too. In the neutral area the partner and employee combination is truly synergistic and partnering the two is key here.

If you fall into the Active Promoter end of the spectrum, pat yourselves on the back for already being an excellent company and then start to employ your superb staff in transforming your company. The partner should be led by these people and any additional resources brought in should mostly be back-fill for your own people.

Process: Documentation Check

Where people are key to getting things done, processes tell them how to do things. If you do not have any, your staff are making it up. This leads to endemic errors, single points of failure, hold-ups when people are on leave, over-resourcing where people are being employed to fix issues caused by others within the organization, and frustration for all.

Again, you will be told you need to bring in expensive consultants to resolve your problems, but if you are serious about a digital transformation this need not be the case. Follow these steps:

1. Get the people who do the work to write down what they do, step by step. Every person should do this, even if they perform

the same task. Then a team leader or manager should review whether they are all the same. If they are not, agree on the way everyone should do it and pass this process to step 2.

2. Get someone from another team to try to repeat this. If they cannot, they should sit with one or two people doing the work and rewrite the process so it can be followed.

3. Wherever there is a hand-off to someone else, write that into the document and the person handed-off should then also write down their process (follow the same method as steps 1 and 2).

4. Gradually link all these processes together. Get someone in to map these, which is boring, and they don't need to know the process (in fact it is better that they don't), but they need to be accurate.

5. The managers and team leaders of the people doing these tasks then need to check that they are accurate. Where you have more than one person doing a specific task, they should all now be following the same method.

6. Once everyone in every department has completed this, you have all your processes mapped. Hand these to your third-party partner when you are ready to begin the transformation.

It does take a little time and some coordination. If you give it focus nearly everything should be mapped in a month (this may miss processes that are irregular, but they should be minor if people cannot remember them). Once completed, you can move forward in the knowledge that you can tell any partner exactly what processes you have in place. A good Dynamics 365 partner will be able to make suggestions for improvements and correctly configure the new Dynamics 365 environment. A great Dynamics 365 partner will be able to show you how to improve, encourage, and enthuse people to make these improvements *and* start your staff on the journey to your digital transformation.

Summing Up

A lot of readiness and planning goes before the digital transformation program can begin. It can be overwhelming for people at the start, as the digital transformation can impact on a number of divisions within the business, their ways of working, and integrating with other departments for information. Our recommendation is to prepare, plan, identify, and manage risks from the very beginning.

Digital Future Checklist

✓ Plan before you leap.
✓ Knowing how your business is run.
✓ Define Benefits and Outcome.
✓ Leadership buy-in.
✓ Selecting an implementation partner.
✓ Preparation and Readiness before the program or project kick-off.

"The key is not the will to win. Everybody has that. It is the will to prepare to win that is important."

—*Bobby Knight*

Notes

1. Capgemini (2017), The Digital Culture Challenge: Closing the Employee-Leadership Gap. www.capgemini.com/consulting/wp-content/uploads/sites/30/2017/07/dti_digitalculture_report.pdf.

CHAPTER 6

Deep Dive: Organizational Change Management for Dynamics 365 and DX

The price of doing the same old thing is far higher than the price of change.

—Bill Clinton

While writing about change management, it is a remarkably interesting subject and close to my heart. I have come across views spanning the spectrum on change management.

On one side of the spectrum—why should we invest in change management? It is not necessary to include change management while we are digitally transforming our business with Dynamics 365. We have internal capabilities to work on employee training and project management, so let us handle change management internally.

On the other side, change management is an integral part of Digital Transformation and without it the projects are bound to fail. Hence the change management cost has increased the overall digital transformation cost to threefold and the timeline is extended.

If you are on either side of the spectrum and if you would like to do your digital transformation again, then you might possibly know what you would do differently. If you are starting your digital transformation journey today, then this chapter will help you to identify any pitfalls from the beginning, explore the significance of organization change management (OCM), and enable you to plan your digital transformation (DX) journey.

The false economy of not investing in Organizational Change Management always exists in the industry.

The best metaphor I can share about making a digital transformation a success is Apollo 13. After a spacecraft explosion, using the lunar module as a life raft, the crew, at least 15 ground-control teams, as well as several contractor groups developed procedures on the fly to slingshot Apollo 13 home. If NASA had not invested in its culture of constant problem solving, Apollo 13 would have ended in disaster. Apollo 13 provides the perfect recipe for enabling thinking *together* outside the box and at pace with:

- Teamwork
- Leadership
- Initiative

Like the Apollo 13 spacecraft failure, organizations report Digital Transformation roadmaps are failing (>70%), and similarly, like the Apollo 13 mission shift, DX needs a shift in mission. Unlike the Apollo space program, organizations have not invested in their environments to create the type of teamwork, initiative, and leadership that enables outside-the-box DX problem solving. As your organization embarks on the journey to ensure a reliable digital core with Dynamics 365, your organization is not DX ready without a DX problem-solving environment. This an environment requiring short information paths between teams working at pace—welcome to the agile organization. Today's hierarchy and silos fail spectacularly at this. "Break down the silos!" is the common cry, but futile legacy habits remain in control.

DX's wingman to change is OCM, which helps transition the organization from hierarchy to networked systems, including leadership, roles, responsibilities, and methods of work. This is a highly complex nut to crack and sometimes approaches fall between two contrasting scenarios:

1. **Slash and Burn.** OCM efforts facilitate the design of a new networked organization. The subsequent "transition" is achieved by laying off and re-hiring staff, as well as hiring new resources into the modernized organization. This drastic transition is often an attempt to fast-track DX while the rest of the industry is failing (see DX interview with ING Bank).[1]
2. **Organic Hierarchy Change with Prototype.** OCM efforts facilitate creating a network organization prototype. The prototype has DX innovation responsibility. The environment is staffed with people transitioning from organizational roles to DX teams and back. The prototype is constantly adjusted until it is scalable (adoption ready). Transition happens with the organization involved. In this model OCM is engaged to facilitate, assess, measure, and influence this monumental change.

This chapter addresses the *organic* approach by running two OCM programs in parallel:

1. **Standard ERP/CRM OCM.** Effort focuses on Dynamics 365 Systems adoption and utilization with a DX awareness culture. The guiding principles are process change and leadership involvement (no change in the project approach).
2. **Supercharged DX OCM.** Effort focuses on building the DX Team and Ecosystem (typically with a Transformation Officer). The guiding principles are to develop "out of the box" thinking tools, methods, and approaches from business, analytics, IT, and lean start-up methodology with the ultimate goal to achieve business agility within a network organization. It should be launched around the ERP/CRM system as tested by users.

Why start both at the same time? Having the DX prototype environment ready at the time of the Dynamics 365 launch gives your organization a competitive edge at DX when the ERP/CRM system is live.

DX success is first and foremost about people, not technology. It requires a tectonic organizational shift from hierarchy to network over time. With the herein suggested approach, OCM enables a prototype, with an empowered cross-functional team (we will call these "Apollo DX Teams"). This is a team that addresses DX methods, strategy, and problem solving at pace.

In my experience, Apollo DX prototype environments are best built when ERP projects are underway. Consider the Dynamics 365 project as an incubator for DX methods of work. Therefore, the goals of OCM are:

- Successful adoption of Dynamics 365; and
- Enabling the DX Transformation Officer with building an Apollo DX program.

This strategy highlights OCM's true impact on the DX roadmap. Not investing in OCM not only puts Dynamics 365 benefits realization at risk, but also puts the DX program at risk. This is a program with much greater transform or perish consequences.

Failings of Tactical OCM

In this section, we will explore the level of change management your organization needs and how the implementation partner can support bringing their expertise by combining with other factors including your expertise.

- Many ERP systems implementation (SI) partners offer OCM. You need to review SI offerings with organization in-house change management capabilities versus effective change management as the effective change management drives results and outcomes. You may need to focus on the following areas of OCM to meet the objective.
- To coach and challenge senior leadership.
- To stay on schedule and on budget.
- Use of OCM tools.
- Adoption and usage.

For small ERP add-ons, the compromise in benefits may be negligible. However, for large-scale ERP implementations, this drives down value.

Projects with improved change management had an increased likelihood of meeting objectives and finishing on time and on budget.

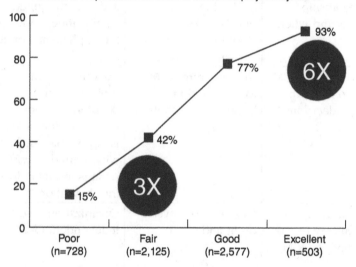

Prosci 2020 Benchmarking Data from 2007, 2009, 2011, 2013, 2015, 2017, 2019

FIGURE 6.1 Prosci 2020 Benchmarking Data

Source: Used with permission of Prosci Benchmarking results. www.prosci.com/hubfs/2. downloads/research-executive-summaries/11th%20Edition-Best-Practices-Executive-Summary-11-2020.pdf?hsLang=en-ca.

Based on Figure 6.1, the following table is an illustration of different scenarios with and without change management. In the short run it might appear as cost-efficient without any investment in OCM, but in the long run it might be a risky option of not involving any change management.

No OCM	SI Vendor OCM	Full-scale OCM
Benefit realization dependent on the technical team who are not skilled in OCM.	SI provides additional resources for OCM for benefit realization.	OCM team responsible for benefit realization and fully skilled change managers have the accountability.
No OCM team to engage or challenge the leadership team as and when required.	Identify risks and engage with the leadership team, but the risks are linked with the implementation team.	Identify risks and engage the leadership team as and when required, as this team is independent of the implementation team.
No data from OCM tools to drive any change decisions.	No data from OCM tools as SI do not bring in OCM tools.	Data from OCM tools drives the decisions. Without tools, transformation is impossible, and what started as cost savings results in lost transformation.
Organization can save money by not investing in OCM tools.	Organization invests on SI and OCM.	Organization invests on an independent OCM.

Why Invest in Strategic OCM Before Starting the Project

"Transforming an organization to be digitally centric is not just about the technology, it is about the culture transformation within the organization. Recognizing transformations are not overnight however, the days of traditional waterfall structures no longer meet the rapid changing world around us."

Renee Dothard,
WW Public Sector,
Microsoft

"Change management is much more than a 'touchy-feely' component of your digital transformation. It should be fully baked into your strategy and plan."

Eric Kimberling,
CEO and founder, Third
Stage Consulting

Today's SI-led ERP/CRM projects are highly efficient and run on tight timelines. Although this preparedness is expected of the SI, organizations do not put the same rigor on themselves in being prepared for the project. Instead, they prefer cliff-diving into the implementation, thinking once it is running the business can catch up with whatever strategic homework they should have done earlier. Needless to say, the critical alignment between leadership and the organization never catches up, affecting:

- Scope (as requirements are not aligned);
- Schedule (too many must have requirements); and
- Benefits to be realized (why are we doing things?).

Without alignment, the project quickly becomes technology driven and the necessary context for the leadership and business (both on and off the project) gets lost. In an ideal state, you turn back the clock by 6 months and start with an OCM practitioner–led (or equivalent) project to prepare the organization for the journey ahead by the following tracts: executive readiness, operational readiness, people readiness, technical readiness, and project readiness.

Although all areas are important to address, we will cover the activities that are the absolute must-haves in order to start your project in this section:

- An executive-aligned DX mission.
- What's the grand vision? How will the organization improve the lives of its customers?

- What's the strategic driver? Customer engagement or digital (product) solutions?
- What external partnerships will the organization pursue? As DX is all about connections, defining what partnerships the company is pursuing may be critical to the ERP scope (e.g., if a company is contemplating a web sales partnership with a third party, it may warrant adding consignment sales to the scope).

Having a clear DX mission statement allows for initiatives that follow, to act autonomously, and not have to ask for approval at every turn of the bend.

- **Executive-aligned benefits.** What are the benefits to be realized after the project? This defines the questions of why change, scope, and when the project ends. The key performance indicators (KPIs) are beneficial goalposts for the implementation to underrate what is important to the business. Executives should create these in a dialog with operational leadership.
- **Organizational metadata.** Data about the organization itself. I call this the Business Operating Platform (BOP) and discuss it in the section "How will you embed any required cultural transformation in the organization?"

    Key to priming the ERP/CRM and DX requirements, failing fast/failing often, beguiling the business into full engagement during analysis, preventing IT from panicking and shutting down requirements, and so on, feeds the assess/influence dynamic for OCM impact analysis and response at pace.
- **Tool up for project skills.** Hold an analysis bootcamp for tools (e.g., Visio (data visualizer), Excel *power query*, *company-wide analytics platforms*), techniques (e.g., facilitation, metadata triage, and analysis), and critical deliverables.
- **Holistic OCM/DX roadmap.** Project teams must be informed on the DX roadmap, as the roadmap may have an impact on project decisions down the road.
    - OCM is more effective when embedded in a long-term DX program. Create a joint roadmap to enable visibility between OCM and Technology.

Today's DX roadmaps are being invented on the fly and most frameworks are firehoses. A practical way to build your own is to map out the transition between your current state and the next state on the IDC Digital Maturity Map (Google for details), a five-stage maturity model similar to CMMI.

The DX roadmap included in this section assumes:

- **Level 1.** Become a Digital Explorer by cutover.
- **Level 2.** Advance to Digital Explorer stage II after system stabilization.
- **Level 3.** Become a Digital Player in the mid-range future.

The top half of the roadmap in Figure 6.2 focuses on business change and transformation activities. The bottom half focuses on technology for IT and DT (Digital Technology). OCM plays a role across both. Looking across the rows from the left, each half subdivides into "garden variety change" and "transformation".

This roadmap differs from conventional roadmaps because it includes both a big picture (e.g., ERP/CRM) and a small picture (metadata sharing tools), and technology-agnostic organizational change. These themes need to be argued by your team, to discover what will work for you. This is the difference between "doing digital" and "becoming digital."

Organization After Implementation and Role Change

"Continuous transformation doesn't always mean something is changing every day, but certainly requires a cadence of iterative and continual adjustments and deliverables towards a transformation target with tangible proof points several times a year."

Tim Ferguson,
Senior IT Director,
Maersk

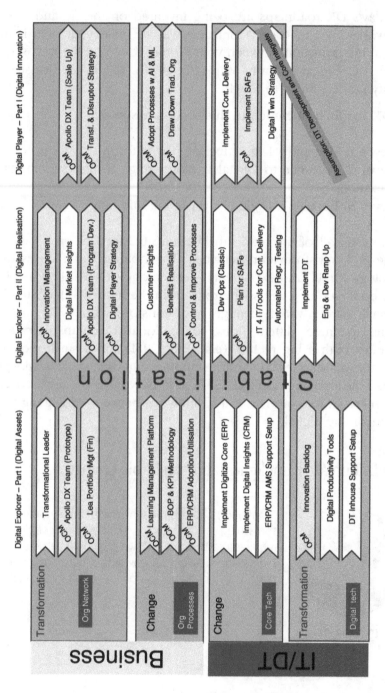

FIGURE 6.2 DX Enablement Roadmap: From Digital Explorer to Digital Player

Source: Sabine Margolis.

"Change management is about preparing, equipping, and supporting our people in change to drive more effective adoption and proficient usage, so that our employees are more successful, the initiative delivers the people-dependent ROI, and the organization grows critical change muscle."

Tim Creasey,
Prosci Chief Innovation Officer

Organizations need to prepare their team in many ways for change management that includes upcoming innovation, updated roles and responsibilities that can drive efficiencies, and a back-filling team where required.

Pros. Being DX ready means the organization generates creative ideas and has analysis and experimentation methods to assess digital technology for business viability.

Cons. Most literature only tangentially mentions that your organization has to fundamentally change to a network of autonomous teams, busting all the paradigms on the need for hierarchy and order.

Changes to the Organization Due to ERP/CRM

As stated in the introduction to this chapter, we will focus on the launching of the DX organization prototype called the Apollo DX program. However, before we dive in, just a few noteworthy Dynamics 365 changes after go [/] live:

- Formal subject matter expert: businessperson in a department who functions as a liaison between that department and IT.
- Shadow systems are sunset as data is located in the ERP.
- Strong reporting flexibility requires a citizen developer reporting strategy to ensure correct data is used for what the individual needs.

- Process transitions from offline to online activity: with an original state the transactions accumulate for later data entry, and with a future state all transaction entries become time sensitive (e.g., WHSE picking). This can be a rough transition as a certain autonomy is no longer possible.

Changes to the Organization Due to DX

Apollo DX Teams

The Apollo DX Team is a construct used throughout this chapter to convey the DX nucleus: a small, cross-functional, and self-empowered team. Apollo DX teams fill the uncertainly void between a business problem/idea and their IT implementation. Their job is to vet the viability of ideas and identify an implementation approach with rapid prototyping and experimentation. *Prototyping results shape the requirements that Apollo DX Teams submit to IT for implementation.* Apollo DX teams form when business opportunities emerge. Assignments typically last between two and four weeks and may or may not be full-time. Once an assignment is complete, team members return to their department.

Apollo DX Ecosystem

The Apollo DX Ecosystem is the environment in which Apollo DX Teams operate. Team membership is temporary and purpose-built by initiative. Three permanent roles manage the environment:

1. **Transformation Officer.** Agile leader of the DX initiative with a seat at the C-suite table. A key facilitator in helping the C-suite change to agile.
2. **Network Operator.** Agile head coach, responsible for several Apollo DX teams, ensures teams form and disperse, and breaks down barriers.
3. **Transformation Lead.** Managers and Senior Managers within the organization who act as OCM Ambassadors of the program.

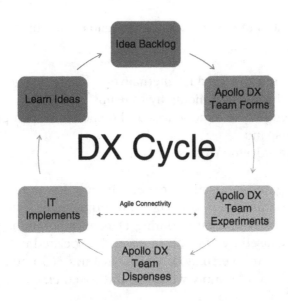

FIGURE 6.3 **High-Level DX Cycle Within the Apollo Teams**

The DX Cycle (Figure 6.3) within the Apollo DX ecosystem highlights:

- Idea backlog capture triage, which vets ideas according to DX mission alignment. Incoming ideas are seeds of innovation, captured and triaged systematically before an Apollo DX team addresses them. *Start implementing this log on the Dynamics 365 project to capture ideas for the Apollo DX teams.*
- Small Apollo DX teams that assemble and disperse, allowing for networks to stay fresh and people to experience agility.
- IT remains the implementation partner, resources expand with in-house systems engineering and programming teams.
- DX cycle has three warning "fail early, fail fast" stages.
- Outside of DX, organizational structure remains hierarchical, for now. The DX Ecosystem is fine-tuned as teams and leadership experience it.
- Organizational change supports the Transformation Officer and all people efforts to improve the information flow network

The intent of the hybrid approach (agile team + hierarchy organization) is to:

- Have a proactive gradual alternative to harsh change;
- Shift decisions from hierarchy to teams in action;
- Shared employee experiences and democratized employee contributions; and
- Allow improvements to snowball.

Exploring and innovating creates a hunger for more.

Note: Communicate the DX transformational strategy to the organization early and often during Dynamics 365 implementation. Job anxiety caused by DX transitions and associated uncertainties is very real and can overshadow your Dynamics 365 implementation. Your people need to know we are in this together!

Gain Meaningful Digital Insights for Change

Somnath Nandi,
Digital Transformation
Leader & Strategist,
Microsoft

"For organizations to be successful at Digital Transformation, they need to gain meaningful insights or digital feedback for change and feedback to continuously optimize operations, empower people, engage customers, and transform products at breathtaking speeds. Microsoft Dynamics 365 infused with AI and its Power Platform is designed for this digital feedback, due to the inherent intelligence built into the solution. Implementing this powerful combination will fast track your digital transformation, as it quickly provides the organization with a holistic 360 view—a 360 view across operations, people, customers, and products to identify meaningful transformation strategies as well as reliable predictions of their outcomes."

Metadata is the secret to measuring change and is critical to engineering the future. Metadata is today's digital junk, highly fragmented and never in a reusable format. However, when accessible in a trusted system, metadata makes guideposts and goals clear. This section uses the Business Operating Platform (BOP) to reflect a centrally accessible and vetted metadata platform. At its core is a business process architecture that functions as the glue to connect all metadata to business context. Key is that the architecture accommodates change over time, a major limitation of many dual purposed workflow/reporting tools today (e.g., Service Now, Jira).

"The information about the package is just as important as the package itself."

—Fred Smith, Founder of FedEx

FedEx is built on metadata. The secret sauce is consolidating fragmented meta into a digital shareable format. With metadata, FedEx exploded, finding never-imagined opportunities, which resulted from opportunistic use of metadata.

Just as the package metadata created context, process metadata creates business context for anything associated with it, such as stakeholders, technical objects, and even business value. Merging all metadata into a centrally accessible reporting platform, or Business Operations Platform (BOP), creates the data repository that can provide organizational context and direction.

- Connecting workflow outputs of siloed IT tools, such as ServiceNow, SharePoint, and Jira adds up-to-date *business context* to IT outputs.
- Connecting siloed people data, such as position, role, systems access, contact info, and supervisor, adds *technology context*.
- Connecting project data, such as future state metadata, impact assessment, benefit realization metrics, stakeholder engagement plan, communications plan, development objects, and user stories, creates *team context*.
- Connecting business value alignment data, which is a simple NEW measure on how a scenario's metadata aligns with your business mission (high/medium/low) adds *priority context*.

The nucleus to connect metadata for the preceding is a hierarchical taxonomy called business process architectures.

Business architectures in analytics systems can grow and change with your processes. Each process architecture includes identifiers. This allows current and future states to share the same architecture nodes when they have the same meaning and new nodes where they differ. This version control sets continuous change into motion, a critical success factor for DX, as well as a critical navigational guide for Business Agility and even OCM. The BOP enables the big picture of change impact on your organization's people, processes, and technology.

The following four steps guide you to developing your very own BOP:

1. **Develop Your Business Architecture.** Everybody has a love-hate relationship with Visio, but with its new integration to Excel it is the perfect "citizen analyst" power tool. Start with Excel templates for your architecture. Then list process steps (end-to-end) in Excel, push the data to Visio, refine the process in Visio, and push it back to Excel. Excel contains the metadata in reusable format and Visio is only a visualizer.

   Example: PTP – Raw Material Purchase[2]

   A great demo of this in action is available at:

   https://www.youtube.com/watch?v=O2qWMFtyT3s.

2. **Business Architecture Refinement: Data Patterns and ID.** Excel Power Query enables you to see the metadata of all the scenarios generated in step 1 as one dataset. This requires a one-time setup to enable a real-time merged dataset (while keeping the data intact on the spreadsheet). Once set up, drop all metadata Excel worksheets in the same folder, as defined in the power query setup. This functionality can be used to refine and cleanse the structure, create the ID, as well as develop a load file for the BOP.

   LinkedIn Learning offers in-depth training on this topic.[3] An interactive demo can be seen at:

   https://www.youtube.com/watch?v=vq9AgAtSvQg.

3. **Assign Business Scenarios to Their Mission Alignment.** Collect the DX mission alignment goals and collaborate with others on how well a business scenario aligns with the constellation of goals. Use high/medium/low for evaluation values. If a scenario's alignment is high, also collect the various mission goals to that process.

4. **Create the BOP in a Data Analytics Tool of Choice.** Acquire a data analytics tool of choice (e.g., Visio/Excel, Looker,

Tableau, even MS Access) with enough scalability options to include vested users: leadership, business, IT, and Apollo DX, for starters.

The tool does not matter; it is metadata or rather business architecture that matters. The magic is being able to connect everything and everyone through the architecture, to share the architecture, and keep everything up to date. This maintains alignment across the board. With the preceding architecture at the center of the BOP's universe, add the following to the BOP:

- DX Mission alignment by scenario (HML)
- ERP Metrics (connect to scenario and process)
- HR Data (Employee/Contractor Info & Dept)
- Systems Info (Access and relationship to process)
- IT Service Delivery Platform data (ticketing, development, testing, etc.)
- OCM Service Delivery Platforms and Strategies
- DX Service Delivery Platforms

Where possible, make the data feed real-time. Everyone will thank you for the resulting simplicity.

Embedding Required Cultural Transformation in the Organization

"When it comes to digital transformation, the biggest mistake leaders make is that they focus too much on 'digital' and not nearly enough on 'transformation.' Get the transformation part right and the digital part will fall into place."

Charlene Li,
Author of *The Disruption Mindset* and Senior Fellow at Altimeter, a Prophet company

Organizations do not change, people do! People do not like to "be" changed; for any change to stick, people must change on their own accord. Culture provides momentum for change, as it offers "multisensory" context for "how things are done." To stay ahead of culture's impact, leadership must actively develop and manage it. For "if you don't manage culture, it manages you."[4] Culture change is directly correlated with leadership engagement as well as their communications and behaviors.

The challenge under DX is to develop an innovation culture, one that embraces change and experimentation and has leadership with a high tolerance for uncertainty. To help leaders transition to the new model, agile leadership coaching should be made available. Furthermore, leadership can accompany Apollo DX teams as they journey through an assignment of high uncertainty to gain confidence in the process. Lastly, OCM is also able to provide communications coaching and feedback to help develop the innovation culture.

Figure 6.4, the only model that even has a chance at succeeding at DX, is the organization that provides opportunity for

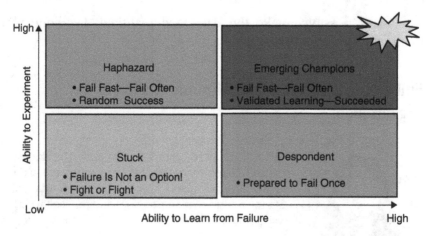

FIGURE 6.4 How to Succeed in DX: Uncertainty-Busting Matrix

Source: Sabine Margolis, S. Phillips (05/13/2020), Time to Shift the Change Management Paradigm: From Managing Change Projects to Leading Change Organizations [Bite Size Agility Webinar], Agile Business Consortium. doi: https://www.agilebusiness.org/page/resource-video-bitesize-change-management.

experimentation and learning. This is the model leadership should keep in mind when dealing with teams who work at the forefront of uncertainty. As long as a methodical approach is applied, a solution to the problem can be found.

Measuring User Adoption, Key Performance Indicators, and Benefits Realization

Measuring Business Value Archetype

Let us test the business operation platform and develop a metric with our newly identified field—business value—which is a new concept that identifies the IT's future business value on work performed today. This metric is intended to be part of an IT Business Value Dashboard (Figure 6.5).

Today's Business Value Dashboards (BVD) are specifically designed to show the IT value in a business context and can provide useful information on desktop support and network usage. However, they fall short of showing the IT value of "future engineering" activities.

To reflect business value, it matters how the numbers are reported with the reporting category and the numeric business value and how it will shape the conversation with various stakeholders:

- Envision many project scope battles of the past (regardless of whether you work in the business or IT). How would the information and dashboard have changed that conversation?
- Envision stakeholders who see this picture on their daily dashboards, a dashboard that lets them drill down on any of the columns to see what scenarios are affected and what objects are being developed. Wouldn't that change the steering committee status meeting?
- What if your OCM team sees this and notes the alarming number of remaining objects. Wouldn't the dashboard and chart help them strike a dialog with the business to see what is truly required?

Objective	Measure Description	Business Value of Development Objects		
Ability to show business value in the work IT performs				
Objective Owner	**Measurement Type**	*Leading Indicator*		
Bill M.	**Measurement Formula**	*(object count * scenario business value)*		
Desired Results	**Unit of Measure**	*None—Count of development objects by Bus. Value H = 3; M = 2; L = 1*		
As a project manager, I want to show the business value of development objects so that my team can deliver what is important to the business.	**Measure Location**	*Code in Analytics Platform (Business Operations Platform)*		
	Measure Owner	*Susan J.*		
	Data Source	*Org Metadata, IT Delivery Systems (Smartsheets, Service Now, JIRA) . . .*		
	Collection Frequency	*Real-time*		
Measurement	**Reporting Frequency**	*Real-time*		
Visual Order of magnitude for value creation & development objects count (investigate the delta between actual count and business value)	**Approved by**	*Vinnie B.*		
	Results Validated by	*Lipi S.*		
	Presentation	BVD: Business Value Dashboard		
	Targets and Thresholds	Green	Amber	Red
	Impl., Revisit & Planned Sunset Dates	xx/xx/20	xx/xx/21	12/31/23

FIGURE 6.5 Functional Metrics Design Form Expanded

Source: Anonymous, (2020), How to Develop KPIs/Performance Measures [Blog Post], KPI.org, https://kpi.org/KPI-Basics/KPI-Development.

- As DX's focus is all about value creation for the future, leadership now has a powerful tool that can communicate their vision into reporting accessibility by everyone in the organization.

Metrics and Data-Driven Culture

With benefits realization metrics defined, OCM can facilitate your organization's shift to a data-driven culture.

- **Best Practices Are Not KPIs.** They may serve as an inspiration but should never blindly become a KPI to measure your organizational benefits as there may be underlying reasons that are driving the KPI.
- **Measure the Process, Not the People.** When people feel they are being measured for their individual performance, especially when the measurement is not on activity solely in their control, they react with a fight-or-flight response. Fight triggers overtime and aggressive behavior and flight triggers resignation. Neither outcome creates an engaged employee.
- **Create a Data Culture Methodology.** A data-driven culture starts in the current state. Assuming the benefit realization of how KPIs are defined, measure these KPIs in the current state ecosystem. This provides an ample runway for the business and OCM to create a KPI analysis method that demonstrates shared accountability. Once established, OCM must actively coach management on their adherence to the methodology and ensure all affected teams have access to view the KPIs. The goal is to empower teams with the problem-solving skills required.
- **Create a KPI Constellation**. Benefit realization KPIs are the North Star to accomplishing the new normal. The majority should focus on process output to validate that all systems are running under the new normal and a few may have ambitious financial goals. We recommend a four-stage approach:

1. Leadership defines the DX mission and high-level ERP/CRM implementation goals.
2. Each operational team creates a few but balanced KPIs by their respective workstream (BOP architecture to the rescue!).
3. Operational teams validate KPIs are in balance across workstreams.
4. Leadership approves KPI alignment with implementation goals.

An operational step validation session. KPIs should ensure they do not artificially force a process out of its balance. For example, avoid increasing throughput while sacrificing quality at all costs. As a guideline, define KPIs across three of the following four quadrants (see Figure 6.6) and always include a productivity metric.

Responsiveness	Productivity
(how fast)	(how much & pace)
• Lead Time Metrics	• Throughput
• Cycle Time Metrics	• How much per Hr/Day/Week
[Threshold Metric]	[North Star of Metrics]
Predictability	**Quality/Efficiency**
(how repeatable)	(how well)
• Forecast Accuracy	• Number of Service Tickets
	• Number of Active Users
	• Number of Process Corrections
[Threshold Metric]	[Threshold Metric]

FIGURE 6.6 Metric Quadrants

Source: Sabine Margolis, T. Magennis (08/25/2016), Driving Change with Data – How to Get Started with Continuous Improvement, Planview Leankit. doi: https://vimeo.com/180219147.

■ **All KPIs must have an expected completion date**. This date cannot be a stretch goal. Instead, pick a reasonable date with ample time for the teams to accomplish, and that also reflects a business-critical **schedule.**

Try to distinguish stretch from status quo goals. Benefits realization can either entail returning to the previous status quo or represent an entirely new goal.

Measure Benefits Realized Post Go-Live

When a workstream accomplishes the benefit constellation, it is time to turn the KPI off! Too many metrics confuse. Your team is now ready to activate new KPIs, especially ones to manage alignment with the DX roadmap. However, proceed with observation; if other team constellations start to fail, your change may be the culprit. However, you don't know until you know. That is part of fail early and fail often until it is right.

CX for DX a New Measurement

Many organizations perceive themselves as customer experience centric (CX), but often it is a small front-office team that manages this experience, disconnected from the rest of the organization. Neither side can communicate how they affect the customer experience. However, back-office operations like shipping have a greater effect on the customer experience than anything the front-office team can offer. KPIs on how your organization affects the customer is an invaluable discussion for the entire organization to have.

However, companies today are measuring backwards. That is "how the customer is performing for us."[5] To become truly CX centric, companies must also measure "how the company is performing for its customers."

A new CX measure category is called "CPIs" for customer performance indicators. CPIs and KPIs are essentially the same idea but differentiate themselves by the customer-centric focus. A CPI aligns with outcomes relevant to the customer, such as payment flexibility or a quick turnaround time of a service. CPIs measures in increments of value to the customer, such as time, convenience, savings, and recognition. CPI development has four tempting mistakes:

1. Adopting the CPIs from other sources: CPIs miss the essence of how your customers perceive you.
2. Relying on expert judgment of internal teams: CPIs based on localized understanding of customer centric.
3. Relying on focus groups: CPIs reflect only what customers did, not what customers really do.
4. Relying on surveys: CPIs reflect only what customers said, not what customers really do.

Observing customers in their "natural habitat" is essential to capturing criteria that matters. Processes and KPIs should be accessed on how they affect CPIs and the connection logged in your BOP. Organizations report this activity as essential to CX transformation success, as the back-office and front-office silos become a thing of the past and the customer experience soars.

Summing Up

DX is about people and how they can experiment with technology to isolate game-changing uses. Organizations must fundamentally rethink their structures, by experimenting with new designs now, as networked organizations are the market disrupting approach. For the alternative, a drastic, force-fitted overnight change from hierarchy to networked, is otherwise inevitable. Good news is that the herein proposed solution offers a viable alternative. It enables the organization to experience what DX means firsthand in a prototype agile ecosystem and helps shape what that change means for the organization. Agility is achieved by a culture with a high tolerance for uncertainty embracing "fail fast/fail often" in daily operations and leadership. The key to change lies in enabling everyone to work at pace. The single most important tool for this agility is pooling your organization's metadata, so you not only see the results of your process (ERP/CRM) but also how it is executed, by whom, what influences it, and how your change relates to CX and business value.

Organizational Change Management for Dynamics 365 and DX
Digital Future Checklist:

✓ OCM for MS Dynamics project means executing both a systems adoption program and developing a DX-ecosystem prototype.
✓ Plan approach before you start the MS Dynamics 365 project.
✓ Initiate the Business Operations Platform (BOP).
✓ Create KPIs that communicate business with BOP.
✓ Mix approaches from business, technology, and analytics.
✓ Ensure OCM and DX have digital tools.
✓ Individual DX experiences are key to DX enablement.

Guilherme Santana,
Head of Digital Transformation Change Management & Communications at DHL Supply Chain

"Digital transformation changes the landscape of every industry. The need to change is a strategic imperative. Clear connection to the organization's strategy goes a long way to on-board people on this journey. Get that strategy playbook out and get started on business context: change purpose, vision, and desired outcome. Only after that can you go the project management route. Keep in mind that change happens through individual experiences, not tools, manuals, or training. It is difficult and does not happen overnight. Your organization is stepping outside its comfort zone, and so should you. Your leadership attributes will become the pillars to sustain the change and build a digital future."

Notes

1. D. Mahadevan (01/10/2017), ING's Agile Transformation, McKinsey. doi: https://www.mckinsey.com/industries/financial-services/our-insights/ings-agile-transformation.
2. YouTube demo on Data Visualizer. www.youtube.com/watch?v=O2qWMFtyT3s.
3. LinkedIn Learning, Power Query Overview – Automate Data Tasks in Excel & Power BI. www.youtube.com/watch?v=vq9AgAtSvQg.
4. Edgar H. Schein (2010), Organisational Culture and Leadership.
5. G. Cornfield (04/30/2020), The Most Important Metrics You're Not Tracking (Yet), *Harvard Business Review.* doi: https://hbr.org/2020/04/the-most-important-metrics-youre-not-tracking-yet.

CHAPTER 7

Fundamentals of Executing a Successful Dynamics 365 Project

Do not judge me by my successes, judge me by how many times I fell down and got back up again.

—Nelson Mandela

Do you follow or have you watched any episode of MasterChef? I have managed to watch a few of them and its quite interesting to find how much preparation and planning goes into the making of one dish. The contestants start with selection of ingredients, planning where timing plays an integral part, defining the dish with combined creativity and innovation and finally the moment of truth, presenting before the judges or guests waiting for the decision. I have seen many contestants—even though they might be good chefs in their own little world—crumble under time pressure, make many mistakes during cooking, not finish on time, or create a dish that was not edible at all. There are also contestants who have taken feedback during the entire process and, with well-thought-out planning and a good strategy in place, have shined as winners.

You can take this scenario and if you investigate the occurrence of events, you can easily identify that the key to success starts with preparation and planning for the end goal in sight with a fixed time-line or fixed resources. The rest is to prepare for your journey, plan, listen, action, and adjust your roadmap.

The benefits of planning are evident and fundamental. Accomplishing any project lies in the reasons for it and the plans for achieving the goals. It is all about the vision and execution, and a business project such as a Dynamics 365 project is no different.

To execute a successful Dynamics 365 project and leverage its benefits to achieve a full digital transformation will require engagement from all areas of your business. The preparation, planning, execution, and completion of the project to implement Dynamics 365 will have massive benefits for your organization and wherever possible you should involve your own people in this. Get guidance, hire consultants, engage with experts, but make sure you also back-fill staff and redeploy them in this journey to a future state. Otherwise, when all the outside agents leave you, they will revert back to the old ways of thinking and working.

Effective Communication

Try to make your communication plan effective by having a strategy for communication. What do you need to communicate? Who and in what frequency do you need to communicate? You may identify that you may need to tailor your communication to different groups based on their interest and influence levels.

Your communication should regularly indicate the following:

- The reason for the project (your business case for change).
- The roadmap (timescales, planned activities, dependencies, assumptions).
- Highlight any known and identified risks that need to be addressed.
- Do not hesitate to communicate about the unknown risks that you may come across during the journey, but there will be an impact assessment and a plan to mitigate them. Encourage feedback on a regular basis.

You need to consider the following to encourage and engage all stakeholders:

- Respond to feedback received, as silence is a demotivator when we are talking about digital transformation programs and projects.
- Regularly explain the plans and actions with a progress update.
- Recognize imperfections and that some areas of the business may start to feel left behind.
- Thanking people for their patience, validating getting what you want.
- Recognition is a motivator if done right, even for those waiting.

Have you thought about collecting your business metrics, which will drive your future goals and enable you to measure against the current business capabilities? These serve future purposes:

- They set the baseline against which you can measure future stabilization.
- They indicate the complexity/scale of the cutover tasks.
- They provide focus on data/processes that need to be cleaned up.
- They provide a benchmark for benefits realization.

Help others to understand what is going on. Communication is critical and will help you set the direction, culture, and habits of the project and beyond.

One common fallacy is to think about the solution ahead of defining the business needs and the business. Challenge these needs to ensure that they are real and strategic, not just how things are normally done in the current state. A Dynamics 365 solution can make your business run more efficiently by following standard practices for the most part, identifying any unique or specific business requirements related to regulatory, country-specific, or product-related issues, and will help you identify the gaps and your competitive advantage.

A warning: Creating endless lists of requirements based on the current ways of working and customizing the solution is not cost-effective or best practice, and may not be future proof for upgrades and patches. In fact, based on customer feedback sessions, we have seen CIOs rank this as their number one mistake.

You should know as much about your business and your requirements as possible to get the most out of technical and consultant support. Select a partner or a specialist who can provide advisory services and who is equipped with industry-specific process frameworks tailored for Dynamics 365. Let them suggest how to run standard processes in the system. Identify critical gaps and then determine a suitable way forward based on the gap requirements that your business teams come up with. This avoids the "because this is how we have always done it" mentality and gives permission to be creative around real needs.

Importance of Design Thinking, UX Design, and Customer Journey Mapping

Often referred to as "outside the box" or "outside in," Design Thinking has attracted interest because you can apply its methods to promote innovation. It is an iterative process that tries to understand the user, question assumptions, and redefine problems to identify alternative strategies and solutions. Design Thinking is regarded as a system of three overlapping themes:

1. **Viability.** The business perspective of design thinking.
2. **Desirability.** The user's perspective.
3. **Feasibility.** The technological perspective.

Innovation increases when all three perspectives are considered.

UX Design is user-centric design, bringing the user to the forefront and encouraging thought processes that include empathy for the person using a system. It is not to suggest that business needs and processes are not considered, but is more about considering the user experience and how improving that improves the business. There are five phases to Design Thinking:

1. **Empathize.** With users
2. **Define.** Users' needs, their problem, and your insights
3. **Ideate.** Challenge assumptions and produce ideas for innovative solutions
4. **Prototype.** Begin creating solutions
5. **Test.** Your solutions

These steps are not linear. They can occur in parallel and are often iterated over, generally starting with the empathize step.

What is the relationship between Design Thinking and UX Design? Both are user centric and driven by empathy. UX designers use many of the steps laid out in the Design Thinking process, such as user research, prototyping, and testing.

Despite these similarities, there are distinctions to be made between the two. The impact of Design Thinking is more strategic; it tries to understand user needs, technological feasibility, and business requirements to discover possible solutions. Design Thinking is embraced and implemented by all different teams across the business, including at the executive level. Design Thinking focuses on finding solutions, while UX design is concerned with designing these solutions and making sure they are usable, accessible, and pleasant for the user.

Benefits of Design Thinking

Integrating Design Thinking into your process could add huge business value, ultimately ensuring that the processes designed are not only desirable for users but also viable in terms of the company's budget and resources. With that in mind, let us consider some of the main Design Thinking that we need to apply in the Dynamics 365 implementation teams and the business:

- **Implement "out of the box" standard.** Do not start from a blank canvas for Design Thinking; instead start with the "out of the box" standard wherever possible. This helps in significantly reducing changes to standard Dynamics 365 by reducing the amount of time spent on re-design and configuration in Dynamics 365.

- **Start early user engagements.** Improves people retention and loyalty on the product with early engagement of users, familiarization with product designs, and boosts a user-centric approach.
- **Cultivates innovation.** Design Thinking fosters a culture of innovation that extends well beyond the project team by challenging assumptions and established beliefs.
- **Can be applied company-wide.** Design Thinking is not just for the Dynamics 365 project. It leverages group thinking, encourages cross-team collaboration, and can be applied to virtually any team in the business.

Using Design Thinking, Lean, and Agile Together

Design Thinking is how we explore and solve problems, Lean is our framework for testing our beliefs and learning our way to the right outcomes, and Agile is how we adapt to changing conditions with software development lifecycles.

Mauro Porcini, SVP & Chief Design Officer, PepsiCo

"Design thinking lives at the crossroad amongst empathy, strategy, and prototyping. With empathy we understand people's needs and wants. We then transform those insights into an actionable strategy, considering the business, and technical and cultural implications of our ideas. Then we start to prototype, with a sketch on a napkin all the way to a functioning 3D model. The prototype is not just a simple visualization of the idea, it's actually a tool to facilitate relevant thinking, to enable conversations, to validate hypotheses, to test the strategy, to engage the user, to generate cross-functional work, with speed and agility. Too many times, too many people, in too many books, from too many stages, have reduced design thinking to the mere idea of processes, tools, and frameworks. Successful design thinking is much more than that. Successful design thinking is all about people and the quality of their thinking and of their feeling. Or in other words, it's all about human beings that with intellect and emotions, with intuition and analysis, with brains and guts, with optimism and curiosity, understand the needs and the desires of other human beings, and then imagine, define, and produce the most meaningful solutions for them. Design thinking is all about *people in love with people*."

"If you want to successfully manage project time-scales in an Agile environment, the key is to create an agile team culture that takes ownership and accountability for all the decisions that may have an impact on time and budget. During the course of a project there will be many occasions where several approaches can be taken to solve a problem or create a solution-different design option, nuances in how something can be managed technically, tooling decisions, and so on. If the team has a good sense of accountability and ownership over the 'time' element of what they are doing, these occasions will naturally be highlighted throughout the project by team members to the entire team. Team members stop making siloed decisions, big or small, about the approach to take and start openly communicating the different options, so that the time-impact of each can be determined properly, with collaborative input, collective understanding and able to assess the overall impact on resource and budget. The key is shared ownership and accountability over 'time'; once you have this you will find that time-line 'surprises' happen less, changes are known in-advance, stakeholder management is easier, and you have a much happier, calmer team."

Kathryn Moore,
Senior Product Owner,
Mercedes-Benz

Design Thinking is a solution-based approach to investigating and solving problems. Its focus is on generating ideas with a specific problem in mind but keeping the user at the heart of the process. Agile ties all of this into short and iterative sprint cycles, allowing adaptability in the face of change. In an agile environment, ideas are improved and built upon incrementally. Again, cross-team collaboration plays a crucial role. The best practice approaches and methodologies taken from Design Thinking, Lean, and Agile cut out unnecessary processes, valuing the contributions of all key stakeholders for continuous delivery and improvement, and delivering early benefit and values to business.

What Tools Can Be Used to Help With Design Thinking?

There are many tools that are used in Design Thinking, which include: Personas, Empathy Maps, Stakeholder Maps, Customer Journey Maps,

Service Blueprints, Rapid Prototyping, and Business Model Innovation. Below is a suggested tool to use at each stage of the Design Thinking process.

- **Empathize using an Empathy Map.** Empathy mapping defines a user persona and characterizes your target users to make effective design decisions. Pay attention to users' needs, goals, expectations, behavior, habits, and so on (see Figure 7.1).
- **Define User Journey Mapping.** User journey mapping is a way of deconstructing the user experience into a series of small steps. This is commonly used while working with Dynamics 365.
  - A retrospective map should be used to track the way they usually behave.
  - A prospective map should be used to outline how you expect users to behave with a new process or system.
- **Ideate.** This is a way to encourage getting fresh and innovative ideas, which is also most exciting because it offers the possibility of imagining the unimaginable and making it real.

    There are several rules to follow here: set a time limit, stay on topic, be visual, and build on each other's ideas.

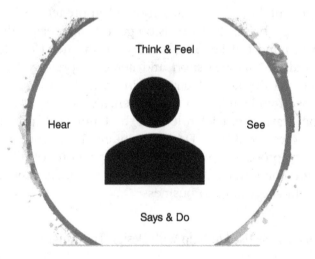

FIGURE 7.1 Empathy Map

The ideation process can help you with:

- Asking the right questions.
- Thinking unconventionally and beyond the obvious.
- Discovering surprising possibilities for your product.
- Coming up with innovative solutions.

There is no such thing as a bad or unwanted idea; consider everything.

- **Prototype.** This phase benefits from the Agile methodology and includes software development methods for collaboratively building business solutions. The core Agile concepts include:
- Iterative development
- Risk management
- Transparency

Another useful tool for use in the prototyping phase is the Service Blueprint. This visualizes the relationships between different service components—people, propositions, and processes—that are directly tied to points in a user journey.

The Nielsen Norman Group (www.nngroup.com) user experience specialists created a map split into four lanes: (1) user/customer actions, (2) front stage actions, (3) back stage actions, and (4) support processes.

Using Design Thinking concepts and having a User-Centric approach to the implementation of Dynamics 365 and your Digital Transformation will give a different perspective to the project and the planning. Use this as part of the digital transformation when implementing Dynamics 365 and consider your users as well as the business processes and the concepts of innovative thinking and challenging assumptions will stand the project in good stead as it moves forward.

Establishing Clear Design Principles at the Outset

"If you don't know where you are going, you'll end up someplace else."

—*Yogi Berra*

This well-worn quote stands the test of repetition because it is so true. It applies to many things, not least plans, processes, and design principles. In the last section we covered Design Thinking and UX Design but in the digital transformation roadmap it is pertinent to lay out the design principles at the very beginning. Without clear communication on design principles to the project team, users' group, and business group you could end up with something hugely different from your vision.

There are several design principles to think carefully about when considering your Dynamics 365 implementation:

- **Redesign from the ground up.** Without the need to support out-of-date business processes or a legacy code, designers are free to learn from industry experience. Security, separation of duties, newer standards, and more recent legislation can be incorporated in the initial design. Designers create uncomplicated business processes and code, which then supports easier implementation. Design your business processes to fit with industry norms and best practices, and most of your business will run without any problems and your people can then be released to work on adding more value.
- **User-Centric Design (UCD).** Use UCD principles and you could achieve remarkable solutions. The user interface provides a mechanism for customizing the vocabulary of terms used by the system in its communication to the user, helping users understand what they are doing in the context of their own business area. Use the hints and tips to support the correct processes that you have documented. Effort early in this area will have a big impact on compliance, positivity, and costs.
- **Identify and go with "out of the box."** Design your forms keeping to an "out of the box" standard and, where possible, minimizing changes from the core product design. It will eventually help in software upgrades and running patches.
- **Single code base.** Supporting all customers on the same Dynamics 365 code improves Microsoft's efficiency. Effort is directed toward improving the software; no time is wasted adding features or patching security bugs in old releases. This lowers their cost structures and should enable them to continue to produce

and improve a stable, forward-thinking, and flexible platform and modules. Thinking the same way allows the business to concentrate more on giving its customers what they want, and less on how to resolve internal processes and problems.

- **Operates in the cloud.** Microsoft, like other vendors, has really stopped offering software for customer servers. Without access to the source code, your programmers cannot modify the code (although they are almost infinitely configurable). Software restricted to configuration can be considered a limitation but prevents enterprises from storing up problems through ill-advised special features. Cloud software reduces programming costs plus the costs of massive infrastructure upgrades that exist with many on-premises ERP systems. However, this means you must keep on top of changes and improvements that are coming down the line.

- **Frequent small updates.** Cloud software relies on regular small upgrades. While many are transparent to users, some will require configuration changes after analysis by the internal business process team. With cloud-based ERP systems reimplementation is rarely required and is only likely with major acquisitions, divestitures, or business model changes. It removes the organizational need for system changes every decade or so. It means you can focus on what is important to your business and there will be no blaming the "old system" or the "new system."

Mistakes to Avoid

From experience, one of the mistakes that we have seen is engaging UI designers while mapping a business user journey and spending a few months' resources and budget working on the UI designs. This is where the organization does not have any experience working with Dynamics 365 and has not yet engaged any implementation partner but has started mapping the user journey. Please avoid the UX design upfront as you would be amazed that Dynamics 365 as a product comes with all the Design Thinking taken into consideration and, as part of implementation, you need to stay as close to "out of the box" as possible.

Shortening Project Timescales Through Empowered Decision Making and Collocated Teams

It is possible to use "follow the sun" methods to keep working on the project for 24 hours a day. This requires empowering your teams and a clear understanding of the target state with clear objectives that have been broken down into well-defined sections. If done well it allows for "out of the box" thinking that encourages creativity and can accelerate the program, but if done badly it costs time, money, and people.

Before you start your digital transformation consider which aspects must be done locally, which can be done globally (if 24-hour working is required), and how much you will need to empower others to make decisions. This is not a time for micromanagement, but equally you must not lose control. This is even more relevant in 2020 during the pandemic situation of Covid-19 with remote working practices as our new normal standard.

Self-Organizing Teams

Avoid the typical structure; instead set it according to activities and know-how. For example, structure along features:

- Data security in the onshore
- UI for accounts payable in the offshore
- Error reporting in the nearshore

Design out incompatible interfaces through creative thinking. Encourage feature groups to achieve business value before the end of the project.

Speeding Up Feature Development

Don't split features across teams. The feature provides a joint goal and enforces team spirit. If you empower the feature team they can gather (or gain) everything else required. This ensures that they work together and complete valuable sections in an iteration. Make sure all the teams are keeping each other informed, as gentle competition alongside collective responsibility will add further benefits.

Supporting a Feature Team Perspective

Depending on technology and the project size, you will need one architect supporting each feature team (or one architect supporting several feature teams if they are small, colocated, and similar), but there is only one chief architect. A technical service team or teams at the beginning will ensure the outputs are tested together.

Every feature team needs the business product owner's support and there may need to be multiple business product owners in this setup, so there must be close coordination between them. As features are implemented you can disband the teams and reduce the architects, so that at the end you should be left with a single lead architect and a technical support team who will understand every feature and integration.

Development Cycles

Don't prolong development cycles, as two-week iterations have been proven to work in the development phase. Listed here are key considerations of the development cycle:

- Frequent feedback should steer everyone in the right direction.
- Short cycles reduce risk.
- Balance feature accomplishment with risk reduction.
- Ensure delivery at the end of each iteration.
- Keep the same heartbeat across all sites, one or two standups per day to ensure teams stay in sync with each other.
- Holidays will require adjustment; it is often worth using these for other things (e.g., an onshore bank holiday gives the offshore and nearshore teams time to focus on something else).
- Hand the features completed to the technical support teams for execution into test and let them get on with testing and raising change requests.

Iteration Review and Planning

Plan the start and end of the iteration with an event that is acknowledged as a ceremony and encourage open conversations for receiving feedback and discuss ways for improvements. Listed here are some key considerations for review and planning based on best practices:

- Ensure iteration turnover is in the middle of the week to allow for start and end phases to complete.
- Pre-planning happens in the middle of the iteration to reduce friction between one iteration and the next.
- Product owners and architects decide on which features are given to the assorted teams.
- Each feature team plans individually but is guided by the product owner.
- Outcomes are visible and accessible in a prominent place.

For dispersed teams:

- Get together in person from time to time.
- Use different communication media if the teams are based in different countries (e.g., phone, webcam, MS Teams video, and audio conference).

Integration and Build

In your planning, try to allocate time for solution releases to different environments. Listed here are key considerations of planning that you need to build in your planning:

- Before expanding the solution release across sites ensure the integration and solution build is working at one site. The later you address problems the more difficult they get, so do not underestimate complexity and effort.
- Assign 15% of your time to create and manage artifacts as deliverables.
- Assign 10% of your development effort to releases.
- If a release iteration (sprint) is required for a bigger delivery, then each delivering team should send a representative (in person) to the integration site.
- Integration sites should alternate to ensure cohesion and remove any centralization or bias.

Trust

Using a dispersed model requires a great deal of trust on all sides, and mutual respect goes a long way to maintaining this. While widely dispersed teams are more difficult to manage there are some key methods that will help.

Closeness engenders trust, so face-to-face is preferable even remotely via video conference. The frequency and duration depend on the physical or sociological distance, and it is also a good idea to rotate people around sites.

Communication

Because trust is based on mutual respect, use different locations and change the meeting leader. Pay attention to vocabulary; a nightly build happens in the day for some people, the morning roll call is not always in the morning, and no one wants to work at a "remote site." It is harder to re-establish trust than to establish it. Misunderstood emails break trust, so keep the communication between sites personal. Have an ambassador at each site who is respected by all and can help keep people working together.

Documentation and Planning

When working across teams that are spread across the globe (or the country), documentation and planning are crucial to making sure the hand-offs are clear and timely. Stand-up meetings are important, but there must be a culture of actions documentation and dissemination to make sure everyone comes away with the same understanding. Misunderstandings increase risk and waste time. Plan all meetings and team interactions as far in advance as possible to reduce the time taken by them. Keep documentation in a way that reduces the friction of access from anywhere (on MS Teams or SharePoint, for example).

Culture

If you are going to locate teams across the world to take advantage of the 24-hour working opportunities, then cultures and the differences (and similarities) between the people working in the different environments will come into play.

Bridging cultural differences is quite integral as you deal with different cultures everywhere. You need to take into consideration the differences in culture due to geography, language, nation, political differences, values, and beliefs of groups. It is not that people are not used to this, but it just requires thought when dealing with a culture they are unfamiliar with. Try to respect each other and the history of different cultures.

Agility provides a culture of its own and commonalities can bridge the distance. Diversification allows us to have different perspectives on the same thing and to learn from each other. There is a significant positive side to distributed development.

Pragmatic Approach to the Agile Implementation of Dynamics 365

What Is Agile Project Management?

Traditional project management methodologies such as Waterfall, PMI's PMBOK, and PRINCE2 are all highly controlled and outline distinct stages for project planning from start to finish.

The Agile philosophy needs to be tempered with structure, planning, and considerable focus. Agile project management accepts uncertainty and places a higher value on responding to change over having a rigid plan. Agile planning urges you to work on something small, perform it quickly, get feedback, assess what is and what is not working, and adjust your plan from there. The key word here is planning, which is too often glossed over.

Principles of Agile Project Management

The core tenet at the heart of Agile project management is the idea of "inspect and adapt," which means last minute changes are welcome at any stage of the project cycle. The Manifesto for Agile Software Development outlines 12 principles:

1. Customer satisfaction is the highest priority, which you can ensure by delivering them valuable software early and continuously.

2. You welcome changing requirements, even late in development, for the customer's competitive advantage.
3. You deliver working software frequently, such as every few weeks rather than months.
4. You must have close, daily collaboration between the business people and the developers.
5. You build projects around motivated individuals, who deserve support and trust to get the job done.
6. Face-to-face conversation is the most efficient and effective form of communication.
7. Working software is the primary measure of progress.
8. Development should be sustainable. You must be able to maintain a constant pace indefinitely.
9. You must give continuous attention to technical excellence and good design.
10. Simplicity—the art of maximizing the amount of work not done—is essential.
11. The best architectures, requirements, and designs emerge from self-organizing teams.
12. Retrospection—the team should regularly consider how to become more effective and adjust accordingly.

Why Use Agile Project Management?

Agile project management is popular because it mirrors real life. Businesses move quickly, things change, and teams need to adapt to these changes. The 12th principle outlined in the Manifesto—Retrospection—helps teams understand what did and did not work and to adjust their workflow accordingly. This encourages teams to constantly improve.

Other benefits of Agile project management include:

- Testing early and often quickly detects issues, bugs, and defects before they become critical.
- Improving customer satisfaction because you keep them involved in the process every step of the way and integrate their feedback within the project.
- You almost remove the risk that your project will completely fail, because you always have a substantial working product.

Within an agile way of working, managers, leaders, and executives must empower project teams to make decisions.

All stakeholders engage with a process that is collaborative, iterative, and transparent. A feedback loop updates everyone on what needs to be improved. The team deliberates issues together and proposes a solution together.

You need to adopt agile decision making that enables the work to be ongoing and the team to make decisions faster.

Working in an agile methodology means making iterative progress as an empowered and self-organizing team. The project team delivers what the customer wants in the most efficient and successful manner, regularly checking with the customer to make sure they are on track.

Here are five tips for agile decision making that you may like to adopt.

1. **Gather iterative feedback.** Showing the work and getting feedback regularly reduces the chance of a major misunderstanding.
2. **Balance alignment and autonomy.** Your agile team needs to be empowered and as well-informed as possible when making decisions. However, make sure the goals are clear and in the front of the team's minds.
3. **Get comfortable with good enough.** One huge mindset change that is needed is getting comfortable with "good enough." The requirements documented are "good enough." The readiness to start is "good enough." You can work toward "great" during the execution process.
4. **Place time limits on decisions.** Project managers love timelines and due dates. Agile decision making needs timelines. Set deadlines for when analysis must be stopped because it is likely to be good enough.
5. **Don't get sloppy.** A regular meeting rhythm builds trust with senior leaders, improves the strength of the team, and builds the team's confidence in their decision-making skills. Give updates, brainstorm for improvements, plan the next block of tasks for a sprint, and get iterative feedback on what has been delivered.

Incorporating Traditional Planning Approaches with the Flexibility of Agile and Scrum

Agile is not considered a methodology but is an overarching philosophy or belief system. There are many different methodologies with which you can implement Agile principles. One of the most prevalent Agile methodologies is Scrum.

We are going to discuss 10 comprehensive steps of Agile project management with Scrum, but you should always consider this in the context and dynamics of the team you are working with, and you may need to add a few more additions to the list by keeping in mind the delivering value.

1. Make a list of all the things you and your team need to do. This is your "backlog." Get into the details and try to break down tasks into their smallest parts and make them visible.
2. Create a Task Board to list all the things you will accomplish over the next week or two. This is your "sprint" or "iteration."
3. Plan your Task Board. This is "iteration planning" or "sprint planning." On the Task Board, you should map out and plan multiple iterations.
4. Assign someone on your team to each task in your sprint. Ownership motivates.
5. Prioritize the tasks in your upcoming sprint. Agile project management favors categorizing tasks according to four priorities: critical, high, medium, and low.
6. Estimate how long each task will take. As people go through their tasks they need to consider the amount and complexity of the work and any risk or uncertainty in the task.
7. Start! Communicate with the team, keep them up to date on where things stand.
8. Hold daily meetings (10 to 15 minutes maximum) with your whole team (face-to-face). Scrum calls these "dailies" or "stand-ups." This is an opportunity to discuss issues as a group and decide on the best course of action.
9. When you finished your sprint review, analyze what worked and what didn't. This is "retrospection." No mistake should be glossed over as they help the team's workflow to constantly improve.

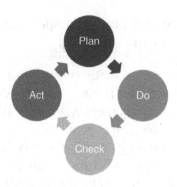

FIGURE 7.2 The PDCA Model

10. When the sprint is complete, move it to the bottom of your board and start the new iteration at the top. Keep repeating this process and make sure you keep the boards constantly updated. Didn't finish everything? Move it to the next one. If a task from a previous sprint needs looking at again, just drag it into your current sprint.

These are 10 steps but they still boil down to the frequently seen diagram shown in Figure 7.2.

Scrum methodologies are catered for in Azure DevOps and all the above steps can be managed there.

"There are many ways to do Scrum right, but there is one definite way of doing Scrum wrong, and that is—doing it by the academic version of Agile. Context is more important than Content in any process implementation."

Nitin Malhotra,
Senior Director, Head of EPMO (Enterprise PMO), Chipotle Mexican Grill

Embrace Change: Deliver to Time and Budget

Here we will explore work methods you can be confident in and that strike the right balance in the midst of change.

- **Traditional or Waterfall Methodologies.** This is a useful methodology to use as the wrapper for your Digital Transformation. It sets up the structure and encourages good planning, a carefully considered project charter, and clear roles and responsibilities.
- **Iterative Work Management.** This method uses a hybrid approach, including shorter work periods (sprints) and adding responsiveness to change as the work progresses. It is especially useful during the configuration phases as setup and test cycles can be worked through quickly.
- **Collaborative Work.** Cross-functional teams should be created without restrictions such as location and language and assigned to delivery tasks and "out of the box" thinking. It is especially useful when you are challenging the status quo and want to look at outdated or unnecessary business practices.
- **Lean-Agile Delivery.** This is used to get departments and cross-functional teams to consider their processes and what they do and don't need in the Dynamics 365 implementation.

As organizations adapt to new work methodologies, new approaches to planning, funding, and analysis will develop, shifting to "just enough" governance and a Lean approach to portfolio management. While annual plans and project-based funding have their place, they are often being replaced inside the project with incremental or iterative funding practices that allow for shifting priorities, new ideas, and emerging requirements.

There is no such thing as a perfect system and you don't want one. If your system is perfect, how unlikely are you to let go of it? A good-enough system allows for constant improvement and change. A Dynamics 365 system that is 80% of the way is one that is reducing your business costs significantly and already increasing your flexibility. Don't wait for a perfect system; it will cost you more than going live with an imperfect one.

As an example of this, an engineering company in the United Kingdom with no previous ERP system implemented one badly because their largest customer insisted on them having an ERP if they were to continue doing business.

The focus soon came on the need to work collaboratively; teams had always been able to do their own thing, but the new system forced them to work together cross-functionally. This led to improvements in working practices, communication, and understanding. As the implementation is reworked by a new partner, the organization benefits from the experience. Implementing badly is not recommended but it shows that a system does not need to be perfect to achieve benefits.

Maximus Ndaboka,
Technology Specialist,
Nestle

"In 2009 when I was working for a mining company in Africa, we were assigned an ERP project implementation from A to Z. A team of four young dynamic developers knew nothing about Agile approaches found themselves in a complex environment.

We found out that even the executive leadership was unaware about Agile best practices and executing projects with Agile approaches. The project failed, why?

The *strategic planning* from top management didn't include any face-to-face meetings with our direct business stakeholders on a regular frequency. We didn't build any relationship with our client stakeholders and didn't have any feedback on the ongoing build of the project. Tasks were time consuming.

When it was time to deliver the project, we had never met with any client business stakeholders and what we had was only the list of specifications. There were many things to consider that we didn't even think about: new needs raising, changes, adjustments, and a new go-live schedule. The project was an ultimate failure. Then we were supposed to take another 6 months to include all these new features, needs and changes, but unfortunately this traditional approach didn't allow that. From that time, we saw the importance of Agile approaches.

We then knew from that experience that traditional strategic planning models don't work, certainly not in the rapidly changing world we live in today and, I would argue, fundamentally they never did. Traditional leadership practices are outdated and ineffective in today's workplace.

What are the weaknesses with the Traditional Strategic Planning model?

1. **It's linear.** The world is volatile. Markets are volatile. Businesses need to adapt rapidly. None of this lends itself to a linear approach.
2. **It is often complex, laborious, and time-consuming.** Never has the need for rapid deployment been greater than it is today. What is needed is a straightforward, non-complex approach.
3. **It is static and lacks agility.** The "digital revolution" shows that things are changing rapidly and business leaders need the ability to respond in kind. What is needed is a process that is agile enough to respond rapidly to unforeseen turns of events.
4. **It does not leverage failure.** We should learn to leverage our failures in real-time rather than view them as shortcomings. What is needed is a process of experimentation, failure, learning, and agility.
5. **It is more often than not implemented top-down.** Great ideas in an organization come from the bottom up, from its rank-and-file members, and not from top to down. There is a need for listening to feedback from everyone and adapt."

A Different Approach

"In 2019, I was involved in the Microsoft Dynamics implementation for the Heineken Group in Congo, and that was the biggest Opco in terms of complexity. Every morning, at 8:30 a.m., we were standing around a table, looking on the white board containing sprints. This is called a 'SCRUM Meeting' and is a 15-minute time-boxed event for the development team to plan for the next 24 hours.

The three daily standup questions are:

1. What did you do yesterday?
2. What will you do today?
3. Anything blocking your progress?

The team gets on the same page in terms of who completed specific tasks. You discover this: *What still needs completion? Based on yesterday's results, do our plans change today?*

As results. The team is transparent if it is on track to complete the sprint goal. Teammates get a chance to help each other by removing blockers/impediments.

Then at the end of the week, we do what we call 'Sprint Retrospective,' where even the business customers are invited to validate together with the team their specifications so that the changes, suggestions, and adjustments discussed during that weekly meeting are directly taken into account and recycled into the *next sprint*.

With this approach, leadership is very Agile and many mistakes are avoided as we are continuously learning, listening, and adopting."

In Conclusion

"Agile organizations are both stable and dynamic. They work through a network of small, empowered teams; use rapid decision and learning cycles; use next-generation-enabling technology; have a *'north star'* embodied across the organization; and focus on customers, embedding customer centricity in all they do. They have tried and tested practices that can fluidly adapt and adjust to market changes, innovative technology, customer feedback, and government regulation. They are open, inclusive, and non-hierarchical, evolving continually without the frequent disruptive restructurings required in more mechanistic organizations and they embrace uncertainty and ambiguity with greater confidence. Such organizations, we believe, are far better equipped for the future.

This new kind of agile organization requires a new and fundamentally different kind of leadership. Because leadership and how leadership shapes culture are the biggest barriers to—and the biggest enablers of—successful agile transformations."

Summing Up

In this chapter we have looked at the approach to the project and what elements of project management principles are worth following, and what levels of change can and should be accepted as you progress.

In Chapter 8, we will talk about how you can maximize the help you get from inside and outside the organization and the project teams. In this way, we will both consider the eventual users of the system and the customers.

Digital Future Checklist

✓ Communicate well and often.
✓ Develop and then Test, Functional Test, and UAT Test.
✓ Cleanse your data early.
✓ Design with the Customer at the heart of the system.
✓ Use the right project tools in the right areas.
✓ Embrace change, but do not let perfect get in the way.

"Think big; think disruptive. Execute with full passion."
—*Masayoshi Son, Japanese Businessman*

Customer Stories

HICKORY FARMS OPTIMIZES SEASONAL SALES AND CUSTOMER SERVICE USING DYNAMICS 365

Challenge

Hickory Farms is a holiday food gift retailer of cheese, meats, fruit, and nuts with 150 full-time and over 4,000 seasonal employees and multiple selling channels. Ninety percent of its business is generated during the holiday season, starting in late November. Since 1951, the Chicago-based company has enriched family gatherings with delicious meats, cheeses, and sweets.

Hickory Farms had 20-year-old systems for their catalogue, kiosk, and online businesses that were built up in silos as the business grew over time, and many integration points between the legacy systems. Hickory Farms describes their sales channels as wholesale operating as a traditional company selling products, online/catalogue with three paths to order—ecommerce, call center; and mail, brick-and-mortar stores; and corporate gifting. It was incredibly challenging for Hickory Farms to focus on delivering a valuable and personalized customer experience with all the disparate systems and lack of one single view.

Solution

Hickory Farms decided that a software as a service solution would be a fit-for-purpose solution and would provide the flexibility, scalability, and efficiency the business needed to serve all channels and drive growth across all channels. Hickory Farms chose Microsoft Dynamics 365 for Operations on Azure as a solution and selected RSM as a Technology consulting partner to deliver the solution in a two-phase approach.

Hickory Farms is excited with their systematic, scalable, modern cloud-based Dynamics 365 system that is updated to stay current and provides a single version of the truth across all sales channels, an integrated view of performances across all channels, and allows them to run the business more holistically and faster and can be managed and optimized by their staff.

Outcome and Benefits

"With Dynamics365, we'll have a single version of the truth across all our sales channels and can run our business more holistically."

Matt James: Chief Operating Officer, Hickory Farms (used with permission of Hickory Farms)

Hickory Farms" growth strategy has been to position the brand and business to grow in Q1–Q3 in three channels—wholesale, ecommerce, and corporate gifting. With Covid-19, they have shifted their focus and leaned even more across these three channels and are able to drive growth and a huge increase in their off-season business and in their corporate gifting, which were all remote.

Hickory Farms have achieved:

- Majority of gift sales occur in two months.
- Workforce grows from 90 to 4,500+ every holiday season.
- Serving customers through three distinct sales channels.
- Efficiency and transparency in one comprehensive solution: Dynamics 365.
- Allowing them to scale as needed given the Azure backbone and to go 100% remote for almost all of their staff with no infrastructure concerns and no VPN requirements.

STE. MICHELLE WINE ESTATES CRAFTS PREMIUM CUSTOMER EXPERIENCES WITH DYNAMICS 365 COMMERCE

Challenge

Ste. Michelle Wine Estates, one of the largest premium wine companies in the United States, prides itself on superior consumer experiences and has 4,000 competitors in the United States alone. Ste. Michelle Wine Estates recognized that delivering on a promise of luxury requires consistent engagement with customers across all shopping channels, and wanted to customize the tasting and purchase experience and to use technology to bring the "wow factor" to the brand experience.

Ste. Michelle had some experience on the Microsoft Dynamics Retail Management System (RMS) that was reaching end-of-life, and the different data they had about consumers was not centralized and also prevented making valuable connections between different points in a customer's purchase journey. Another challenge in their industry was that each state has different laws on how products could be shipped into those states, and their systems need to have the flexibility to accommodate that.

Solution

At the National Retail Federation 2019 conference, Ste. Michelle came to understand about Microsoft's offering for comprehensive, omnichannel capability and realized the need of a platform that could bring all the information into one accessible place and the capability to draw out insights across all different channels—physical tasting rooms, websites, email campaigns, social, and paid media channels.

Ste. Michelle recognizes that the implementation timeline of Dynamics 365 Commerce was extremely aggressive, so their first brand went live in Commerce on October 1, 2019, and by the end of January 2020 all of the other brands were moved over. With the new capabilities, they are making ordering more seamless and personalized, with consumers enjoying purchasing products, discovering new wines, and exploring features like wine clubs.

The CEO of Ste. Michelle had been very clear over the last year about the need to digitally transform, focus on being consumer centric, and leading and sponsoring the strategy.

Outcome and Benefits

> "What's exciting about Dynamics 365 Commerce is that it opens up so many possibilities for us to extend the reach of our imagination about what a luxury consumer experience can be."
>
> **Melanie Baker, Senior Director, Direct to Consumer and Retail Operations** (used with permission of Ste. Michelle Wine Estates)

Due to COVID-19, Ste. Michelle had to reconfigure their e-commerce fulfilment from a central location to a distributed model that Dynamics 365 made very easy, having a minimal impact on their consumers. Ste. Michelle has taken the learning from each store and brand go-live and acted upon the learning for the next go-live.

Ste. Michelle is continuing the innovation journey and continuous improvements to optimize for mobile viewing. Consumers can use smartphones to place an order while in the tasting rooms. Despite all challenges and reworking on the original plan during COVID-19, we have managed to engage with our clients across their preferred channels.

Ste. Michelle has achieved:

- Increased the growth in the direct-to-consumer channels by 40% compared to competitors.

- Able to identify active consumers beyond those listed in the current database and reach out to them in a personalized way through our various contacts.
- Deepened loyalty with existing consumers.

IN SEARCH OF FLEXIBILITY, AGILITY, AND PROVIDING A FOUNDATION FOR BUSINESS GROWTH, TILLAMOOK MOVED FROM MICROSOFT NAVISION TO DYNAMICS 365 FOR FINANCE AND OPERATIONS

Business Challenge

Tillamook County Creamery Association (Tillamook) is a farmer-owned co-op of about 80 farming family owners on the coast of Oregon. Tillamook continues to grow and works with best-in-class business partners, including other milk suppliers, co-manufacturers and distribution centers. Tillamook's growth and geographic expansion across the country led to the decision to have a flexible, reliable system to support dairy production and seamless integration with other systems.

Tillamook was operating on an earlier version of Microsoft Dynamics Navision that was heavily customized, preventing a clear upgrade path. Tillamook decided to engage in a formal request for a proposal reviewing various products like SAP, Oracle, Infor, and Microsoft Dynamics 365 for Finance and Operations (Dynamics 365). Tillamook selected Dynamics 365 because of the cloud offering, flexibility to stay current with upgrades, while still having the ability to modify the system to their specific business needs. Another influence that shaped the decision was that Tillamook's software partner RSM had a Diary module in Dynamics 365.

Solution

Tillamook took the approach of an "out of the box" solution first and customizing only where necessary instead of replicating the existing process. Tillamook and their partner RSM worked collaboratively using Azure DevOps for the sign-off on all "out of the box" and customization requirements. Upgrading from Dynamics Navision to Dynamics 365 was an 18-month implementation using a hybrid project management approach. However, once the configuration and development started, it was based on Agile disciplines with iterative functional and integrations testing for 12 months. Data Integration with about five other systems (i.e., EDI, Manufacturing Execution, Transportation, etc.) was the most complex part of the project, having one- or two-way data flows with each. Reporting was leveraged using Power BI capabilities. Data cleansing and data migration was carried out by Tillamook with guidance from RSM.

Tillamook went live with nearly all Dynamics 365 modules in November 2019 followed by three months of stabilization and an additional eight months to optimize gaps by automating any labor-intensive processes. They had a rigorous change management plan and execution during the implementation, ensuring that everyone was prepared for change. The people at Tillamook really made it successful.

Outcome and Benefits

"The biggest benefit for us is a cloud-based system that we can stay version current even with modifications and also the ability to easily access the system from anywhere there is an Internet connection. Dynamics 365 has given us that flexibility and agility with our business."

Travis Pierce, Director of Information Technology, Tillamook

When COVID-19 hit in March 2020, Tillamook was well prepared with the Dynamics 365 solution and their business operation did not have any impact with many team members working remotely from home and collaborating across the Dynamics 365 platform.

Tillamook's Dynamics 365 system has supported:

- Addition of new customers and more sales order volume
- An increase in demand due to COVID-19 that saw up to 30% sales increase depending on the product category
- 200 Users using the Dynamics 365 system remotely
- An increase in third-party suppliers

Tillamook continues to work on further enhancements in 2021 for Workflow Automation, Credit Management, Project Accounting, EDI with suppliers, and enhanced data integration with their Transporting system.

BREVILLE EXPANDS CULINARY EXPERIENCES BY ENTERING NEW MARKETS 80% FASTER

Challenge

Breville is a world leader in small kitchen appliances with creativity. Breville takes the time to understand both food and the user and help customers master every moment. Founded in Sydney in 1932, Breville has become an iconic global brand that enhances peoples' lives through design and brilliant innovation, delivering kitchen products to more than 70 countries around the globe.

Breville's existing Microsoft Dynamics AX 2012 application was region specific and included a lot of customizations, resulting in high maintenance and support costs, needed a longer time to enter a new market, and hence was unsustainable. Breville decided to move to Dynamics 365 global template system and processes with a vision of growth, innovation, and customer-centric approach.

Solution

After Microsoft introduced Avanade to Breville, this partnership agreed to implement an "out of the box" Microsoft Dynamics 365 with its standard processes and tools delivering with faster speed, better support, and better uptime.

Using the Agile methodologies principle, the solution focussed on building MVP (minimum viable product), created a core global template, and deployed the solution to multiple countries in consecutive wave deployments. The solution integrated warehousing, new regulatory processes, new functions to regional sales channels, integrated Power BI with Dynamics 365 for efficient access to data and analytics, providing a holistic view of the customer.

Outcome and Benefits

"These innovations not only improve our overall business performance, but they will also vastly improve the overall customer experience to help them master food moments. We have been able to deliver some incredible working processes that actually performed quite well in live environments around the globe."

Jeff Suellentrop, Vice President of Enterprise Architecture and Programs at Breville

"Our attitude toward this program was to break out of the traditional paradigms. We wanted to reimagine the way our core systems are designed, built, and deployed. This reimaging has permeated through the organization and changed how we think about tools and software."

Nathan O'Donnell, Breville's Global Program Lead, Business Systems

In FY20, Breville Group delivered strong revenue with a double-digit growth against a turbulent backdrop of US tariffs, Brexit uncertainty, exchange rate volatility, and COVID-19. Breville's top-line growth included the successful expansion into Spain and France.

Having a Dynamics 365 global template and virtualized team, Breville continued deployment in new regions and did not need to slow down deployment when COVID hit in March 2020.

Breville achieved:

- Entering new markets 80% faster and efficiently, no longer constrained by time and resources
- Agile continues business enhancement
- Transparency and visibility into the supply chain enhances the communication with customers on product availability, shipping, and delivery time

PART III

Driving Innovation and Improvements with Dynamics 365

This part focuses on go-live of the Dynamics 365 solution and how to prepare the organization before and after the go-live. This part also ends with real-life customer stories from organizations on their business challenges, solutions, and the benefits they have achieved.

Chapter 8: Does everyone understand their roles and responsibilities while working in a project or program? Do you understand how to measure user engagement and customer experience? Do you know what should be included in user documentation or how to leverage the community? If you have said no to any of these questions, then dive into this chapter.

Chapter 9: Often the engagements, discussions, and decisions related to application support are kept toward the end of the project lifecycle, future upgrades, and the process post go-live. This chapter will help you decide when is the right moment in the timeline to start these conversations.

Chapter 10: This chapter shows you how to build a culture of continuous improvements and periodic changes, making the best use of Dynamics 365 and instilling the right habits.

CHAPTER 8

Makers and Shakers of Dynamics 365 Transformation

You can have everything in life you want, if you will just help other people get what they want.

—Zig Ziglar

I remember explaining to a family member that the reason her mother had rejected her offers of help was not because she did not need or really want it, but because she could not bear the thought that she might be in some way beholden to her. This is not a sign of self-contained strength but one of deeply held weakness. We know how much we really benefit from the help and support of people around us, whether they are family, friends, or co-workers. These ties between people do not just bring about shared experiences; they also strengthen the ways we work together within an organization, whether this is a team or a family. Asking for and getting help as part of a project is far from a sign of weakness, but is a way of binding people together in a shared vision and working toward something larger than ourselves.

Running a team, a department, or a company cannot be done by one person. High-performing teams (and companies) work together to be efficient and effective, and a Digital Transformation team is no exception. In this chapter, we will look at all the places you can and should get support from and identify all the makers and shakers in the organization.

Help from within will not just come from the people taking responsibility. Business users can be a critical resource for help in making sure your digital transformation and Dynamics 365 implementation are successful. We start with the support you can expect from the people who have a more formal role in the transformation.

Project Charter: Roles and Responsibilities

The project charter (or project model or definition, if you prefer) is the statement of scope, objectives, and people who are participating in a project. It starts the process of describing the roles and responsibilities of the participants and outlines the objectives and goals of the project. The charter should also identify the key stakeholders and define the authority of the project manager. The charter has much more in it than details of what the people will be doing in the Dynamics 365 project, but without them you will not have a positive implementation.

Because it is people who will implement your digital transformation through the implementation of your Dynamics 365 system, you need to make sure everyone knows what is expected of them. This is fundamentally what the roles and responsibilities in the project charter is designed to do. These duties are not nominal ones; they are absolutely not to be considered honorary titles that confer no additional work, and they are all critical to the success of the program.

One of the key parts of any project statement is to establish the authority assigned to the project and/or program manager. This must be sufficient for them to be able to control, direct, and implement the changes required but not so uncontrolled that they are not accountable to the Senior Leadership Team.

Other responsibilities assigned as part of this document are as follows:

- **Who determined and directs the reasons for undertaking the project?** Detailing these and who has set them (and can change them if necessary) ensures everyone is clear about why they are doing what they are doing. It also clarifies ultimate accountability.

- **Who has set the objectives and constraints of the project and what they are?** This is likely to be the next management level down from the preceding and therefore has more detail as to what the project will achieve by department. If you don't have a clear target, your project is going to miss the mark, and the people setting these targets will need to be signed up to them enough to put their names to them.

- **Who sets the directions regarding any constraints listed above?** You want to have at least an outline and the right 'go-to' people to determine how you are going to deal with project constraints. If you don't determine this now, you will have to agree on this later.

- **Who are the main stakeholders?** It is always crucial to note the stakeholders in any project, for they are the ones who you will be communicating with and managing their expectations. The sooner you are clear who they are, the sooner you can build a productive relationship with them.

- **What are the in-scope and out-of-scope items and who has decided these?** Scope describes the broad limits of your project, such as its start date and when it concludes. When either the in-scope items or those out of scope need to be updated, you will want to be able to talk to the people (or roles) who decided these in the first place.

- **What are the potential risks in the project and who owns them?** Identify all risks and their owners that could arise in the project so you are not taken by surprise. This should be detailed in a risk register and risk management plan in your project plan, where you detail how you will resolve those risks and who on the team is responsible for catching and fixing them. The owners and the fixers are likely to be different; you need both because there may be decisions around risks to be taken. For example, a risk that will be very costly to resolve may be accepted by an accountable owner.

- **Who will determine whether the project benefits have been achieved?** The project will bring plenty of good outcomes to both sponsors and stakeholders, but it is often not clear who says whether a benefit has been achieved. The people who decide this should be identified at the start, avoiding any misunderstandings around who identifies that a benefit has been achieved at the end.

- **Who will have spending authority and at what thresholds?**
  While your project or program manager should have spending
  authority within the project up to certain limits you will also
  want to set levels of authority elsewhere (or dual authorities
  in the case of absence). These will include a higher authority
  as well as the authority of people outside the project to make
  spending decisions if needed. Documenting this ensures clarity
  for anyone unsure of where the responsibilities lie.

Overall, because it is people running the project, it is important
to ensure there is clarity at the outset as to who is responsible and/or
accountable. People do move around in a project, so we would suggest that wherever possible the responsible role is detailed rather than
the person. However, this should not be the case where decisions such
as the reasons for the project or the objectives of the project have been
taken. These should be assigned to named individuals; if they change,
the next person in the role should agree to and sign up to the original
reasons or objectives. In this way accountability remains firmly set and
this helps to ensure the project remains on track.

Accountability and the Roles in the Project

The following table covers the accountability of the key project roles
from a governance perspective.

Project Sponsor	Steering Committee	PMO—Project Management Office	Project Manager
Sets the strategic direction, oversight, and stakeholder cohesion	Sets the operational direction and is accountable for managing business issues and monitoring risks, quality, and project timelines	Supports the operational direction and is responsible for monitoring and reporting on risks, quality, and project timelines	Sets the tactical direction and ensures the project activity happens in line with the objectives set by the previous three

Project Sponsor	Steering Committee	PMO—Project Management Office	Project Manager
■ Project champion ■ Approves the project charter ■ Business case owner ■ Accountable throughout the project ■ Sets the project priority within the business/ organization	■ Determines how the project goals and objectives are measured ■ Approves the plans and metrics ■ Monitors and controls the project to ensure alignment with the charter ■ Escalation point for project deviations ■ Creates consistency in project and program governance ■ Maintains best practice and follows up with lessons learned; provides traceability for governance ■ Manages interdependencies		■ Executes the governance plan ■ Tracks the ROI and budget ■ Manages the progress and performance of the plan ■ Carries out the communi-cations plan ■ Manages the stakeholders

How the Project Charter Will Help Underline Responsibilities and Accountability

While it is true you are going to cover this ground on a granular level later in the project, this is your first opportunity to agree on who will be broadly responsible for sections of the project, and there is a reason why it is more general and comes before everything else. The following are three main uses of the document:

1. You need it to authorize your project.
2. It serves as a primary document.
3. This document will stay with you throughout the term of the project.

There is a process for writing a project charter, which starts with knowing what the vision of the project is. That vision statement must be specific and clear, capture the purpose of the project, define the end goal for the project team, and determine the ownership.

Critical Role of the User on a Dynamics 365 Project

The user in a Dynamics 365 implementation is likely to be the one with the business focus, having a detailed view of their own team or department and often cross-functional perspectives as well. Users with cross-functional knowledge are particularly prevalent in organizations that already have experience of integrated ERP systems. If Dynamics 365 is your first ERP system, then bringing your users together as part of the project is even more critical and their involvement will bring significantly more benefits.

User Engagement

User engagement differs from user experience. User engagement is the ongoing, value-driven, emotional relationship between the user (internal or external) and the business. It is not the memory of one moment, but the sum of all moments—the user's overall emotional connection arising from the totality of experiences with or within the company. This covers a great many interactions, such as booking leave, placing orders, putting away stock, as well as the actions that they might take—acting on reports, targeting the top 20% of the organization's best customers, congratulating suppliers on a great performance, and so on.

If you provide a positive user experience throughout the Dynamics 365 implementation, your people will become more engaged. Highly engaged staff are advocates of your brand. They refer friends, talk positively about the organization, and are more loyal. However, negative experiences damage the memory of the entire involvement and therefore the implementation within a company. This can ultimately lead to disengaged users, who can act on their dissatisfaction by undermining the goals of the project and being negative with other members of the team and the wider organization.

Understanding the difference between the user experience and user engagement is critical. User engagement goes beyond managing individual experiences from each touchpoint with Dynamics 365 to include all the ways you will motivate your staff to invest in an ongoing relationship with the project and the goals of the Dynamics 365 implementation and Digital Transformation. More and more user interactions spanning across more and more touchpoints will shape the amount of engagement an employee has with your Dynamics 365 implementation and the resulting system. Knitting together each experience and focusing on the user journey will generate greater engagement and a positive ROI.

Measuring User Experience

It is clear that the user experience is integral to their engagement, as better experiences generate better engagement. But how does a company measure the user experience to identify gaps? What are the areas that need improvement?

Get feedback. An overwhelming 90% of users want to provide feedback about their experience with you and your project, while only a small percentage are often given the opportunity to share. This frustration can be easily fixed through regular surveys and immediate feedback in sessions with people. These can provide a wealth of information. However, they will not help if you fail to analyze and act on the responses.

Understand churn. Churn is natural in business, but understanding when churn happens can help you prevent it in the future. In any change program you will get staff turnover, because you are disrupting habit structures that are keeping people in your business. You want to make sure that you keep the people key to your digital transformation, which requires an understanding of why they want to leave.

Solicit ideas and comments on ways of working and features. This is best done in community forums where people can request new features, share new ideas about processes, or share problems they are trying to resolve. If there are recurring topics, it may be a sign you may need to do additional research into configuration in Dynamics 365 or process design within the organization.

Analyze support ticket trends. Review your support tickets for recurring issues that are causing angst and/or are taking significant agent time to resolve.

Dynamics 365 will unify and measure your data, allowing you to easily glean valuable insights and then take informed action to improve business proficiency, boost engagement, and strengthen loyalty. To ensure these benefits are appreciated through the digital transformation, get and keep customer (user, employee, and stakeholder) engagement throughout the process.

Customer Perspective Adds Value to the Project

In business research the concept of Customer Value (CV) is the term known for years to salespeople as adding value to the sale. The idea is that rather than affixing a price to a good or service, you investigate and understand the actual value something has to a customer and then sell your product based on this.

CV is an essential prerequisite for long-term company survival and success. If you understand the way customers judge and value a service or product, you can achieve a competitive advantage. Scientists and practitioners have long recognized the power of CV in identifying value for customers and managing customer behavior. The objective of CV research is to describe, analyze, and empirically measure the value that companies create for their customers and to link these insights to further marketing constructs. More recently, research has also begun to link CV with concepts such as customer lifetime value (CLV) or customer equity in order to assess the return on marketing actions and the financial impact of CV on the company.

The research clearly shows that the best people to explain customer value in any given product are the customers. They may need some guidance, there may have to be discussion and monetary prices assigned to a given value, but it is the customer who best articulates this.

So what should this mean for your Dynamics 365 project and the Digital Transformation of your business? The project customers are the best people to determine the value of your processes, configuration, and work instructions allied to the implementation of Dynamics 365. They will give you perspectives that a business leader, project manager, or department head will not have and be able to articulate enthusiasm for the improvements being made throughout the transformation. If you ignore this resource, you will lose an opportunity to make the implementation and transformation the best it can possibly be.

Prepare Interactions with Stakeholders to Get the Best Value

Generate a Comprehensive List of Value Elements

Value elements are anything that affect the costs (including time and opportunity costs) and benefits of the configuration or process in the user's or stakeholders' eyes. These elements may be technical, service, or social in nature and will vary in their tangibility. How well a form configuration reduces keystrokes, for example, would be a technical element, as would providing an emailable invoice; designing correct data inputting would fall under the service heading for the receiving departments; and ease at communicating with each other in the application might be social. The list should capture all the potential effects that a process might have.

The team should identify as many elements as possible to gauge accurately the differences in functionality and performance a configuration or process provides as compared to alternatives.

Gather Data

The next step is obtaining initial estimates for each element and finding out what each could be worth in monetary terms. Focus groups made up of representatives from each functional area in a company are an effective mechanism for uncovering data. Sometimes the only way is to discuss the current process, the expected improvement, and brainstorm the reductions in costs.

Validate the Model and Understand Variance in the Estimates

After building the initial value model, the project team should validate it by conducting additional assessments in other areas. Conducting further assessments enables you to refine the value estimates and understand better how the value of the Dynamics 365 configuration or business process varies.

Understanding of Value to Use

The project can use their understanding of value to strengthen the implementation in several ways, for example, in tailoring processes and configurations to the needs of multiple departments, focussing training programs, or guiding the development of new ideas. Finally, it can better sustain stakeholder relationships by documenting its delivery of superior value over time and by discovering new ways to continuously improve the system in a way that adds real value.

Guiding the Development of New or Improved Products and Services

Most research conducted to provide an understanding of user requirements and preferences does not address the question: "If we do X, what is it worth to that user or group?" Knowing that an improvement in some functionality is important does not tell a project how much value a user, stakeholder, or department actually assigns to it. Value models provide that information.

A note of caution: the project team must take into account the fear of change when evaluating any value attached by the individual users. An improved process that reduces user effort can be seen as a way to reduce headcount. While this fear can be mitigated through the development of interesting work and removing drudgery, it is important to take these concerns into account.

Sustaining Stakeholder Relationships

At the core of all successful working relationships are two essential characteristics: trust and commitment. To demonstrate their trustworthiness and commitment to stakeholders, progressive projects periodically provide evidence to customers of their accomplishments. The process of gathering the real value of improvements provides the information needed to inform all stakeholders of these improvements. The distance travelled, for example, is often and easily forgotten by the users of a new system, but communicating this from time to time is important and builds the relationship between the user community and the Project Team.

Delivering Value and Getting an Equitable Return

The principle of user value management is to supply superior value and get a fair return for it, as both superior value and a fair return depend on value assessment. Equally compelling, though, is a comment made by a senior manager at a company that does business based on value: "Selling only on price! Where's the fun in that?" When there is market pressure on price, this manager recognized that his business unit needs to respond by demonstrating that it has something different to offer, something that will provide superior value. Assessing and truly understanding value in a project means that when there are difficulties and roadblocks the total value rather than the raw return is the focus that your stakeholders will have, and this will help keep the project on track.

Customer Experience (CX) Is Key to Acceptance and Engagement

As your customers will mostly be the users of the system, these are the people you should focus on to keep engagement in the project and ultimately gain acceptance of the outputs and the implementation. Make the experience great and you will have system champions and people willing to go the extra mile to help you improve the system and the company further. Alienate them and you will have an uphill struggle in all aspects of the project, including the implementation and the digital transformation. As we have seen in this section, the way to a user's heart is through engagement.

Why Users Should Create Dynamics 365 Documentation

Apparently, Steve Jobs said, "if you need to write a manual for your software, you have done something wrong." His point is if you design your software to be as clear and easy as possible to use you will not need documentation. However, an ERP is much too complex a system to take this view in all cases (although it is a good rule of thumb to keep in mind). Good user documentation can make or break the success of your Dynamics 365 system. The design, presentation, and evaluation of your user documentation is a really important part of developing software. Sadly, it is also an area that is much neglected.

User documentation refers to the documentation for a product or service provided to the end users. It is designed to assist end users to use the product or service. This is often referred to as user assistance.

Start by determining exactly what assistance you want to document. For example:

What	How	Why
Business processes	In Visio	Clarity of what we do
User instructions	Work instructions	Clarity of how we do it
Reports	Reporting instructions	Clarity in what is reported and how
Off-system documentation	Standard operating procedures	Clarity on how we remain compliant with the law, etc.
Support guides	FAQs and quick guides	Immediate help with the system

These need to be kept up to date, so add an expiration date to each document that requires it to be reviewed and approved before the date is extended. This will help to keep the documents fresh; it is a role that should be assigned to someone in each department.

Traditionally, user documentation is provided as a user guide, instruction manual, or online help. However, user documentation is increasingly being delivered as an integral part of the application wherever possible. Within Dynamics 365 this is an ideal way of giving prompts, directions, and help, but there will also be a broader need for work instructions for processes and ways of operating within and across teams. Both should be considered as integral parts of the application for your organization. Both should have significant or exclusive input from users who will be operating the system.

These days, users are also used to multiple ways of accessing information about the best practice use of any given application including:

- FAQs
- Video tutorials
- Embedded assistance (e.g., tool tips or dynamic page content)
- Support portals

User documentation is important because it provides an avenue for users to learn:

- How to use the software, especially if they are new to the business.
- Features of the Dynamics 365 system that will improve productivity.
- Tips and tricks of the application that will make people's lives easier.
- How to resolve common errors that may come up.

With good user-created documentation, it is possible to ensure even smoother processes within the software.

There is also the "Task recorder" capability within Dynamics 365 that can be utilized for automating the process of creating user manuals. For example, during UAT when super users are verifying key processes, they could record the system steps at the same time, using these to create manuals. The steps for this are as follows:

1. Record the steps using Task recorder.
2. Upload to the LCS (Life Cycle Services) BPM library.
3. Generate Word documentation including print screens and navigation using the LCS built-in capabilities.

Not only can the task recordings be used for creating manuals, they should also be played back by the users to provide an interactive tool for guiding other users on how to complete specific processes.

What Are the Essential Elements of Great User Documentation?

An excellent user documentation always contains the following:

- **Plain language.** Writing in plain language about a product or service you know front-to-back is more difficult than you might think. You know all kinds of jargon, acronyms, and other "insider" info that customers don't. It is natural for you to use it. A good way to avoid this and the confusion it creates is to get your users to create the documents.

- **Simplicity.** If your user materials intimidate your customers, they are much more likely to call your support team than try to solve their questions on their own. They are also unlikely to have a good customer experience. Customers who use documentation written by their peers are much less likely to have this problem.

- **Visuals.** The best user documentation perfectly illustrates the adage "show, don't tell," or "a picture is worth a thousand words"; using pictures to augment your text minimizes the length and complexity of your documentation. System users like quick reference and having pictures, diagrams, tables, and bulleted lists is superior here. Visual content, including images, annotated screenshots, graphics, and videos, quickly shows someone how to use the system. They don't have to read about it—they can see it!

- **A focus on problem solving.** This is one for the help files and pop-ups in the Dynamics 365 system itself. Often a particular input or data from earlier in the process will throw up an error. Explain what it is and how to fix it at this point. Informative errors get read; opaque ones start a bad habit of ignoring the error.

- **Accessible content.** Create accessible content. Ensure that electronic documentation adheres to accessibility standards for people who may be blind or visually impaired, deaf or hard of hearing, or have cognitive disabilities. Remember, many of your customers need support to understand and fully access your user documentation. Dynamics 365 has this accessibility built in when you use the in-system help files.

- **Good design.** Design materials with your customers in mind. Make it usable and friendly. Encourage your user documentation creators to avoid long paragraphs of text or pages that are packed too full of content. Use white space to help break up any monotony and help make learning a new product less daunting. Use consistent fonts and complementary colors across multiple documents. If your organization has a style guide, make sure your documentation adheres to it.

Evaluating what user documentation to use:

Method	Advantages	Disadvantages
Integrated help files	■ User guides ■ Really fast ■ Easy to use ■ Can be accessed as you work	■ You might not get the level of detail you want ■ The user might be new and not understand the help ■ Need to be really succinct
Online support	■ Larger amount of information ■ Easier to update ■ Can access from any device ■ Can be faster	■ Cannot be accessed offline ■ Unless it is integral to the system, it can be hard to relate to a specific issue
Printed manuals	■ Easy to find ■ You can browse through them ■ You do not need a computer	■ Slower ■ Can be lost or destroyed ■ Harder to search ■ Go out of date
How-to guides	■ Answer specific questions ■ Are team or department specific ■ Are short and accessible	■ May not be clear to new people ■ Need to be updated if processes change

Documentation and training should go hand in hand but the training does not have to be formal if you have invested in good user created documentation.

There are two big bottlenecks identified following ERP implementations: the failure of employees to master the new tools, and the time taken finding and fixing errors made by employees because they are not clear on how to use the system.

Getting the ultimate users to create the documentation from the start introduces the system to as many people as possible as you go through the project. Human errors can be resolved, or at least miti-gated, by having work instructions and by using the in-system help files to prompt people in the right direction as they use the system. The lack of adoption of ERP systems always prevents companies from achieving the expected process improvements. With user-created documentation and correct work instructions, you will increase the adoption of your Dynamics 365 system and realize more business value from your investment.

To sum up, some of the benefits of having your Dynamics 365 documentation written well are:

- You retain valuable knowledge when consultants or employees leave.
- It brings standardization and transparency to your business processes.
- It ensures better employee onboarding. Documentation and in-system help are effective means of communicating information about the system and at the point of use.
- Dynamics 365 work instructions allied to your business processes helps you measure progress toward departmental and company goals and keep track of your key activities.

Role of Microsoft Customer Success Manager

In the run-up to your Dynamics 365 go-live, Microsoft will appoint a Customer Success Manager (CSM) to work together with you and your Microsoft partner, initially on change and user adoption, but in the future on getting the most value out of all the Microsoft products you use. You keep your Dynamics 365 Customer Success Manager relationship for the life of the association you have with Microsoft.

For Microsoft the CSM's focus is on all the services and capabilities included in the Microsoft 365 offering—Dynamics 365, Office 365, Power Platform, Security, and so on. The role is a post-sale, adoption- and change management–focused role. In the most basic sense, the CSM is there to help you use what you have already purchased.

Why Does Microsoft Have This Role?

Microsoft says that the Customer Success Manager role was created based on feedback from their top customers:

- They want help realizing the full business value from the investments they have made.
- They want expert, proven guidance on how to deploy Microsoft technologies.
- They want a single point of contact for technology utilization and value realization.

To meet these needs, Microsoft lays out three stages where the CSM helps achieve value for customers:

1. **Envisioning.** The plan for a successful rollout
2. **Onboarding.** Moving to the cloud with confidence
3. **Driving Value.** Realizing business value faster

Jonathan Rowley,
Senior Customer
Success Manager
Business Applications -
UK, Microsoft

"Microsoft allocates Customer Success Managers to the largest Enterprise projects across the World. These resources are skilled in Adoption and Change Management as well as the Dynamics 365 product and its roadmap. All customers should actively engage with these resources when made available as they act as a single point of contact for the Customer into the complex Microsoft machine.

Customers that fully embrace Microsoft's approach to Customer Success generally have better outcomes than those that do not engage and provide the right access to the Customer Success Manager.

Microsoft's Customer Success Managers and Microsoft FastTrack, as well as its Support functions, are critical to a Customers Dynamics Journey to Success."

Envisioning

To ultimately realize value, you must first define what it is. Typically, this takes the form of goals, objectives, vision statements, and strategies in an organization. Envisioning is probably at the top of the needs list, because enterprises start with the end in mind, and figuring these elements out first is a key precursor to success. In the digital transformation you are going through (and therefore the Dynamics

365 implementation) you cannot know if you are successful if you have not defined at some level what success looks like.

A critical part of defining what you want is understanding what you bought. When you buy Dynamics 365 you get so much functionality you need some help (and often a bit of time) to realize the full potential of the system. Businesses often make their initial purchase based on one or two core needs. The business justification and return on investment can be met through the cost savings related to improvements in reporting and financial management, reviewing, and simplifying core processes and automating alone. However, your Microsoft CSM should then be helping you get even more out of the system.

For Microsoft, helping customers at the envision stage means:

- Working with you to establish long-, medium-, and short-term goals that align with a broader vision and strategy.
- Helping determine training needs and options for the core team and key stakeholders. It is necessary to ensure that team members who will be the most involved have a deep understanding of what capabilities they have at their disposal.
- Providing insights, experiences, success stories, and use cases for how to best leverage each product and service. They should be able to give you insights into the best use made of Dynamics 365 elsewhere, without necessarily trying to sell you anything extra.
- Assisting with establishing key performance indicators, that is, how success will be tangibly measured.
- Helping you throughout the deployment and beyond, including making recommendations on the appropriate amount of change management that should be factored in.

Onboarding

Every business's journey through a digital transformation will not be the same. There are some wrong turns and rocky roads that you will want to avoid. The CSM should help to provide deployment guidance as you go through the process.

Some of this guidance will be of a technical nature. Some will be working through configuration options. Some of it will be ensuring that the roadmap and schedule are achievable. Some, of course, will be assisting in figuring out "what to use when." The largest and most difficult part of any guidance, though, will be your organization's need for change management.

From an organizational perspective, knowing when to change and when not to change is as important as knowing what to do during the process of change.

Some of the ways your Microsoft CSM should be able to provide deployment guidance will include:

- Getting the right technical resources and subject matter experts within Microsoft to help with any deployment-related concerns or questions.
- Helping you make the best use of Microsoft's FastTrack[2] service, which provides migration and adoption assistance to customers with current and eligible Dynamics 365 licenses.
- Where necessary, assisting with proofs of concept and pilot activities.
- Supporting the removal of "blockers" (issues hampering deployment).
- Providing use cases, experiences, insights, and success stories for driving adoption by all of the user base.
- Ensuring that the vast resources from Microsoft, and potentially other partners, are used as desired. This includes: training resources, communication templates and samples, implementation checklists, videos, and other acceleration programs.

Driving Value

The Microsoft CSM does not leave and go to work with other customers once the deployment is completed. They continue to support you post-deployment and should help you to increase the value of the Dynamics 365 deployment over time. The CSM should stay engaged and continue to consult and advise. This is where being the primary point of contact brings the biggest benefit to you. Your point of contact works as a trusted advisor and partner to help achieve your documented goals.

Some of the activities related to driving value include:

- Being your advocate within Microsoft. This may include sharing successes as well as challenges to ensure the right level of visibility is reached.
- Reviewing usage and trends to identify opportunities for improvement aligned with your organization's vision and goals.
- Identifying options and good practices for increasing adoption of Dynamics 365 (or other Microsoft products you use).
- Identifying new services and capabilities that are available to determine if there is new value for you. While you should not rely only on your CSM to tell you of upcoming improvements being released into Dynamics 365 that you could use, they should be able to highlight the most significant for you.
- Ensuring that you continue to take full advantage of all that Microsoft has to offer.

The Customer Success Manager is responsible for helping Microsoft's customers be successful. Although that is going to mean something slightly different for each customer, you should take advantage of this role to get the best advice, support, and connections into the Microsoft behemoth as possible.

Leverage Your Community

The Microsoft ecosystem has a robust offering of peer communities and user groups. Often people assume they should wait until they are users (i.e., after go-live) before participating in the User Group. That is so far from the truth. The most important time to get engaged in the community is before the implementation project. Having hundreds or thousands of other people who are willing to share their mistakes and successes ensures a much better plan and execution.

Dynamic Communities[1] offer some of the most widespread and well-known user communities. There exists an array of communities and special interest groups that gather veterans and newcomers together to share knowledge and experiences with each other.

By participating in online forums, virtual roundtables and events, as well as local groups, international groups, and almost any industry, job role, or other topic that you can imagine, companies are able to glean intelligence to optimize their implementation and avoid mistakes that others have made before them. Although every organization's implementation is unique, there are enough commonalities that are shared that make this resource invaluable.

Best practices for efficiently finding value from the community include:

- **Assess your organization and inventory to find the key areas that will need to be addressed during your implementation.** Create a list of attributes applicable to you such as your industry, market, geographies, products/services, and business models. At the same time, assess the key users during your implementation. What job roles are they in? What issues do you anticipate will be the greatest to overcome during your implementation, such as unique processes and cultural change challenges?
- **Participate across the company.** Don't make the mistake of having one individual serve as the user group representative. Communities are meant to be digested by many perspectives. All key users should make time to engage and glean value from their specific group or subgroup.
- **Scan the community offerings.** Once you assemble your attribute list, you will quickly be able to seek and identify the specific communities and groups most applicable to you. Do web searches for user groups. Ask your partners. Ask Microsoft. The choices are many.
- **Subscribe to communities that make sense.** There will be many. Don't expect to find everything you seek in one place. For example, CFOs will find the most value in spending time with other CFOs. Technical architecture will be the theme of other groups. Your geography will have some groups more active than others in the region. Some individuals on your team feel most comfortable in using asynchronous online forums, while some people find it best to have synchronous face-to-face (or at least voice-to-voice) conversations. Use your attribute list to match up the groups that serve you best.

- **Discern the group you join.** The models vary across community groups. The common models out there have pros and cons:
  - The organic forums that pop up in social media places like LinkedIn, Google, Yahoo, and Facebook are often valuable. They are almost always asynchronous (online only) and wide open. Users engaged in these will see a variety of perspectives, but are mostly anonymous. Relationships don't come easily in this format. Like anywhere else, facts should be checked and vetted. The information seeker will most likely have to wade through many inapplicable postings, as these are usually open to everyone.
  - Organized groups such as Dynamics 365 User Group[i] are typically administered by a staff of professionals. These independent groups can usually be relied on for efficient participation across a wide array of topics. They almost always bear a nominal membership fee for full engagement, although some offer "freemium" content as well. In addition to membership fees, these organizations sometimes rely on advertising and other means of covering the costs of delivering these services.
  - Some groups are offered by partners and consultancies. These often offer valuable content; however, discernment should be applied to make sure you understand the goods or services offered by the proprietor of the group. Often these groups are opened for sales and marketing purposes that end up pitching the item that is for sale. Again, they can be very valuable as long as you go in with your eyes open to the agenda.
  - Microsoft-offered communities. Microsoft offers some online groups as well.
  - Events and conferences are plentiful. Some of the most valuable information and relationships are obtained through attendance at conferences throughout the year. Many of the groups mentioned here will host a get together (virtual or in place). These real-time engagements add an element of meeting others that prove to be valuable relationships and friendships that can be relied on for sharing knowledge outside of the typical event or forum.
- **You get out what you put in.** Active engagement in the community requires give as well as take. The premise for user groups is that peers share knowledge freely with each other. Obviously

brand new implementers have less to share than those veterans who have gone through the process, but it is important to share your experiences as they are occurring or help those that come behind you.

- **If you can't find exactly what you need, invent it.** If it is important to you, chances are it is important to others as well. Some groups allow specific sub-communities to be formed by simply raising your hand to help provide the topic generation and dialog. Many people find personal growth and thought leadership opportunities through speaking on stages and delivering training through the communities. Even the shiest personality can find a place to contribute through blog writing and forum posts.

Regardless of the place or the level of engagement, don't miss the opportunity to take advantage of the rich ecosystem that exists.

Summing Up

The strength of any project is the people involved with it. No leader can succeed without them and for any success to be recognized there must be people there to do so. In the same way as the matriarch of a household understands who she can trust to manage things without her intervention and when to ask for help, a project sponsor needs to feel able to do the same.

In the first section we looked at this with the assignment of the roles and responsibilities within the project and the use of the project charter.

A critical and often-missed person in any project is the customer. In the second section, we looked at their role and how having a customer focus can help to make the project a success.

The users of any new system are one of your best resources, and getting them to write their own documentation (within guidelines) will ensure both buy-in and good-quality user guides. You miss this opportunity at your own cost.

Testing a new system or even changes to the system must be done in a structured way, but this does not mean doing it in isolation. We looked at the various types of testing and how to get the best out of it by using the people resources you will have.

In Leverage Your Community, we considered how your cutover would benefit from practice to ensure that even very complicated changes to your integrated systems can be smooth on the day.

Finally, we looked at the third-party help and support you can get with Dynamics 365. It is particularly important that you use the resources of the organizations and user communities who know the product best and have been involved in some way in every installation and migration that has ever occurred.

Digital Future Checklist

✓ Use the Project Charter to detail who is involved in the project and what they will do.
✓ Think of the customer in every aspect of the project.
✓ Get the users to complete the operating manuals and how-to guides.
✓ Test often and systematically.
✓ Practice the cutover plans.

"When your dream is bigger than you are, you only have two choices: give up or get help."
—*John C. Maxwell, Author of* The 21 Irrefutable Laws of Leadership

---

Notes

1. Dynamics Communities, https://www.dynamiccommunities.com/.
2. Dynamics User Group, https://www.d365ug.com/home.

CHAPTER 9

What Does Post Go-Live Look Like?

We all have a choice. We can create transformational action that will safeguard the living conditions for future generations. Or we can continue with our business as usual and fail.
—Greta Thunburg, Activist

Whether you agree or disagree with Greta Thunburg's view of the future she is correct; there is no more business as usual when you want transformation. However, you do need a stable platform to build from and this needs people who understand the day-to-day operations of your business.

Back in the late twentieth century, there were several business leaders who were lauded for being the turnaround kings of business. A man who personified this style of business management was "Red" Adair, who was an oil well trouble-shooter and firefighter of the period. The press loved him and he was instrumental in putting out some of the worst oil fires, including some in the second Gulf War. His style was very much to parachute in and solve apparently impossible problems with a flair and energy that was often copied by businesspeople at the time. He was clear on what he was not good at (or particularly interested in), which was the aftermath, the clean-up,

and the getting back to normal. This is not seen as exciting or glam-
orous and you certainly are not going to be trending on Twitter over
the consequences, but it is much more important to the company
even than the project. What a waste the effort of all the people
involved in the organization's digital transformation and the move
to implementing Dynamics 365 would be if the post go-live is not
considered and managed well. That is like building the foundations,
walls, and roof of your house and then not bothering to put windows
into it. It would not take long before you would have to knock it
down and start again. What you want is to make it secure and watertight and then add value by putting in the internal structures. In addition, what Dynamics 365 brings is the ability to do all this AND be
able to move the house and/or change its orientation and/or expand
it—the evergreen foundation to your future business needs.

In particular, the Value Add with Continuous Innovation section
will cover the adding of value to your newly implemented Dynamics
365. This is the beginning of your entire future in your digital transformation. It is not the first in this chapter because you are not done
with the critical operations planning (the end of the beginning) but
it is your opportunity to start thinking outside the "normal" IT box.

A project is often a slightly messy, constantly evolving, and exciting thing. After you have implemented your Dynamics 365 solution,
while you are in the throes of your continuous improvement cycles
as part of your digital transformation, you will want some structure
around how this will work. If the Dynamics 365 implementation has
gone well, you will have all the environments and habits in place and
you will just be iterating over improvements cycles.

In the following section we cover the monitoring of your systems
so there are no sudden surprises, how (and why) you will set up
your Dynamics 365 environments for continuous improvement, and
how to use the useful information already being gathered to direct
your Dynamics 365 roadmap.

The Windows: Planning for Operations

Following the implementation of your Dynamics 365 system, you
will need to underpin the ongoing improvements to the business.
From a systems perspective this means having complete control of

the business-as-usual operations. This requires good Dynamics 365 operations management. This supports system monitoring, security management, integration management, batch management, device management, performance management, and so on.

There are a number of models you can adopt to achieve this: from the traditional leave it all to your IT department, through the more nuanced layered approach that has some aspects with IT and some with applications support team, to the entirely managed service model that outsources the entire operation. Each has its own challenges and benefits. The important point is not to sleepwalk into a decision. Make sure you look at your needs as a business, your current in-house expertise, your skills with managing third parties, and your strategy for the future.

The first things to decide are who will direct your Dynamics 365 operations management and what service level do you need to have (24/7/365)?

Martijn Brons,
Global ERP Director,
Howden Group

"During a digital transformation initiative or project avoid the pitfall of focusing all the effort on the Go-Live. Instead spend at least the same amount of attention and time, if not more, on preparing for how you will do business in the future. This should include all elements, including business processes, future support, and maintenance. Before transitioning to new business processes ensure that you have completed all due diligence so that everyone accepts and understands the future ways of working. As far as future support and maintenance are concerned, consider how a shift toward a cloud environment will need to be managed, including skills, activities, release processes, etc. etc. It is impossible to spend too much time on preparing for life after Go-Live."

Manage Your Dynamics 365 Operations?

IT?

Having your IT department solely responsible for operations management keeps the responsibility in one place, but can also remove the understanding of the business needs from the equation. Unless your

IT department has consistently shown it has an understanding and is supportive of the business requirements and does not have the attitude that the customer gets in the way of a smoothly operating system, there is no reason not to leave the support of Dynamics 365 management to the IT team.

IT and Applications Support?

Your Applications Support team should be made up of people who have a business understanding as well as a technical one. They will be experts in their own business areas and have significant knowledge of the Dynamics 365 system from a functional perspective. These people will be looking at all aspects of the business operation of the system and will be closest to the customer base. The requests for help in the form of issue resolution, training, data problems, and change requests are likely to be hitting this team first. For these reasons, if you want to ensure that the Dynamics 365 system is operating to the best advantage of the business, it is useful to give this team some responsibility for the day-to-day operation of it. However, if you are going to split the responsibility, you will need to set an RACI (responsible, accountable, consulted, and informed) for the teams. Refer to Figure 9.1, which reflects a template of an RACI model per area.

In this way, the aspects of Dynamics 365 that will directly affect the business operation will sit with the application support team, but the technical and security management of the system will sit with IT. There will be a requirement for each team to work closely together and keep the other informed of changes.

	IT	**Application Support**
System Monitoring	R,A	I
Security Management	R,A	C,I
Integration Management	A,C	R,I
Batch Management	I	R,A
Device Management	A	R
Performance Management	A	R

FIGURE 9.1 Support RACI Template

While there is currently no good evidence to say it is not good practice to have your applications support team part of IT, we would not advise this. As an illustration, IT responds to operational demands like network, security, and patching, while applications support is focused on delivering functionality and enhancements. Having all these demands within one team will lead to application requirements being de-prioritized, especially during any IT crisis, slowing down the business transformation process. The tension you need between the two teams can be undermined by the IT management, and it is better to have them separated but to ensure both the IT Operations Manager and the Applications Support Manager work closely together. Each role is greatly enhanced by the other's perspective, so this should not be a problem.

Infrastructure Management and Monitoring

Cloud-based systems such as Azure and Dynamics 365 require just as much management as their on-premise counterparts. Nearly all the old infrastructure monitoring is now done for you, so this is no longer needed in the same way as for on-premise and you do not need to worry about system and network dependencies, but you should be monitoring resource usage to remove as much cost as possible. The overall management is different, and the focus is on cost reduction and efficiency rather than making sure that systems are operational.

Azure Monitor gives full visibility into the health and performance of your Azure workloads, apps, and infrastructure with monitoring services, such as log analytics and application insights. Your IT teams can easily collect data from any source and get rich insights, such as understanding CPU disk and memory utilization for your virtual machines, view applications and network dependencies across multiple virtual machines, and track application performance. It supports interactive queries and a full-text search, allowing IT to perform root-cause analysis with advanced analytics, including machine learning algorithms. Using Azure Monitor should enable the fixing of issues before they become problems using alerting and fix automation. It is also possible to integrate with other ITSM (Information Technology Service Management) tools. There are other tools available for monitoring your applications and cloud-based infrastructure such as Solarwinds and their competitors.[1]

Security

Security in the cloud is no longer just your organization's responsibility; you also have all the resources of the cloud provider behind you and it is their reputation on the line too. In Azure you also have the Azure Security Center, which allows you to centralize your security policies and integrate them with existing processes and tools. Supporting this in the modern cloud computing era is the use of advanced analytics, which can detect threats and deploy security controls, reacting more quickly than your staff can to reduce the risk.

Integration (Data and Applications)

Dynamics 365 can be integrated with other Microsoft solutions as well as a myriad of third-party applications such as web portals, BI applications, and other systems. This works both for small and large organizations, as the integration does not require extensive configuration and can be accomplished using integrators and add-ons. Such integration is critical to Dynamics 365 and is part of the evergreen concept that most ERPs now have. The use of Power Platform to support the near system applications and integrations also ensures that the Dynamics 365 continuous improvement from Microsoft is kept available as changes to the system should be unnecessary.

The Dataverse is also used to support the flow of data to and from Dynamics 365 by using the data integrator, which is an application-agnostic platform that can scale across various sources, allowing two-way data flows. There are other tools that allow data integration such as APIs, Excel, and web services and also a dual-write capability to provide easy synchronization of data changes between Dynamics Customer Engagement apps and the Supply Chain Management/Finance, to name a few.

Batch

Batch management can help reduce the impact on the system from long-running or less frequently required processes. Most tasks in Dynamics 365 can be run as part of a batch job but some are particularly worth setting up; for example, batch jobs that print reports ready for morning tasks (such as pick and put away lists for the warehouse shift), processes that perform maintenance on the Dynamics 365 environment, such as tidying up log files or removing data falling outside GDPR, even sending bulk electronic documents such as purchase orders or invoices. By using batch jobs, you can ensure that you make the most efficient use of available processing during typical working hours.

Devices

If you use phones and tablets to access Dynamics 365 and you already have access to Office 365, then you have Mobile Data Management (MDM) available to you. MDM allows you to secure data on iOS, Android, and Windows devices and this allows you to selectively wipe company data from these devices. This is especially useful if you are going down the bring your own device (BYOD) approach to phones and tablets. You can go further with your device security by adding Microsoft Intune and get additional device and application management capabilities for phones, tablets, and PCs. This includes the ability to restrict actions such as cut, copy, paste, and "save as" to applications managed by Intune—helping to keep corporate information even more secure.

System Performance

If you are running Dynamics 365 on Azure, you should be using Lifecycle Services (LCS) to monitor the performance of Dynamics 365 and Azure. In LCS you can check your Azure performance by looking at the diagnostics that are loaded there; this will help you with determining whether it is Azure or Dynamics 365 that is having a problem. However, if you have correctly sized your environment and performance has been fine up to now, then the first thing you should be looking at is any changes that have been made to Dynamics 365 (assuming Azure is showing no problems).

Data Performance

Within the administration module of Dynamics 365, there is a Data Performance feature, which shows the queries that have been run in your environment that could be improved or queries that have taken

more than three seconds to resolve (also called long-running queries). If the view is empty that means that your queries are already
running smoothly. However, if you see something here, you can optimize it using the "Optimize" button. This can reduce the time it will
take to resolve a query. It is one way that Microsoft has improved the
ability to find performance issues in Dynamics 365.

Best Practices for Dynamics 365 Operations

Here are some practices suggested for the operations of Dynamics
365 post go-live. As the system is still being adopted in the organization, you can plan some frequent activities as a health check of
Dynamics 365.

- **Report only on exception.** Too often we have seen the deluge
  of reports on how well the systems and applications are doing.
  This is a boost to the IT and applications teams as they can
  look at all these reports and say everything is doing well, but
  among all these there may be the odd error or warning that is
  a precursor to something more concerning. Our recommendation is to report only on errors and warnings. Now this is often
  also something that then gets ignored because the same errors
  or warnings keep coming up, so you absolutely must have a
  good practice habit of looking into and ideally correcting every
  error or warning. If you are going to accept that something
  keeps coming up and you are not going to do anything about it,
  then suppress the alert (not best practice but better than ignoring them). By following this practice, you will see any errors
  that must be dealt with and encourage your teams to react to
  all messages.
- **Alert before failure.** As mentioned, you should not ignore any
  errors or warnings, as these are ways that will alert you to possible problems. You need to make necessary actions to the alerts
  you receive before you are near to a failure. This sensitivity will
  serve your IT and applications teams well because they are much
  more likely to achieve the 99.99% planned uptime that all IT
  departments are (or should be) working toward.

- **Data Compliance Reports.** By far the most data errors come from people not following the agreed and documented process. If your applications team set up and report on the adherence to process you are much more likely to have people following it. The Dynamics 365 system can be set up to show when processes are being ignored or misunderstood. Our recommendation is to set up a periodic activity monthly or quarterly in order to review the quality of data using these reports and take the necessary action to cleanse any polluted data.

Value Add with Continuous Innovation

This section is all about planning for continuous innovation; for example, platform updates, application upgrades, Azure innovation, and Power Apps innovation. Post Go-Live is about ensuring an efficient, scalable, and auditable mechanism for business-as-usual activities, as well as supporting continuous innovation and improvement, where new thinking is required for your Software as a Service (SaaS) Evergreen ERP or CRM system.

In the past, system manufacturers innovated slowly from their customer's perspective. The infrequent deployments, characterized by extensive customizations and complex integrations, could not adapt new capabilities without expensive, disruptive upgrade projects. The result was that most organizations faced long delays and increased expense before they could realize the benefits of new capabilities. Organizations took their eyes off the customer while they implemented these significant deployments, costing a great deal financially and in opportunities lost. With One Version, Microsoft Dynamics 365 innovation will be delivered rapidly and regularly, and companies will be able to opt in to leverage the new capabilities as soon as they are released. This continuous innovation delivers service updates for mission-critical enterprise business software such as Dynamics 365.

Platform Updates

You may have been used to the downtime and overtime that came with an update to your systems. This is no longer a cost to you.

All updates to your Dynamics 365 and Azure environments will happen with little or no downtime and in most cases no impact at all. The significant overtime bill should also be a thing of the past. Now, with the correct planning your IT team and external partners will be preparing your system in advance. They will have a clear idea of any issues that may occur from a platform update with sufficient time to make any changes that might be needed arising from alterations you have made to Dynamics 365 during an implementation.

As part of this continuous update process, you will no longer be in the uncomfortable and frankly risky position of having to remove the focus your entire business has on the customer to upgrade your core business systems. This is a highly valuable position to be in and one that will allow your company to continuously innovate in the margins while having your core systems kept permanently up to date.

You will have heard that cloud operations mean you do not need as many IT staff. Reducing your technical staff is not a wise course of action, however. You will still need technical people, just differently skilled people. What you are looking for will be cloud specialists who have an innovation attitude tempered by a risk-averse mindset. These should not be impossible to find, as cloud operations and Dynamics 365 lend themselves to both states. The key is to resource this properly. Although you will see a reduction in infrastructure, this allows for an increase in proactive planning. Make innovation part of the culture. You will be able to move faster and further if you are confident that your system is always being managed correctly and kept up to date. For example, what organizational best practices and patterns could be baked into the Post Go-Live and BAU (Business as usual) teams to ensure that innovation is supported? Now you have technology backed innovation with a background of features being continuously developed offering high value but low cost to your organization what are you going to deliver or adopt first?

Can We Customize and Extend Dynamics 365?

The answer to this is "it depends." New customization models can be achieved solely through a Dynamics 365 configuration. Within Dynamics 365, once a customization has been moved to the new model, the core product can be updated and the combined system of product, configuration, and extensions continues to operate smoothly. Extension software, such as the use of Power Platform applications, can also provide essential building blocks that allow for significant opportunities for flexibility at the edges of Dynamics 365.

The new customization model is a critical enabler of the new application lifecycle, and it powers another critical change for the entire update ecosystem. A typical Dynamics 365 implementation also has one or more Independent Software Vendor (ISV) solutions within it. In the past, when a product update was published, each ISV needed to merge their solution with the new base, and in many cases this had to be done first and then your own customizations put in. This was onerous and took considerable planning. With the new customization model, this sequencing challenge can be eliminated. There is no more code merging and, as a result, you no longer need to sequentially apply each ISV solution. You can simply take the product update with your ISV extensions and your own extensions directly. ISVs will follow similar new development process guidelines to manage their updates.

What Does This Mean to Us?

The process for updating Dynamics 365 and planning and then testing these updates is becoming simpler over time, but this is a complete shift in the mindset from the previous model as there is more emphasis on automated testing and an upgrade is much less likely to cause issues. As before, it needs to be managed, but the chances of error by your IT people and the resulting downtime are being reduced with every release.

Dynamics 365 Upgrades

The process of receiving updates is relatively straightforward. You will be able to sign up to an early adopter program where you can preview the updates. Updates received via this program will not be supported in a production environment; it is purely for preview and early testing. This is where your teams will check out the update and make sure everything is working successfully for the implementation you have. It is a good idea to automate the initial part of this process (see Chapter 6) and again we come back to the mantra of reporting by exception.

At the time of printing the update schedule, your likely response to it looks something like Figure 9.2.

Bear in mind you have the option to pause up to three consecutive updates, but Microsoft services the current update and the immediately previous version.

In the first week of availability for an update, you will have the ability to proactively update sandbox environments and test, prior to self-initiating a production environment update. If, however, you take no action in Month 1, automatic updates will occur in Month 2. This would first include notification of update, sandbox update, and finally, the production update. You do have the ability to specify an update time (e.g., Friday, Saturday, Sunday) for the production update. The new update model will include production downtime on the selected update day—anywhere from 20 to 45 minutes, but zero downtime updates are often the case. There are rollback capabilities as well, should you discover an issue after you have applied the update.

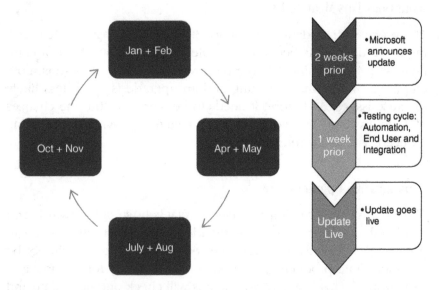

FIGURE 9.2 Updates Are Delivered per Year in the Following Cycle.

Source: Used with permission from Microsoft Corporation. https://dynamics.microsoft.com/en-gb/business-applications/product-updates/

And before you or your IT teams panic about the amount of testing this will require you to complete monthly, there are testing tools that will greatly reduce the testing burden. Also, the upgrades are progressive, so additive of new functionality, and therefore much less likely to break existing functionality. If you have task recordings of your business processes saved to a business process library in Lifecycle Services (LCS), and you should, then the process can largely be automated.

Azure Innovation

As you will have seen over the last few years, the emphasis from all cloud-service suppliers is on innovation. Azure is no different in this respect. What you can expect from Azure is the continuation of this and the expansion of Artificial Intelligence (AI) capabilities and technology along with the IoT (Internet of Things) will advance this further. The intelligent cloud is ubiquitous now with the public cloud and AI technology combining to enable the creation of increasingly clever applications and systems. People (your customers) are getting real-time insights and experiences already, delivered by highly responsive and contextually aware apps.

Combining the virtually limitless computing power of the cloud with intelligent and perceptive devices at the edge of your network allows Microsoft to leverage this framework for building immersive and effective business solutions. By uniting the massive computing power of the cloud with increasingly connected and perceptive edge technologies, these technology companies are creating possibilities we could only have dreamed of just a few years ago. These opportunities apply to millions of connected devices, virtually limitless data, and a growing number of multisensory, multidevice experiences. This is not only happening in Azure, but the combination of Azure, Dynamics 365, and other applications such as those in the Power Platform will ensure you stay up to date with technology as well as in control of your own innovation journey.

Power Platform Innovations

Microsoft Power Platform is an umbrella term given to four distinct applications: Microsoft Power BI, Microsoft Power Apps, Microsoft

Power Automate, and Power Virtual Agents, as discussed in the earlier chapters of this book.

In the context of a major implementation of Dynamics 365, the role of the Power Platform is to empower the wider organization to assist the innovation and transformation, to move faster, enabling complementary apps, insights, automations, and integrations to be created at speed without the need to wait for traditionally longer delivery cycles.

Automating repetitive, time-consuming tasks improves employee satisfaction and drives productivity, by allowing staff to focus on more valuable skilled work that drives business growth. Power Platform unlocks much of this potential by offering easy-to-use yet powerful capabilities that integrate with SharePoint Online, Office 365, Dynamics 365, and Azure, as well as hundreds of third-party applications. Power Platform automates processes and workflows, allowing organizations to build end-to-end business solutions.

This interoperability helps organizations maximize their data and content assets, automate existing processes, and enable entirely new, intelligent ways of working across these four areas:

1. Power BI enhances the visualization of data and insights gained from analytics. The creation of interactive reports that can be embedded into other services enables those without a data science background to manipulate and understand information without being able to change the message the data has embedded within it. This is unlike Excel, which allows users with an agenda to take raw information and manipulate the way the information is presented. Correct information leads to better-informed business decisions.

2. Power Apps make it simple for anyone to create a custom application that solves a particular business challenge. Point-and-click tools mean that little or no coding knowledge is required, and pre-built AI modules mean that it is possible to make intelligent apps without the need to train models or hire specialists.

3. Microsoft Power Automate makes it simple to automate business processes. Power Automate can be viewed as the link between disparate platforms, allowing information to "flow" between applications and data sources for automated workflows.

4. Power Virtual Agents allows you to create your own virtual agents without the need for developers or data scientists. Integrate Power Virtual Agents with the products and services you use every day using hundreds of prebuilt connectors, by building custom workflows using Power Automate or creating complex scenarios with a Microsoft Bot Framework.

How Do the Applications Work Together?

Each constituent element of Microsoft Power Platform is a powerful tool, but when combined with one another, and through integration with Office 365, Azure, Dynamics 365, and other applications, Microsoft Power Platform delivers great value and benefits to the business.

In fact, Microsoft sees the Power Platform as an enabler for the rise of citizen developers. This is their term for the people within your organization who, when exposed to the opportunities available to them from Power Platform applications, will create innovation and build integrations that improve the working environment for everyone.

Microsoft's view of the Power Platform is that it will enable the building of modern relevant business apps fast, empowering business power users, who understand their business needs best, to create solutions quickly without the need for code. This puts the creation of business applications within reach of subject matter experts who understand the business processes and needs, so that they can compose and co-create applications quickly to meet those needs using visual configuration-based tools. The ability to measure with Power BI, act with Power Apps, and automate using Power Automate creates an integrated framework for these applications. Additionally, the underlying infrastructure behind this supports the power users' use of the Azure platform services, and the Dataverse and integration capabilities will allow the cross-application enrichment of data.

While citizen development will empower the people who feel the pain of manual repetitive tasks to create apps that automate processes, relying on the inspiration of enthused PowerApps fans may not be enough. The broader organization needs to understand that there is an "app for that" to fill gaps in digital processes where a custom development project is too expensive or the commercial applications on offer are not the right fit. It is also important to get IT on board with app creation to encourage the subject matter experts in the business unit to take ownership of the Power Platform and roll it out. To support the citizen developers, it is worth following a Center of Excellence (COE) model. This is a combination of the application owners from the business and IT developers, who can provide governance, tooling, training, guidance, and automation to productionize the business developed applications. The COE toolkit provides dashboards that highlight the use and adoption of the platform, enabling Centers of Excellence to get involved in mentoring and curating the applications that have started out as requirements and prototypes created within the business.

A member of staff could create a custom application based on SharePoint lists that allows a head of department to request an IT project. This list would be sent to an IT manager for approval and, if approved, the project is assigned to a project manager who is then notified. Meanwhile, a business analyst could assess the viability of a project using a Power BI report embedded in SharePoint. All stages of this workflow are linked through Microsoft Power Automate.

Another example is custom chatbots. Power Virtual Agents offer the ability for anyone to create a bot to handle internal queries or basic customer service functions. Data can be harvested from Azure or Office 365 and fed through other applications.

Integration with Microsoft Teams, the new default communication tool within Microsoft Office 365, adds another dimension to collaboration. Dashboards, custom applications, and automations can be added to Teams, ensuring that the most relevant information is made available to individual groups.

Simple interfaces that mask powerful capabilities are a powerful combination for any organization embarking on a digital transformation project. By application integration and added intelligence, Microsoft Power Platform can unlock the full potential of your organizations' people and assets.

Andy Cheng,
PwC, Director,
Data, Technology
and Innovation

"Moving to Dynamics 365 for Operations and Supply Chain Management cloud-based enterprise application provides unique advantages not available in traditional on-premise ERPs, such as flexible cost structures, scalability, and comparative ease of system consolidation. Successful companies must now learn how to maximize value from a cloud-based implementation and address a different risk profile. Business operations can be streamlined and standardized, which enables businesses to make rapid, more insightful decisions.

"While these new technologies can provide measurable benefits and promote development and growth, the opportunity to maintain an always updated environment adds a challenge that requires validation of all changes going into a covered environment. Frequent updates require continuous monitoring to prevent the chance that your controls framework is impacted. The question that needs to be asked is, 'How can my organization effectively utilize the features and functionality of a SaaS Dynamics 365 environment, all while minimizing risk, to implement an efficient, focused, process to validate all updates going into my environment?'"

Key Considerations for Dynamics 365 Platform and Application Update Cycle

"Customers going through a regular update cycle for their Dynamics 365 environment should apply a set of considerations to their update cycle. While each customer's environment is unique, the following are core considerations Dynamics 365 for Finance and Operations customers are responsible for:

- **Impact Assessment.** Through review of Microsoft-issued release notes and tools such as Microsoft's Impact Analysis tool, customers should understand the parts of their environment impacted by the change and assess any greater impact on their system, including any regulated functionality or data. This exercise will help the customer define what testing is required and how it may affect data and processes under regulatory requirements.
- **Risk Assessment.** Using the Impact Assessment, customers should evaluate the areas of their environment impacted by the update and assess these areas relative to the risk to the organization (e.g., compliance,

operational, financial). This could include an evaluation of a population of the company's risk and control environment and related IT dependencies to the Impact Assessment to identify high-risk areas impacted by the change.

- **Velocity of Change.** Reviewing and acceptance of updates based on the desired strategy and risk tolerance of the organization. Microsoft provides customers updates on a monthly basis that can allow customers to update up to 10 times a year, or, based on risk tolerance, business, and timing, customers can pause updates up to two consecutive service updates. Customers should document formally their approach and velocity for applying changes so the approach is defensible in the case of a regulatory inspection or audit.

- **Customization/Extensions.** Identifying integrations or other customizations deployed to understand *where*, *when*, and *how* the customizations may be impacted. Unique test scripts for these customizations may be required prior to implementing a change in production based on impact from an update.

    Microsoft has worked with a population of ISVs to confirm compatibility of updates with ISV solutions. When assessing the impact of updates on customer's ISV solutions, customers should speak to their ISV vendor to understand their partnership with Microsoft as part of One Version and obtain any necessary documentation showing testing by the ISV vendor supporting compatibility with each update.

- **Evaluation of Internal Controls.** Evaluating the configurable control to evaluate whether the internal controls function as expected remain relevant to be triggered as part of the normal course of business after changes have been applied, or have been adjusted appropriately and tested prior to migrating the update to production

- **Evaluation of End-to-End Impact (Regression).** Performing a full risk-based validation of impacted functionality per the customer's validation methodology is recommended."

Managing Your Product Backlog Post Go-Live

Managing the Product Backlog beyond go-live is quite beneficial and integral for the Dynamics 365 roadmap.

At the point you go live and for a while after, there will be areas of functionalities your teams may highlight as issues, problems, or changes they feel are required to the new Dynamics 365 system. Ideally you want these to be recorded somewhere (probably in your

IT Service Management application). Issues should be reviewed and triaged; there may be issues that have no current resolution, but there is likely to be a workaround available or there may be items that are good ideas and changes.

Both the issues list and change request list are useful to you and your D365 applications team. Issues as incidents should be triaged and handled if they are a priority, but change requests should have more information added to them. If you do not already have a process for managing change proposals that come from the business teams, it is a good idea to create one.

The process should focus on the benefit to the business of any given change and should request this information in some detail. It is important not to make the activity of raising change proposals too easy or too difficult, but should encourage thought and proper consideration to avoid frivolous suggestions, but not be so onerous that good ideas get dismissed as too hard to put forward.

Incident Management: 3 W's

Whether you or your organization follows ITIL maturity models or not, you can create your incident management process with three W's—what, where, and who. Listed here are some key considerations when creating an incident management process:

- In a large IT organization, you will have an Incident Manager, who can help administer the incidents logged and assign to the relevant team inhouse, or externally if it is managed by a third-party supplier. In a smaller operation it is a good idea to give this role to someone who has a business-oriented focus. The process needs to be fully documented and to be agreed in principle about what, where, and who of the process will eventually help your organization to measure against the defined process.
- Define "what." The process flow needs to be clearly stated and communicated with identification of the business stakeholders and any third-party supplier involved with an RACI matrix of roles and responsibilities. In the early phase, the post go-live process needs to be followed so it becomes a routine and business as usual.

- Define "where." As part of the process, you need to mention where to log all incidents and define set rules based on SLA (service level agreement) on the threshold of resolution time. Manage and review these lists periodically, setting governance calls.
- Define "who." Without a clear definition of the process, it might be exceedingly difficult to understand the ownership and accountability of the incidents. The RACI matrix covers who is responsible, accountable, consulted, and informed and hence removes any ambiguity on the ownership of incidents.

The business also needs to prepare for any good ideas or any change requests that may arise during the early phase post go-live of the project. These requests need to be raised as change requests and to be part of the product backlog, which can be reviewed and prioritized with an impact assessment on timeline and costs.

You want the list to be tackled in order of cost savings; don't just tackle the "quick wins" as they are often not quick and not always a win. If an acceptable work is in place and the ROI for removing it does not stack up, don't do it. Alternatively, have a look at the problem differently; can a resolution be found another way?

A good approach is to use DevOps "boards" to track backlog items, and then ensure these are grouped into achievable sprints for delivery. This keeps the list transparent and open, and simple to report on progress against those items. The backlog (in the form of a Kanban style board) in Azure DevOps encourages everyone to contribute and indicate their progress, making it a collective responsibility, rather than an administrative burden

Managing Dynamics 365 Change Backlog

If you are encouraging transformation within your organization, you can end up with a deluge of suggestions and pet projects. You need to get a handle on these, partly to be able to see the forest for the trees and partly to encourage more ideas. People who have ideas that are (even briefly) considered will come up with new ones as well. The key is to make the process simple but not too easy; forcing people to think about the actual requirements as well as the benefits to the business and should start to achieve this.

How you define and deal with any backlog boils down to two factors: (1) the source of the demand, and (2) the stage of development the project is in. It is generally accepted that there are two different types of backlogs: (1) a backlog of desire (things that users would like), and (2) a backlog of commitment (projects that are approved but not started). Innovative organizations need to pay attention to both. If internal customers cannot get an idea on someone's radar, they will eventually stop trying. Even worse, if projects have been promised but not delivered, then expectations have been set and not fulfilled. It may be that it has not been planned properly, or that managers are not tracking projects well, or that developers are taking time to assess the ins and outs of a project, but all users see is that they have yet to get what they were promised.

One way to look at the backlog is to consider the whole spectrum of projects that people are currently working on but have not finished, in addition to the ones ready to go. If you have a list of 100 projects that have funding and that people are working on, then outside the top 100 are projects that are next in line. When you finish project 3, you bring in project 101. If you don't have the right staff with the right skills available for the next project on the list, then skip to another. You may have a backlog of months of work but reprioritizing every two weeks will mean that some items never make it to the active list. This is not necessarily a problem as long as the list is being managed.

Often when you are managing the backlog you still get a change that will take resources that comes apparently from left field. One recent example for many companies will have been the General Data Protection Requirements (GDPR). Now, these had been known about for some time but came as a surprise because they were not understood. A well-managed change backlog will know where the resources are being spent and be able to reprioritize or, at the very least, suggest additional resources in the case of an unavoidable change coming in. This does not mean, however, that the noisiest person in the room should have their changes moved higher up the list; anything that comes in and disrupts the in-progress changes risks stopping innovation in an organization and should be strongly resisted.

Your applications (Dynamics 365) support team is a resource to the business like any other and needs to be managed as such. To ensure this happens to the best advantage of the business, you must take away the constant demands on their time from requests for changes. The way to do this is not to put in a blocker, a manager who is happy saying "no" to every request that comes in. Doing this risks your new innovative organizational mindset. Instead, the answer is never "no" but should be "follow the change proposal process and get the business management team to prioritize it." In this way your business managers get to see the proposals, your support team get on with their prioritized work, and the organization benefits from innovative ideas and planned changes.

How to Manage Change Requests

Suggestions regarding the operation, processes, or look and feel surrounding Dynamics 365 and the other applications that are associated with it are an opportunity to engage the user base. Set up a process that can be understood by all for completing a change request form that is then considered by the head of that department, then a group of department leads, and finally a small group of mixed business and applications people who can determine the priority and the impact of any suggestion on the system (see Figure 9.3).

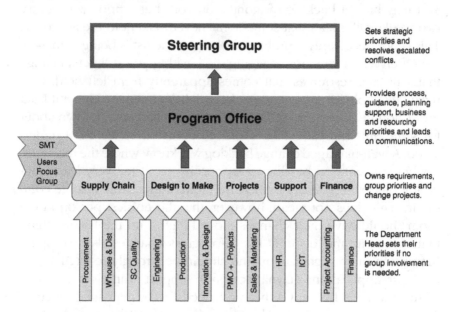

FIGURE 9.3 Change Governance Structure

In Figure 9.3 you have the department heads managing any changes that are restricted to their own area; they do not need to refer to anyone else as long as they have the budget and resources to make the change being suggested. The group leads will take responsibility for changes that only affect the departments they are overseeing. The Program Office will take the lead and provide the budget for any organization-wide changes. Finally, the Steering Group sets the strategic priorities, oversees the governance, and provides budgetary oversight.

At each stage of the change request journey, the person passing it up the chain should add value by considering the benefits and the costs and making the case for the change. At the point it reaches the Program Office, it should have a costed Return on Investment or at the very least a benefits analysis with values applied where possible. It will then be the Program Office's responsibility to get the budget and make a recommendation on priority based on resource availability.

There should always be change requests bubbling up through the organization, some of which will be great ideas that will make your organization more competitive or efficient. The trick is recognizing these, consideration, and scrutiny along with support and eventually budget, which will bring the best ideas to the fore and make them happen.

Keeping an updated change backlog with the business priorities and ROI directing the order these are addressed in post go-live is obviously beneficial. It is also a great way of starting to embed the innovative ways of working you want to instill within the business.

Summing Up

To start with, we looked at making the business renovation watertight and adding in the windows. This means creating the support structures that will underpin your future transformational actions.

Following on from this base, we covered the preparations needed that will allow you to add more value to your Dynamics 365 implementation. This is a combination of upgrades and innovations coming from the use of the Microsoft Power Platform.

How you manage the list of issues, problems, and changes that have been identified pre and post go-live was the next focus. Our recommendation is that everything cannot be fixed; prioritize key items related to the business, create a change request process, and log all new ideas and changes so this could be revisited in future for impact assessment and can be added as part of continuous innovation or improvement features.

Digital Future Checklist

✓ Get people interested in making the system stable *and* moving it forward for your business to support the solution.

✓ Do not have the same support structure as you did before your digital transformation.

✓ Use the benefits of constant change to add value, keep the system stable, and the peripheral applications dynamic.

✓ Review the quality of data in the system periodically and take the necessary cleansing action as required.

✓ Maintain and manage the backlog of requirements for impact assessment and consult and inform the progress.

✓ Set up a governance structure that drives innovation and business need.

"We cannot solve your problems with the same thinking we used when we created them."

—*Albert Einstein, German Physicist*

Note

1. Solarwinds and Their Competitors. https://www.gartner.com/reviews/market/it-infrastructure-monitoring-tools/vendor/solarwinds/alternatives.

CHAPTER 10

Dynamics 365 Support and Continuous Improvement

Strive for continuous improvement, instead of perfection.
—Kim Collins, Athlete and World Champion

The end of the Dynamics 365 implementation project is not the end of the story, far from it. Apart from the practical overlap between the project team in hyper-care and the support team spinning up, the whole point of a digital transformation is to embed continuous change, and an appetite for it. However, on a practical level, how do you support your Dynamics 365 environment and your business users? There is the traditional route of getting people to log requests with the support teams and then implement the ones that have the biggest clout or shout the loudest. The problem here is this can lead to a slide back into siloed thinking and working, and is counter to the values of cooperation, collaboration, and customer focus you are trying to encourage.

There is another way, one that companies are finding out for themselves gradually but that we have honed and implemented in multiple businesses, and which has been proven to work well. This is based on the premise that the business drives IT and not the other way a round, but the business teams have to work together to ensure the strategic priorities are always followed and the Dynamics

365 (and related applications) support team helps the business with the technical possibilities and testing the business requirements. The intention here is to remove the focus on IT providing broad technical support and move toward the business being self-supporting in the ERP, with technical expertise and some governance being provided by applications specialists.

Here are some suggestions for checks that are worth thinking about now you are post go-live and into hyper-care:

- Is the business stabilized? Base your answer on pre-agreed measures (as mentioned in Chapter 5) prior to the hyper-care period, which should have been agreed with the business on how you will measure stabilization. These need to be measured throughout the project so you can benchmark what good looks like.
- Do I have a support organization set up, trained, and available, including a local support framework as well as a formal system support framework? This should consist of your Application Support and Business Process Lead creating a center of excellence between them.
- Is the business mature enough to manage the daily tasks in the system and are the support processes needed to resolve issues/requests and enhancements embedded?
- Is the organizational design in line with how it was defined during the project and have all organizational design changes been made?
- Have you completed a post-project assessment (lessons learned + a survey), evaluated the outcomes, and acted on the key points?
- Is the benefits realization plan available and in progress? Do you have planned checkpoints to evaluate whether the system is being use efficiently and effectively? (See also the section on Benefits Realization later in the chapter.)

The key components for BAU that absolutely must be in place are:

- A local support framework consisting of a site ERP lead and functional experts. At a minimum these are responsible for:
  - Training new people.
  - First-line support.

- Testing new functionality.
- Raising issues to the formal second- and/or third-line support and tracking them.
- Considering system enhancements and providing detail to build new functionality.
- Supporting any local interfaces with local suppliers.
- Managing data issues.
- Measurements to ensure you see problems before the customer does:
  - System health.
  - Key business and system metrics (so not only real business metrics but also metrics that are pointing to system issues).
  - Data maintenance/accuracy. (Are the correct processes being followed or is incorrect data being entered into the system?)
- Processes to support continuous improvement, based on both (evolving) business strategy/demands as well as improving system use/efficiencies. Maintain analytics on issues that arise to see if it is a process, training, or software issue.
- Testing capabilities for new releases and functionality.
- An effective second- and/or third-line support process.
- Relationships with partners to ensure ongoing understanding of new functionality/trends/changes in licensing, and so on.
- Tracking the benefits realization plan (see the section on Benefits Realization).

Bear in mind, however, that this is a minimum and the center of excellence you are aiming to build on involves close collaboration between the business teams and the application support team. It is this that will bring you the most value if you get it working correctly. For this reason, in the next section we will make some suggestions as to how you can ensure these components are in place in a framework that will ensure business focus.

Recommendation for the Dynamics 365 Business Team

You will need to find the right people to fill a number of key business and IT roles. The business roles do not need to be full-time, but it is a value-added position if your organization is large enough. It is very likely that these people will come from the project team or others who have been close to the implementation of your ERP. Therefore, as you get toward the end of the project you should start to identify and put in place people who can fulfil these roles.

A key business role is as follows (you can call it what you like, such as Business Solutions Lead, but I have used Process and Systems Lead to explain that they have responsibility for both the department's process mapping and understanding, and all the systems used in the department). If you are a larger business, then a process owner could be something else, purely responsible for establishing a common way of working across legal entities and continuously striving to make improvements to the process. The systems lead takes the responsibility for all the systems that the department or workstream are using, but from a business perspective.

The process and systems leader is a senior position reporting to the department head or director and has the following responsibilities:

Responsible at own level for:
- Validity of process
- Delivery of outcomes
- Compliance to process
- Reporting versus targets/SLAs
- Measurement of process performance
- Operational delivery collaboration
- Change sponsorship and authorization
- Resourcing User Acceptance Testing (UAT) and Subject Matter Experts (SME) input to change

Responsible across levels for:
- Analysis of process performance
- Proactive identification of best practice
- Optimization of the process–system interface
- Effective IT/application support collaboration
- Alignment with other process and systems leads
- Gaining sponsorship for the process/system change
- Prioritization and governance of the process/system change
- Management and delivery of improvement projects

There are other critical roles that are required but may not be full-time positions. In the business teams it is worth having a group of subject matter experts (SME) that come from all areas across the business teams and act as the initial go-to people in their own departments. Their existence supports a single way of working in the team or department and they can also filter the less useful requests for change and focus on the ones with the biggest return. In addition, they are a resource for testing any changes that become available in their area of Dynamics 365.

Recommendations for the Dynamics 365 Application Support Technical Team

In this section we will look at an example of the Application Support Team and different roles within the team. You might need to consider the Dynamics 365 Solution specialist and Analyst roles within the team.

The Dynamics 365 Solutions Specialist is a technical role with a specialist in a business area to align with the process and systems lead or leads.

- Responsible for the provision of technical specialist support to assigned business areas: working with partners and customers to conduct root cause analysis, evaluate and generate ideas, design solutions for improvement, and contribute to effective implementation plans.
- Project management expertise for transformational support projects in relation to the implementation of technical deliverables.
- Responsible for the successful delivery of technical solutions, including testing of new and existing applications and performing post-resolution follow-ups to ensure problems have been adequately resolved.
- Manage and oversee enhancements and defect resolution. Communicate application problems and issues in a timely manner to key stakeholders and lead on the resolution plans including the prioritization, scheduling, and administering of work as required.
- Manage a team of Dynamics 365 applications analysts who technically support the wider user base in implementing functional improvements and fixes.

- Develop and maintain relationships with key stakeholders including process and systems leads, IT, and management teams to help identify technical opportunities, mitigate risks, and deliver technical change/improvements in the most effective way.
- Participate in the design, development, and delivery of software applications, training programs, and individual classes.
- Manage the knowledge transfer to other team members to ensure there are no single points of failure in application understanding or support capability.
- Input into third-party contractual relationships. Maintain excellent communication channels and ensuring effective delivery, always to the best advantage of the organization.
- Ensure technical knowledge is kept up to date, keep abreast of external trends and developments, and demonstrate commitment to their own professional development.

In the technical team it is worth having an analyst role as well as the specialist one, which allows you to employ less experienced people and train them up and gives a structured path for promotion in the team.

Depending on the size of the applications team and the number of integrations there are with Dynamics 365, it would be best to have this team responsible for Dynamics 365 as a core system but also be experts in the integrations with other applications. In particular at go-live, there may be issues with integrations, while it should be the responsibility of the project delivery team to resolve these during hyper-care, as they should hand over the integration documentation and environments to a centralized team, in this case the applications team.

Other useful roles would include a release manager and a specialist security and licensing role that is responsible for both the licensing maintenance and setting up the security access roles for the business. Both the release manager and the security specialist roles should report directly to the applications manager. (These roles will liaise closely with the process and systems leads but are technical roles where as the process and system leader's role is a business one.) There should also be a development lead covering all aspects of the integrations and technical architecture. Depending on the size of

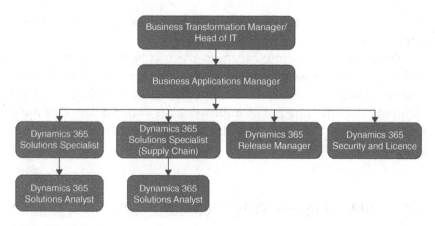

FIGURE 10.1 Example of an Application Support Team

the organization, this could be an in-house person or someone who does this role for you as part of a partner organization.

A suggested structure for the application support technical team can be found in Figure 10.1.

This example structure could also accommodate the hybrid or external models by substituting some (or all) of the specialist roles below the business applications manager role to external third-party resources. However, this does have the risk that you are relying on the manager to understand all the business needs of the organization and be able to translate these to technical people not embedded into the organization. The finance and Supply Chain Management roles should be seen as a baseline and additional roles should be added depending on your industry. For example, in a retail project you might also have a Dynamics 365 solution specialist for sales and services marketing automation. In a professional services industry, you might have a project specialist (including time reporting and expense). In discrete manufacturing you would have a manufacturing role.

The symbiosis between the solution specialists and the process and systems (or business solution) leads will create a center of excellence within your organization. The business focus aligned with technical resources who understand and can support the changes required will bring you significant improvements over time. Application support should be seen as an integral part of the business team rather than an IT team, and this will be an indicator of success if it happens.

Not putting a structured team in place is likely to lead to a lack of focus on the cross-functionality of the system, for a single well-structured and well-led team will be able to bring significant benefits, including the coordination of improvements and avoidance of ineffi-ciencies. Without this team you risk a continuation of siloed attitudes and working practices.

How to Support Dynamics 365 Implementation

Do you have capability to support in-house? Do you have a budget to outsource? How to evaluate what is best for you?

The project go-live is the beginning of a journey of continu-ous improvement, idea implementation, and keeping ahead of the competition. How you support the implementation will determine how possible all these things are. Attitude is everything in your sup-port team(s).

There are multiple aspects to the support of Dynamics 365 (or any other ERP), including an understanding of the business and overall direction as well as the technical considerations of configu-ration, changes, and how they impact your business, the way the cloud-based system is kept up to date, and how new functionality or bug fixes are implemented. Each of these requires knowledge and planning, so the support model is as important as the processes you follow for developing the systems in line with business strategy and, most important, customer focus. There are a number of models to follow and each has pros and cons. I have detailed here examples for each model, but the decision is yours based on your capability assessment (see Figures 10.2, 10.3, and 10.4).

It is important to point out that many of the cons in any of these models can be mitigated, but you must recognize them to be able to do this. For example, the intangible part in the in-house model suggesting that "low staff turnover can lead to narrowed thinking" can be mitigated by regular off-site training and/or ensuring there is involvement with Dynamics 365 user groups.

PROs		CONs	
Tangibles	Intangibles	Tangibles	Intangibles
Knowledge of your business practices and procedures.	Helps IT to become a better business partner.	Risk of single points of failure.	Retention may be challenging for technical staff.
Control over people processes and systems.	Responsive to organizational needs.	Technical AX skills sourcing difficult to find and keep.	Low staff turnover can lead to narrowed thinking.
Talent and knowledge kept inhouse.	Staff progression opportunities.	Investing in people is costly.	May not drive department ownership of data and practices.
	Not contract driven.	Time taken to recruit.	
	Drives up quality and innovation	Internal salary grading may constrain market rate pay leading to loss of staff.	
	Organisational culture buy-in.		

FIGURE 10.2 Pros and Cons of In-House Support

Whatever support structure you decide to follow, you will need to feed the business requirements through to these people. Setting this up is important because you want the technical support team to focus on the real business needs and not on the whims of those who shout the loudest. To this end it is worth having some structure in the way the initiatives come from the business teams. What you are looking for is a funnel that prioritizes and approves business requirements and changes and the knowledge in the approvals group of the strategic direction and priorities.

PROs		CONs	
Tangibles	Intangibles	Tangibles	Intangibles
Can flex numbers (if available in 3rd Party).	Any decisions to downsize has less impact on current staff.	Unproductive while learning organisation's systems and practices.	Integration of multiple systems compromised – blame culture.
Skills sourcing is 3rd Party responsibility.	May drive department ownership of data and practices.	Costs high, quality and understanding compromised.	loss of control over processes including business and IT change – supplier may dictate these.
Off-site resources can reduce the need for office space etc.		Flexibility decided by quality of contract.	Knowledge leaves the organization.
Responsible for delivering Dynamics 365 application management.		No control over staff quality and turnover.	Limited business culture buy-in.

FIGURE 10.3 Pros and Cons of Outsource

Initially the application support team will be focusing most of its time on investigating issues that have arisen post go-live. As time goes on it should shift focus to the continuous change based on the digital transformation initiatives that come through the business teams. For this to be successful there needs to be a focus from the business on their processes and how 80% of the business is run. As these processes settle down into business as usual, then the priority will become change initiatives, with the customer at the forefront of the reasons for these.

Your applications support team will need to be able to see the current processes and how these will be changed going forward in

PROs		CONs	
Tangibles	Intangibles	Tangibles	Intangibles
Can flex numbers (if available in 3rd Party).	The business owns the end-to-end service process.	Contract and Employment Law compliance.	Us and them attitude can occur.
Talent and knowledge can be kept in house.	Staff progression opportunities.	More management effort.	Retention still an issue for permanent technical staff.
Knowledge of business practices and procedures.	Business culture buy-in.	3rd Party flexibility decided by quality of contract.	May not drive department ownership of data and practices.
More control over turnover and personnel.	Responsive to organizational needs.	Exposes external pay rates.	Risk of "blame game," no single actor is responsible for the support service.
Difficult skills sourcing can be 3rd Party responsibility.	Cross-service learning is possible.		

FIGURE 10.4 Pros and Cons of a Hybrid Support Model

order to validate the impacts of any requests. An ERP is a highly integrated system and changes to it can have broad impacts that will have to be considered. A way to achieve this focus on the core processes is to have business managers change the process and systems lead aspect of their role, which means they oversee the business processes in the areas that they control. It also means that these people can control and agree on the change priorities that get passed to the application support team from the process and systems leads (or business solutions leads if you prefer this title and structure).

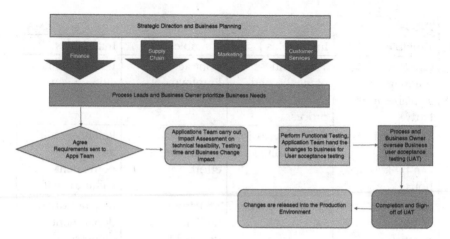

FIGURE 10.5 Simplified Process Flow of Business Teams and Applications Team

Figure 10.5 is a simplified flow of business knowledge, prioritization, and change flows that are recommended to ensure the business drives the Dynamics 365 application, and not the other way around.

The advantage of having business oversight through the process and systems leads in the key workstreams is that this focuses on the change requirements. There are a number of checks that should be done at each stage, but this basic flow ensures that the business can get what it needs and has to think about what this is. It also ensures that each change is technically checked and released as part of the plan that should be in place as per the Dynamics 365 improvements and patching cycle that will go on in the cloud environments.

How to Continuously Improve

How can Continuous Improvements be managed so you get the best benefits?

Improving your Dynamics 365 implementation (or any other ERP) is an ongoing exercise and should be driven by a combination of process improvements identified by the core teams and customer-focused changes that can come from any source in the business. There is a constant danger that the focus is only on the short term and does not give the bigger picture, but if your change cycle is too short this will drive this behavior. You need to recognize that a longer change cycle allows for proper business planning, systems and process testing, and seamless implementation. This cannot happen if too little time is allowed. However, on the other side, you don't want too long a cycle that does not allow for change in a reasonable time. Experience has shown that a quarterly business change cycle gives the ideal flow for both the business teams and the technical teams to manage and, if planned 12 months or more in advance, allows for short-term and long-term change planning. In addition, there should be monthly technical release cycles managed by tools for regression testing (such as RSAT) to allow for the testing of the expected two release waves, as well as the more regular bug fixes and performance improvements from Microsoft, and any internal technical changes or critical bug fixes coming from the last business release.

It has been the habit of organizations to buy an ERP system with the intention of keeping it up to date and as vanilla as possible in order to ensure the upgrade path is kept open. Then business priorities have taken over and the ERP has been changed to the extent that the upgrade path is difficult and expensive, and the business has ended up with an ERP they cannot upgrade. At this point the decision has been made to "look into" a migration and this process has slipped year on year until a business imperative has required a new system. This will now change. From Dynamics 365 onward Microsoft will be keeping the system up to date for you and new functionality will come along that you can use at regular intervals. The downside of this is you will need processes in place to be able to not only look at your business needs but also test the changes that are automatically applied to ensure your Dynamics 365 environment is not negatively affected. This changes the mindset and encourages the best practice of continuous testing and improvement. Dynamics 365 has inbuilt tools and third-party applications that will help you automate the continuous testing you will need to have in place, which will also support your improvement cycle. The only thing now is to create a cycle that the business can work with.

Figure 10.6 is a simplified cycle example.

Cycle 1	Dec	Jan	Feb	Comments
Plan				Plan the business year and outline changes
Build				Build the initial changes needed
Functional Test				Test continuously
UAT Test				Test the business changes & improvements
Release				Business release
Learn Lessons				Learn from the business release and adjust
Cycle 2	Mar	April	May	
Plan				Plan the next Quarter changes
Build				Build the initial changes needed
Functional Test				Test continuously
UAT Test				Test the business changes & improvements
Release				Business release
Learn Lessons				Learn from the business release and adjust
Cycle 3	June	July	Aug	
Plan				Plan the next Quarter changes
Build				Build the initial changes needed
Functional Test				Test continuously
UAT Test				Test the business changes & improvements
Release				Business release
Learn Lessons				Learn from the business release and adjust
Cycle 4	Sept	Oct	Nov	
Plan				Plan the next Quarter changes
Build				Build the initial changes needed
Functional Test				Test continuously
UAT Test				Test the business changes & improvements
Release				Business release
Learn Lessons				Learn from the business release and adjust

FIGURE 10.6 Example of a Plan and Simplified Cycle

The shades of colors represent the continuous improvement and building on the shoulders of previous releases, where the clearer colors in Cycle 4 represent the culmination of the year's improvements. However, you will be continuously improving further into the future. Continuous testing is required to ensure you can cope with the flow of Microsoft patches, improvements, and releases. The highlighted months are when you will (currently) get the main Dynamics 365 wave releases and these should be integrated with your own release cycles.

There is a difference between Dynamics 365 Customer Engagement apps and Dynamics 365 F&O. If multiple Dynamics 365 apps are deployed on your site, these need to be taken into consideration when establishing the necessary application management roles. The current cadence for Microsoft releases is as follows for the different areas of Dynamics 365:

- **CE.** Weekly bug fixes automatically deployed and two major releases each year.
- **F&O (One Version).** Eight updates per year, where a minimum of two updates per year is mandatory. It is possible to opt-out for three consecutive updates but the next one (the fourth) will be mandatory.

As mentioned previously, major updates are called wave 1 and wave 2 and are aligned across the entire Dynamics 365 platform with releases in April and October. Release notes are given three months in advance.

From a continuous improvement perspective, it is worth taking into consideration Microsoft's one version approach and the fact that you need to establish a one version strategy. Should you take each technical update and "stay current," which means eight updates per year, or should you "plan to pause" and perhaps only take a minimum of two updates on a yearly basis? Microsoft recommends taking all updates, but what is best for your company? Create a pros and cons list for the two options and then make a decision and establish a plan for how to manage this. As part of the one version strategy, you also need to decide on how to address regression testing, as one version updates are mandatory but regression testing is not. It is highly recommended, as not doing so adds risks you do not need to take, especially if you have made significant configuration changes from the vanilla setup.

All new functional updates, with a few exceptions, are released as inactivated, meaning that they are implemented but not turned on. To leverage the Microsoft innovations that are continuously released into the platform, you need to establish a feature management process where you evaluate new features, determine if they provide any business value, and then decide if and when to turn them on. Your applications support team should be staying up to date with these features and making the process and systems leads aware, as the feature management process should be part of the feedback loop in the release process, and features should be switched on as part of the quarterly business releases.

As always, the adage "I think you'll find it's a lot more complicated than that" is absolutely accurate here. You will need your applications team, IT cloud management team, and all business teams to work closely together on the plan and execution. It will be necessary to train people in the management of cloud-testing environments and the Dynamics 365 release cycles and then coordinate with the applications team. The perceived extra expenditure here will be worth it. You will no longer be spending to upgrade your ERP and can now concentrate on digital transformation, customer focus, and core strengths.

Review the Changes Periodically

Keep on top of the changes coming from Microsoft and your Independent Software Vendor Partners and make best use of them and plan to review the changes periodically.

As part of the planning described here, you will also want to keep on top of the opportunities being offered by both Microsoft and any independent software vendors (ISVs) you are using. To do this it is important that you manage your ISVs and ensure they are keeping you informed of the changes they are planning and encourage them to make the improvements you want to see.

Additionally, it is best practice to do the following:

- Check you have the right environments set up as it is best practice for Dynamics 365 (and development in general) to have at least four environments: (1) development, (2) test, (3) UAT, and (4) production. This keeps development away from your live environment and ensures there is a testing flow toward the live system where you can capture anything that might negatively affect it. In addition, you should have a sandbox environment for the update previews from Microsoft to go into so that you can test in parallel. If you are not doing any development, you only need to have sandbox and production, but it is recommended that you have other test environments for troubleshooting as well. Proper management of these environments will keep your cloud costs down.

- Download the release notes when they become available: At the moment this is about two to three months prior to each release. Reading these will tell you what the next release includes and give you a sense of scale and the changes being made. You will then evaluate these against your system to ensure compatibility and to test any additional functionality, benefits, or fixes. The release notes are fairly extensive, but your technical teams, both IT and application support, should also be checking for summaries and comments coming from the Dynamics community.
- The most time-consuming task will be testing the updates. It is best to set up the preview as early as possible, and the more you can automate this, the better. If anything is causing an issue, then you will need to diagnose and fix it. The earlier you know, the better.
- Make sure the customizations, integrations, and third-party solutions you have in place are supported; anything unsupported is likely to break during an update. Your Dynamics 365 partner can help with this and Microsoft has tools you can run to check your system.
- The updates are done to introduce new features, functionality, improvements, and benefits to Dynamics 365. An update might introduce a new functionality that removes the need for a third-party tool or might simplify an internal process. Evaluating the updates will help you discover benefits.
- Finally, stay up to date with the roadmap. Microsoft has one Dynamics 365 and Power Platform roadmap[1] now, so keeping an eye on this will give you a heads-up of what might be in the next release.
- Stay in touch with changes through Microsoft's Early Access Programs, so encourage your application specialists to be part of these. Early access is for non-production environments and is offered as a way to learn about and gain experience with the updates.

Build in Data Checks

You need to plan for business process checks, data checks and balances, and the direction of influence into the Dynamics 365 Resource Planning Departments.

The schematic in Figure 10.7 shows the flow from left to right of the requirements from the business teams (or groups of teams,

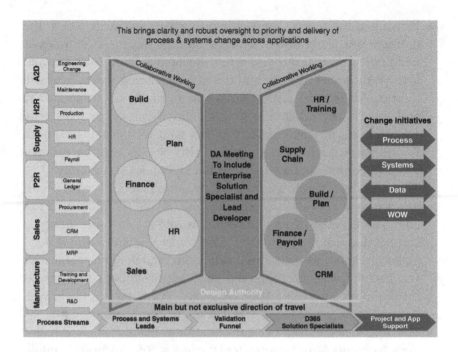

FIGURE 10.7 Example of Requirements of Business Teams

such as Hire to Retire, H2R, Acquire to Dispose, A2D, and Planning to Report, P2R) via the process and systems leads and through the funnel of the design authority that agrees on the technical outputs defined by the business priorities. The changes required in Dynamics 365 that come from process, systems, data, or ways of working shifts as required by the business strategy also feed into this. It is suggested here that the most senior (enterprise) Dynamics 365 solution specialist and the lead developer are included and that the business applications manager or a senior business manager chairs these meetings.

The terms of reference for the design authority should consist of:

Attendees
- Business applications manager (chair)
- Process and systems leads (or a nominated lead)
- Dynamics 365 solution specialists (and/or the enterprise solution specialist)
- Lead developer (often wears many hats including technical architect, integration specialist, as well as lead developer)

Objective

The objective is to evaluate all the business requirements and the changes being proposed in Dynamics 365 from ISVs and/or Microsoft, and any bug fixes. You need to agree on the business priorities and the target release dates. (Typically, as a proposed change in Dynamics 365 will affect other external systems as well, or an external system requires a change in Dynamics 365, these impacts should also be assessed.)

Inputs

- Business requirements.
- ISV changes and improvements (if any).
- Microsoft fixes and improvements.
- Bug fixes (both internal and from software partners).
- Feedback on progress from the solution review board and any actions specified.

Outputs

- Prioritized list of business changes with target release dates, resource plan, and communication actions.
- Agreed communication actions for the ISV and Microsoft improvements.
- Release plan for bug fix and other changes.
- Communication plan for other affected systems and integrations.

It is also worth having a solution review board (SRB) that involves the technical team (Dynamics 365 solution specialists, analysts, release manager, and Dynamics 365 security specialist). This group keeps track of the improvements and changes being developed or tested to ensure all is on target, and will technically evaluate progress and report to the design authority any issues that may affect the agreed release dates.

User Groups and Communities

Continuous improvement is no longer something done entirely in the comfort of your own company offices. While there is the Microsoft communities page,[2] there is also a proliferation of user groups, user communities, and technical bloggers that can help bring ideas in from other people in diverse organizations or consultancies. There are specific user groups for Dynamics 365, such as Dynamics 365UG[3] or AXUG,[4] where you will find like-minded people who are having the same challenges as you and often have found solutions to the common ones. Encouraging your technical team to become part of these groups and to attend meetings in your local area that are run by people in them is a good way to expand their knowledge and help your business. Additionally, there are bloggers who are trying to sell their consultancy services but often blog useful hints and tips about Dynamics 365.

Benefits Realization

Apart from the important information that you get from determining, tracking, and costing the benefits so far in your digital transformation, it is also important to show people how far you have come. It is likely that you will have already looked at some of these when going through the go-live acceptance criteria, but there will be a great many benefits that will have been missed. Consequently, it will be worthwhile taking a step back and gathering all the advances to your business that have come about.

To do this, list out the improvements (tangible and intangible) plus the financial benefits (where possible) in the following categories:

- Processes understood and improved
- Quality in all departments
- Productivity
- Cost avoidance
- Cost reduction
- Cost efficiency
- Customer service levels
- Staff engagement
- Staff satisfaction levels
- Departmental error rates
- Manufacturing or software development rework rates
- Revenue generation

- Customer retention rates
- Customer growth rates

This process will bring forward all the benefits you have realized that you should be celebrating and also ideas for additional benefits that can now come from the system and your business. Capture these ideas, as they will inform the direction you may want to take in the future. They can be handed to the relevant business process and systems lead or business solutions lead to progress.

There are plenty of resources and whole programs dedicated to benefits realization and the enhancement that can be made to a project by measuring these throughout. However, it is worth mentioning that if you spend too much time in a project getting people to work toward specific benefits that you may have seen at the beginning you can miss the ideas that come up as you go through the digital transformation process. By all means set the benefits you want and review them regularly, but don't get wedded to a direction and lose the culture of transformation. It is that culture we will cover next.

Continuing Culture of Digital Transformation

Keeping the Culture

Improvements should no longer be the result of necessity, but the result of the whole organization's desire to work more efficiently and successfully by continuously implementing and then building on small changes. In a traditional business, this has come from a few key people within the business or by bringing new people who will innovate in a few areas and then leave. The digital transformation model needs to empower anyone to suggest and then implement changes within the framework of the business strategy (and even sometimes outside of it). To achieve this, the culture needs to be communicated and reinforced often. It is imperative that your employees feel empowered and your managers feel fearless and able to put into action ideas from any source. Your Dynamics 365 ERP will increasingly automate the mundane tasks and enable creativity and customer focus, but only if you plan and execute it that way.

Making Best Use of Your Dynamics 365 to Empower People

Employees should be encouraged to bring forward new ideas for optimizing the ERP system to make their own job easier and to increase the productivity of the entire organization. They should not fear reducing their own workload but be encouraged to achieve this so that they can work on new ideas or in areas of particular interest. There will be people in the organization happy to do the mundane, but they will become more and more unusual as they see colleagues benefiting from doing interesting work. The single best way to sabotage your organization's digital transformation is to count the cost of employees rather than the value they can bring. Encourage your employees to make decisions on their own and challenge the status quo in order to make decisions that are favorable to their customers. This is a key behavior that is both empowering and critical to a transforming business.

There will be economic downturns, but empowered employees will come up with surprising ways to weather these if they are allowed to. Remind your employees that they are the catalysts for change and every improvement and idea will strengthen both them and the organization they work for.

Instilling the Right Habits

Improvements must be supported by the entire organization. The groups involved in change management play a key role in this and need to ensure employees are not left to their fate, but are actively helped in the improvement process from beginning to end.

A healthy digital culture is a type of high-performance culture. To understand the essential elements of a digital culture, it helps to be reminded of the three critical attributes of a high-performance culture:[5]

1. Employees and teams are engaged to achieve results. They are committed to their work and to the organization's purpose and goals, and they are willing to go the extra mile.
2. Individuals and teams work in ways that will advance the organization's strategy.

3. The organizational environment, or "context"—including leadership, organization design, performance management, people-development practices, resources and tools, vision and values, and informal interactions—is set up to foster engagement and encourage behaviors that will advance the organization's strategy.

In the same way, as no universal strategy exists, no standard digital culture does either, but a digital culture usually has five defining elements:

1. It promotes an external, rather than an internal, orientation. A digital culture inspires employees to look outward and to create new solutions with customers and partners. A prime example here is the focus on the customer journey; employees put themselves in the customer's shoes and thereby improve the customer experience and shape product development.
2. It prizes delegation over control. A digital culture pushes decision making deep into the organization. Instead of receiving explicit instructions on how to perform their work, employees follow guiding principles knowing their judgment can be trusted.
3. It encourages boldness over caution. In a digital culture, people are encouraged to take risks, fail fast, and learn, and they are discouraged from preserving the status quo out of habit or caution.
4. It emphasizes more action and less planning. In the fast-changing digital world, planning and decision making moves from having a long-term focus to a short-term one. The digital culture supports the need for speed and endorses continuous iteration rather than perfection in a product or idea before launch. The minimum viable product (MVP) becomes the mantra.
5. It values collaboration more than individual effort. In a digital culture, success comes through collective work and information sharing across departments, functions, and teams. The iterative and fast pace of digital work needs a far greater level of transparency and interaction than usually found in the traditional organization.

These elements vary in degree across industries and from companies. For example, the degree of risk-taking that is appropriate at a technology firm will not be the same as the degree that is appropriate at an industrial goods company. Within an organization the levels of risk-taking will vary; the strategy team should embrace risk to a much greater degree than the finance team for obvious reasons. Encouraging risk-taking is not intended to foster recklessness or breaching regulation or company policy, but to support thinking outside the box.

Leaders guiding a digital transformation who are too preoccupied with structural and process changes and overlook the people side will wonder why the effort faltered and eventually failed. It is well established that cultural change is a key factor in a successful transformation. In digital transformation this is particularly important. The behaviors that are needed in a digital culture are a major shift from the way we have all been working. They challenge traditional power structures, decision-making authority, and fundamental views of competition and cooperation among employees and will be difficult to overcome, but if you are to benefit fully from the digital transformation that Dynamics 365 will enable, then they must be overcome and transcended.

Summing Up

Initially we looked at the ways of setting up the support teams to underpin your continuous improvement program. Under consideration were both the business and the technical supporting teams. Then we looked at a few types of support frameworks including whether to insource, outsource, or combine the two models. Moving on to continuous improvement, we looked at the frameworks needed to manage this.

Finally, we looked at how to track your benefits realization to show how far you have come and how to keep the culture of digital transformation you have worked so hard to achieve.

> ## Digital Future Checklist
>
> ✓ Get your support framework clear both for technical and business support.
> ✓ Continuous improvement needs a framework, so make sure it encourages the right habits.
> ✓ Document and celebrate your benefits.
> ✓ Continue the culture you have worked so hard to implement.

"The thing is, continuity of strategic direction and continuous improvement in how you do things are absolutely consistent with each other. In fact, they're mutually reinforcing."
—*Michael Porter, Educator and Economist*

Notes

1. Dynamics 365 Roadmap. www.dynamics.microsoft.com/en-gb/roadmap/overview/.
2. Microsoft Dynamics Communities: Microsoft Dynamics Community – Forums, Blogs, Videos, Support.
3. Dynamics User Group UG. www.d365ug.com.
4. Dynamics AX User Group. www.axug.com.
5. Jim Hemerling and Julie Kilman (2013), High-Performance Culture: Getting It, Keeping It, BCG Focus. www.bcg.com/publications/2013/people-organization-behavior-high-performance-culture.

Customer Stories

SCANIA, A DIVISION OF THE TRATON GROUP, EMPOWERS WORKFORCE, ACCELERATES SHIFT TO DIGITAL TRANSFORMATION, AND IMPROVED PRODUCTIVITY WITH MICROSOFT DYNAMICS 365

Business Challenge

Scania is a leading global provider of transport solutions in more than 100 countries. It is not just about performance, reliability, and economy but also about knowledge of the customer's business. Scania creates a tailor-made approach for a package of services that can help increase their customer's profitability.

Scania's strength lies in meeting customer needs, offering a solution platform that enables and offers choices to customers while ordering the vehicle.

Scania needs a good customer relationship management tool to maintain a good relationship with customers, find the right customers to contact, and keep all data about customer interaction in one place, which can help the salesperson to prepare for a meeting and enhance the visibility of a global sales pipeline. Scania decided to move on to the Dynamics 365 solution for Sales, Service, and Marketing and seamless integration with Microsoft technologies.

Wholesale and retail operations are quite complicated and with legacy applications (mix of bought solutions like Epicor iScala and their own developed solutions) reaching the end of life, they must be replaced. This mix of systems has also led to the need for many integrations and high maintenance costs. Therefore, a decision has been taken to go ahead and broaden the use of the Dynamics platform, namely Dynamics 365 Finance & Operations.

Solution

Scania has adopted agile ways of working with SCRUM methodology that was adaptable and flexible, configuring the system in regular sprints and delivering a release of minimum viable products (MVPs) every month. This delivery process and approach has helped Scania to cater to constantly changing demands, reduce time to market, and have a possibility to roll back deprecated functionality.

Scania has streamlined their sales process and retail sales management and implemented Dynamics 365 for a Sales, Service, and Marketing solution.

The Dynamics 365 solution has helped Scania to have a 360° view of the customer, working on opportunities globally together, to be able to sell more instead of cherry-picking customers, finalizing agreement, a structured way of closing, overall sales increased, and improving salesperson's efficiency and performance.

The solution is accessible on web or mobile on offline, which has helped in adoption of the solution. Scania has also rolled out Power BI to have reports and dashboard.

The Dynamics 365 F&O solution is developed in the same way as the CRM solution using the SCRUM methodology. Streamlined processes with a harmonized setup using blueprints lead to more efficiency in the finance and procurement organizations, with bigger possibilities to easily share staff between business units and have reports with drilldown possibilities from the top of Scania Commercial Operations down to each individual transaction in real time.

Outcome

"Dynamics 365 Customer Engagement is helping Scania to identify the right customer to focus on, view the global sales pipeline and implement a standard global sales process to improve efficiency of our salesperson."

Manpreet Gambhir, Journey Lead Sales, Scania

"Dynamics 365 Finance & Operations gives Scania harmonized financial processes. With a common chart of accounts world-wide, management can follow the development in real time."

Peter Edén, Head of IT region EUR, Scania

Scania has achieved:

- A uniformed sales process
- Global view on sales pipeline, with the sales opportunities as one collaborative team
- 360° view of the customer with all details of lead, prospect, details of visits, and appointments in one place
- Distributed team across Sweden and India working globally
- Harmonized financial processes with a common chart of accounts across all units
- Increased possibilities to work across several business units with all units in the same solution
- A modern solution replacing integrations between outdated systems

VIRGIN ATLANTIC EASILY CREATES CUSTOM-BUILT MOBILE APPLICATIONS WITH MICROSOFT POWER APPS AND DYNAMICS 365

Challenge

For Virgin Atlantic, air travel is about much more than just getting from place to place. The company's mission is to be the "most loved travel company" and this aspirational attitude means making every customer feel truly valued. Keeping its 5 million passengers a year happy is front of mind for the airline and its employees.

Virgin Atlantic has a highly mobile workforce, with employees at airports or hangars, on board the aircraft, and in offices around the world, all with different data needs.

It was due diligence to presenting that data in a meaningful way and drive value and benefit when using that data, while considering various options such as time, costs, and right skillsets. For the engineering teams, for example, there was no automation, and no dashboard to visualize their findings. As a result, engineers could not take appropriate action on the most critical items. The engineers were spending time away from their working environment to complete audits on paper.

For other areas of the business, it is about being able to quickly bring a new piece of technology to fruition that will have an immediate impact for either the customers or the customer-facing teams.

Solution

As part of the company's adoption of Microsoft Office 365, they started investigating other elements of Office 365 and discovered Microsoft Power Apps, a cost-effective and efficient tool for building and customizing powerful business applications that will empower subject matter experts creating their own apps. This approach helped increase customer satisfaction, boost employee engagement, and reduce costs.

"We want to be an airline that people love to fly with. From their experience selecting and booking the flight, through to their time on the plane, and all the way until they get to their destination . . . when people leave the airport, we want them to already be thinking about their next trip with Virgin Atlantic. We're always looking at improving levels of employee engagement."

Lee Pope, Solutions Delivery (Microsoft Dynamics 365 and Power Platform), Virgin Atlantic. Used with permission of Virgin Atlantic.

"As someone who is not a developer and not from a technology background, the Microsoft Power Platform has completely changed the direction of my career. In a short space of time, I have been able to design, create, deploy and support multiple PowerApps to our customer facing teams in both the Customer Centres and Clubhouses Worldwide. To see my work being used in the airports by customers, or being used thousands of times a month in our Customer Centres, gives me a huge sense of pride."

Lee Pope, Solutions Delivery (Microsoft Dynamics 365 and Power Platform), Virgin Atlantic. Used with permission of Virgin Atlantic.

Before COVID-19, Virgin Atlantic has achieved:

- Created a 360-degree customer view extending the ability to tailor services and make the travel experience as seamless and enjoyable as possible. Deployed a multipurpose PowerApp to the Customer Centre with over 11,000 monthly engagements.
- Allowed passengers to use a collective 22,000,000 Flying Club miles to pay for spa treatments at Heathrow, Gatwick, and New York JFK.
- Running "in a day" workshops to enable business users to understand and utilize all aspects of the Power Platform.

EUROPEAN PARALLEL DISTRIBUTION COMPANY ABACUS MEDICINE SUSTAINS ITS RAPID GROWTH WITH MICROSOFT DYNAMICS FINANCE AND OPERATIONS AND MICROSOFT POWER PLATFORM

Challenge

Abacus Medicine is a company with a purpose founded in 2004. Abacus Medicine supplies original prescription medicines in Europe through what is generally known as parallel distribution or parallel import.

In the past 16 years, the company has grown rapidly and has an ambitious growth strategy through supplying many types of medicines in many countries. Year after year, Abacus Medicine has reported strong growth, coupled with sound profitability above the industry average.

Abacus Medicine is a highly data-driven business and real-time insight to the data about the warehouse and supply chain across multiple countries is core to its business.

In the past, Abacus Medicine had a highly customized solution using SQL DB, which was fit for purpose when the company was small, but with the expansion and growth over the years, it needed a solution that is robust and scalable, speeds up operations, and enables Abacus Medicine to make data-driven decisions based on real-time insights.

Solution

In 2017, Abacus Medicine started its journey with mapping and streamlining its internal processes across different countries, followed by selecting a vendor. In January 2018, after selecting a vendor, the strategic decision was to move ahead with Dynamics 365 Finance and Operations in the cloud. Abacus Medicine made key decisions around the design approach by leveraging the standard processes of Dynamics 365 where the business could change, and only customizing if the business could not change, aiming for 80/20 principle. In January 2019, Abacus went live with Dynamics 365 in two countries, Denmark and Hungary, including Supply Chain, Purchase, Finance, Sales, warehouse, and integration with other systems.

Along with working on implementing Dynamics 365, Abacus Medicine was also working on another project to comply with the requirements of the Falsified Medicines Directive (FMD), to cover the safety measures including barcode to determine a product's authenticity and an anti-tamper device (ATD).

The roadmap of going live in January 2019 and integrating with FMD regulatory system was very timely and it was possible due to making quicker decisions and leveraging the standard business process of Dynamics 365.

Abacus Medicine has also implemented Microsoft Power Platform and Logic Apps that have enabled it to reduce its manual and repetitive tasks, and Abacus Medicine has included real-time business reports with Power BI.

Outcome and Benefits

"We buy thousands of different products each month from multiple countries in Europe and market them directly to 13 countries. Our success is based on our strong ability to buy and sell in the right markets at the right time. We therefore need to be the most flexible and the fastest distributor in the market. The modernization of our ERP system was a must."

Flemming Wagner, founder and CEO of Abacus Medicine

"The new ERP system needed to be able to follow our business growth in terms of not just users but sites, warehouses, and legal entities levels too. We implemented Dynamics 365 Finance and Operations in the cloud, as it could scale up and down with us very fast. We could also stick to the platform's design and customize not more than 20 percent of the system."

Peter Domonkos, IT Development Manager at Abacus Medicine

Abacus Medicine has achieved:

- More reliable and faster solution.
- Consistent annual growth rates of 30–40%. Revenue in 2019 of euro 421 million.
- Customers receive correct shipments and have quicker financial transactions.
- Go to market has been faster.
- Managers can view real-time business reports on Power BI.
- In the past, inventory took two days per quarter but now requires only two days per year, gaining six extra days each year.
- 250 employees can work simultaneously.

PART IV

Appendices

The appendices explain LCS and DevOps in detail and the importance of each one in the implementation of Dynamics 365. Appendix B provides insights to readers about the FastTrack for the Dynamics 365 process. Also included is a real-life customer story where business challenges, solutions, and the benefits are discussed.

Appendix A: This appendix provides details of LCS, DevOps and how Azure DevOps, Lifecycle services, and RSAT complement each other in the long run, and enable a team across cross-functional and geographically dispersed teams to work collaboratively and efficiently.

Appendix B: Have you ever wondered about fast track and what benefits you can leverage from Microsoft Dynamics 365 Fast-Track implementation? If so, then look no further, as this appendix covers that in detail.

Success Enablers for Dynamics 365 Implementation

Test fast, fail fast, adjust fast.

—Tom Peters

This appendix is here to give you a little more high-level information on a few tools that are available to help you with the planning and operations for Microsoft Dynamics 365. It is not intended to give you the most up-to-date information or to go into much detail because, while enablers such as Lifecycle Services (LCS) and Azure DevOps are important tools, each company will use them differently. There is no one-size-fits-all approach, so the information we are trying to impart is deliberately high level. Reading this chapter will not help you decide whether Dynamics 365 should be your ERP of choice when starting a digital transformation journey. However, if you do use Dynamics 365, this section will help you identify some of the tools that your business is likely to find useful as part of your transformation journey.

There are many different tools that will help you to be successful with your digital transformation. The selection of tools will depend on organizational needs and the success factors that you laid out at the start of your process. In the case of Dynamics 365 and Azure, the most important standard tools from Microsoft include LCS (Microsoft

Lifecycle Services), Azure DevOps (Development Operations), RSAT (Regression Suite Automation Tool), and Power Platform. For the moment we will look at these toolsets separately and describe their benefits. At the end of this section, we will explain how they operate together to support your digital transformation.

Microsoft Lifecycle Services

Microsoft Lifecycle Services (LCS) is a cloud toolset provided by Microsoft that will help you control every aspect of your change implementations.

- It allows all the people involved in the core Dynamics 365 application (and satellite applications such as third-party integrations or internal PowerApps applications) to be able to work together under a structure that ensures adherence to the needs of the business applications lifecycle.
- It can structure the lifecycle methodologies to support compatibility with the business's core system and methods.
- It ensures business continuity by reducing the likelihood of implementing applications that stop software upgrades.
- It removes uncertainty over customizations and their longer-term harmony with the core Dynamics 365 implementation.
- It allows the project and the IT technical team to manage implementations and issues in a way that reduces business impacts.
- It is scalable within the cloud and allows both the business and the project team to manage and therefore pay for only the Azure infrastructure and applications that you need.

One of the major advantages of using LCS is the standard methodology framework that everyone works with. The project team follows the implementation framework and creates and manages artifacts from LCS that will be required in the program. It encourages standardization of all the elements involved with your project. When this happens, it is much easier to track, communicate, and report on progress. LCS offers flexibility and consistency of process and the artifacts.

One of the important tools in LCS is the Business Process Modeler, which helps you define, refine, optimize, and then maintain your business processes. You can then use the content management tools of LCS, generate documentation with Microsoft tools such as Word and Visio, and maintain and monitor any technical debt in tools such as Azure DevOps Services. Additionally, training and testing can be improved by using the Dynamics 365 Task Recorder to create training materials and to automate testing during development.

Main Users of LCS

LCS can be accessed by members across different teams within the project. Here is a list of various roles, but you can decide how you would like to operate within your organization, depending on the volume licensing agreement:[1]

- Project Manager(s)
- Solution Architects
- Migration Leads
- Business Product Owner
- Business Analysts
- Solution Integration (SI) partner—Solution Architects
- SI partner—Developers and Test Analysts
- SI partner—Deployment Leads
- SI partner—Migration and Integration Leads
- Business Architect(s)
- Business Test Lead
- The MS D365 Support team
- IT Administration team

Main Uses of LCS

Here is a list of main areas LCS that can be used in a project:

- Deploying environments
- Code updates to environments
- Moving data around environments
- Business process validation
- Managing support incidents
- Environment monitoring (in the operations phase)
- Performance issues (in the operations phase)

More Details on LCS

There is a lot of online information regarding Microsoft LCS and Azure DevOps that is constantly updated by Microsoft and the specialists promoting and working with both. For this publication we will take you through the current thinking on them and the ways they can help you with your Dynamics 365 ERP and your digital transformation journey.

LCS allows you to implement Dynamics 365 or to maintain it once implemented. It is broken down into three main sections: projects, phases, and tools.

Projects

Either your business team or your partner(s) can use LCS to create or manage plans for implementation of Dynamics 365 and to collaborate on the project(s) that you are all working on. If you use the Dynamics 365 Finance and Operation implementation methodology, you will follow a structured flow for the project that is Microsoft-approved, but you can create and follow your own methodologies and structure. You either create or are invited to projects and the process to completion follows the milestones set up by the PM and agreed with the team.

From LCS you can also create and retire D365 environments needed for the project (such as test environments), look up all the Microsoft documentation that will help your project, and maintain the Azure cloud infrastructure needed by the team on the project. In this section of LCS you can manage the people involved with the projects and see summaries of progress. There is also a document repository linked here that allows you to maintain and update the documents that the project is using via SharePoint.

Phases

As with any Dynamics 365 project or projects there are phases of the project you are collaborating on. LCS helps you define, track, and see these phases and the work that has been done or is still required within them. Typically phases include: analyze, design, develop, or deployment. Additionally, you can see the operations area that is used to manage the Cloud-hosted environments required by each phase.

Tools

There are many tools available to you in LCS including:

- Business Process Modeler helps business analysts define processes or use industry standard business processes.
- License Sizing Estimator helps you determine the licensing requirements of a given setup and to manage your Dynamics 365 licensing.
- Usage Profiler gives you a questionnaire that will help you decide how you intend to use the system and how to design the Dynamics 365 architecture to suit those needs.
- System Diagnostic will tell you of any issues with the systems you are using to support your Dynamics 365 environments.
- Customization Analysis checks (and can apply best practice to) the customizations you are planning to ensure they are compatible with your current version of Dynamics 365.
- Issue Search gives you a powerful search facility within LCS to find all the documents that can help you in any area of Dynamics 365, LCS, or Azure.
- Infrastructure Estimator is based on the answers given using the usage profiler and this tool estimates the infrastructure you will need.

Azure DevOps

Until recently businesses would have at least two teams of people connected to their IT department. One would run the IT operations and the other would plan and/or build the applications needed to run the business. The first were often known as the admin or infrastructure team and the second would be the project or development team. Often these two teams would be in conflict, as the infrastructure team's main objective is to ensure the smooth running of all the systems, while projects would be trying to make improvements by changing or adding functionality to support the business needs. For a successful change program and a stable operation, it is key for both development and infrastructure to work collaboratively and in synergy from the beginning to end. DevOps helps the two work as one, ensuring that your business requirements (for new ways of working and changes to the way your Dynamics 365 environment works for you) are considered and planned for in all aspects of the day-to-day operation of your system.

DevOps as a platform drives collaboration in planning and in all lifecycle stages of the application, setting up workflow for assigning and approval of items to resources keeping an audit trail, security, and compliance throughout, and helps keeping track of ideas and changes driving continuous improvement while in operation (Figure A.1).

Helping to Plan Developments/Changes

DevOps teams will plan out the improvements they need to make. Azure DevOps enables cross-application task planning at low and high levels of detail. The teams can create backlogs, track bugs, manage agile software development, and use Kanban boards and visualizing progress with dashboards. All these activities can then be rolled up into reports and dashboards and made available to senior leaders to track progress as required.

FIGURE A.1 DevOps Lifecycle

Developing the Application(s)

Azure DevOps provides the tools to support development efficiency at all stages of the work. The platform covers all areas of coding: writing, testing, reviewing, and integrating code with other team member's changes. It also helps to automate the deployment into various pre-production environments. To innovate rapidly without sacrificing quality, stability, and productivity, you need to automate standard processes including testing and continuous integration.

Delivering the Changes

Deploying applications and patches into production environments must be done reliably, whether they are application or infrastructure changes. Set out and agree on the roles and responsibilities of the different teams. It is usually a good idea to have Applications Support prepare the release to the point of going into UAT and then have Infrastructure release into UAT (to ensure they have the process correct) and then into Production, following approval from the business teams.

Once the business has agreed on a defined release management process with clear approval points, the technical teams can move improvements between stages until they are live. Automating processes makes them scalable, repeatable, and controlled, leading to confidence and shorter turnaround times.

Operating (Managing) the Applications and Their Environments

This covers the maintenance, monitoring, and troubleshooting of applications in production. DevOps practices ensure that teams work to safeguard system reliability and high availability, targeting zero downtime while reinforcing security and governance. The goal is to positively affect the customer experience and therefore mitigate any issues quickly. To achieve these goals, you need real-time reporting, meaningful alerting, and full visibility into applications and the underlying system.

Azure DevOps gives you the ability to manage all the duties expected of a DevOps team, but most teams will still want to make changes to standard tools and techniques. As we have mentioned previously, it is important to understand and define why changes are needed for your business. If they are, Azure DevOps is one way to manage all aspects of the development lifecycle.

Azure Boards Support Team Collaboration

Azure Boards allows your team to use any method for your development and planning. There are templates for Agile, Scrum, etc., but pretty much any project type can be created. Azure Boards are used for capturing business requirements, assigning work, planning sprints, tracking progress and conducting various type of testing.

Because all the collaboration is done within the Azure Boards, no one is left out of the loop—email is still used but all communication is managed within the boards so everyone can see progress whether they are part of the project or the technical team. Dashboards allow management and executive teams to manage by exception and monitor progress.

Azure Test Plans, Business Process Modeler Tool, Task Recorder, and RSAT Support Effective Testing

Testing is critical in the new world of LCS, Azure, and Dynamics 365. Changes and improvements are frequent and come from multiple sources. It is therefore imperative that as much testing as possible is automated and covers all of the most important business processes. You do not want to be in a position of breaking your production environment because a business process has been missed during a testing cycle.

To make sure testing is as robust as conceivable, planning in Azure can be supported using the Task Recorder in Dynamics 365. From the recordings created by the Task Recorder, the Business Process Modeler Tool can be used to create a structure to be applied to automated testing, and these tests are then used in RSAT (Remote Server Administration Tools; see further information later in this section) to manage tests that only report on failure. Using this method your test team spends their time analyzing the failed test cycles and creating better testing, rather than performing the tests every time a change is made.

Nagendra Sanjeeva,
Senior Vice President,
Architecture and Technology, MasterCard

"We often hear that DevOps is a cultural transformation that is hard to perfect unless it is embraced both by management and the engineering organization. However, not all organizations are ready for DevOps unless applications are architected to be state-less and self-healing, with the ability to run on select standardized technical stacks. DevOps practices on poorly architected systems often become counterproductive with frequent production outages. In the same way, the organization structure must be in place to enable and empower the engineering team that develops the software to be responsible for the run and support of the applications and have opportunities to interact with customers with a clear understanding of end-user journeys."

Other Azure DevOps Services

Azure Pipelines

These are used to automatically build and test code and then make it available to other users. This is useful when multiple developers are working and you want to reuse code in various areas. Here the concepts of continuous integration and continuous delivery are combined to test and build code and send it to multiple developers as required (see Figure A.2). Azure pipelines work with any code language, platform, or cloud. This agnosticism empowers your developments.

Azure Repos

This is where the version control of your code is done. It ensures proper tracking of code changes and can manage multiple developers" work (or one). Version control keeps a history of your developments so that you can review and even roll back to any version of your code with ease. It is more of a technical tool but has business benefits when the code has a problem or is not backed up when needed.

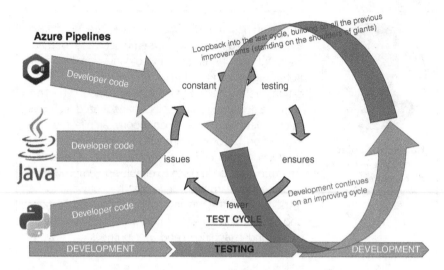

FIGURE A.2 Continuous Integration and Continuous Delivery (CICD)

Regression Suite Automation Tool

The Regression Suite Automation Tool (RSAT) lets functional power users record business tasks by using Task Recorder and then converts the recordings into a suite of automated tests, without having to write source code. How this integrates with other aspects of the tools mentioned is best shown in a diagram (see Figure A.3).

Because the Subject Matter Experts (SMEs) record the test cases used in the RSAT, the end-to-end testing is closely aligned to real business practices. This makes sure that the testing you are doing reflects what is done in a real-world scenario and therefore surfaces any issues before they come to light in the operational environment. In addition, the testing can be automated as far as is possible, although this sometimes requires the use of additional tools such as Power Automate (described later in the Power Platform section).

RSAT is intended to be used for business cycle tests and scenario tests (multiple component tests) that usually occur at the end of the development lifecycle. This is also referred to as user acceptance testing.

Business cycle testing consists of a smaller number of test cases than component or unit testing, which are often also referred to,

RSAT

1. Record Tests
2. Save tests to Business Process Modeller (BPM is part of LCS)
3. Manage/Distribute BPM Library

1. Select BPM Library, synchronize test cases to DevOps
2. Create Test Cases and attach recordings (or use BPM)
3. Create Test Plans and Test Suites

1. Generate tests, update parameters
2. Execute
3. Report and investigate in Azure DevOps

FIGURE A.3 RSAT

more descriptively, as end-to-end tests. In the following graphic you can see where in the hierarchy of testing the RSAT tool is used (see Figure A.4).

Unit and Component Testing

For unit tests, Microsoft does not recommend that you use RSAT. Instead, they suggest you use the SysTest framework and the build/test automation tools. For component tests the developers can use the Acceptance Test Library (ATL) resources. ATL is a library of X++ test helpers. When used with the SysTest framework, it offers the following benefits:

- Creation of consistent test data.
- Increases the readability of test code.
- Provides enhanced discovery of the methods that are used to create test data.
- Hides the complexity of setting up prerequisites.
- Supports high performance of test cases.

The RSAT technology and the RVP (Release Validation Program) are key components to a successful continuous solution evolution. Incrementally building out an RSAT suite of tests, starting as soon

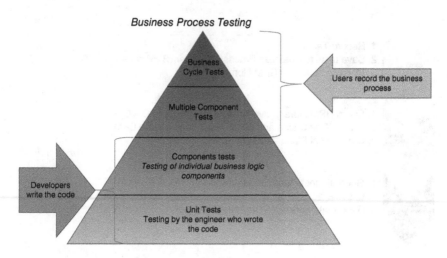

FIGURE A.4 Business Process Testing

as areas of the project stabilize, allows new service updates to be validated with the push of a button and without pulling business users away from their real work.

What Is the RVP?

Basically, RVP uses a number of Microsoft's customers' RSAT suites in addition to Microsoft's own tests to validate new updates before they are published. At some point, Microsoft may not be able to take new customers into their RVP. However, the RVP underlines Microsoft's commitment to quality and their focus on evolution without disruption of the entire Dynamics 365 Customer base.

Power Platform

Power Platform is a huge advance in the way businesses modify their systems to fit their business needs. It puts application development and automation tools into the hands of the business experts, allowing them to meet the real requirements of the organization rather than having to explain to developers what they need. Power Platform consists of a suite of tools that include the following:

- **Power Apps.** Low-code application development, where most of the code needed is easy to program and mimics Excel formulas. This means people who understand the business can develop these applications rather than the more traditional systems developer.
- **Power BI.** A collection of software and service offerings that help users visualize and interact with business data that is collated together. This allows data to be transformed into something meaningful by the people who need and use it. This data is then made available via controlled Datasets as Reports or Dashboards.
- **Power Automate.** Allows business users to create automated workflows and therefore simplify business processes and manage them more effectively.

  Using Power Automate, you can create workflows for common business scenarios from an ever-growing template gallery. These templates are easily customized but you can also create workflows specific to your own organization using the easy editing tools. Power Automate is easily connected to many popular apps and services using the over 200 connectors available. Drive user adoption keeps users on track and ensures data consistency throughout your organization with multistage business process automation. For example, create an automation to ensure all projects are started in the same way, every time.
- **AI Builder.** Automate processes and predict outcomes to improve business performance. AI Builder is a solution that brings the power of Microsoft AI through a compelling user interface experience. It is directly integrated into Power Apps and Power Automate.
- **Power Virtual Agents.** Gives your people the ability to create bots that can automate common enquiries allowing customers to self-help and resolve issues at first contact. Personalized bot conversations with internal users created and curated by Subject Matter Experts (SMEs) can free up those SMEs to focus on more complex issues they encounter rather than answering repetitive or mundane questions. Power Virtual Agents employ low-code solutions that allow the key users to create the bots rather than a developer.

As described, there are a number of tools within the Power Platform that can give you a competitive advantage when used by the key users within your business. The way these are used will depend on multiple factors, not least of which will be your corporate culture, as an empowering culture will generate a greater return than a controlling one.

How Do Azure DevOps, Lifecycle Services, RSAT, and Power Platform Complement Each Other?

The best way to attempt to show this is by using a diagram (see Figure A.5). What this shows are some of the benefits of using LCS, DevOps RSAT, and Power Platform and how these tools overlap and complement each other in the differing teams.

Historically, organizations approached big system deployments as something they executed, finished, and then left alone for years. That cannot be the model any more. If it is, it leads to bad expectations about staffing, ongoing investment, and ongoing opportunity. The successful project today is the one that embraces continuous

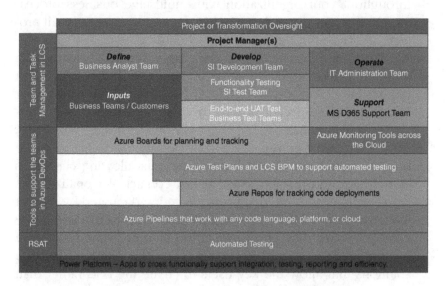

FIGURE A.5 Benefits of Using LCS, Azure DevOps, RSAT, and Power Platform

evolution with first one area of the business and then another. First one set of processes is transformed and then another. Constant attention to the Release Plans for the Dynamics 365 products and the use of the Power Platform helps the business to look for the next opportunity to transform.

Your next big leap forward will be found in the new challenges and opportunities your business faces and the innovations in Dynamics 365 and the supporting and complementary products. Your Dynamics 365 digital transformation may be replacing an older solution that no longer meets the needs of your organization. The act of replacement can be traumatic and expensive and not one you will wish to repeat. Continuous evolution with Dynamics 365 and its supporting success enablers means you can now grow, change, and improve for years to come without having to look at another disruptive system upgrade.

Notes

1. https://docs.microsoft.com/en-us/dynamics365/fin-ops-core/fin-ops/get-started/move-licenses-between-agreement-types.

Microsoft FastTrack for Dynamics 365

We are what we repeatedly do. Excellence, then, is not an act, but a habit.

—Aristotle

The FastTrack for the Dynamics 365 program is driven through the Microsoft engineering team and is focused on providing experiences and learnings from thousands of Dynamics 365 implementations around the world through a prescriptive and recommended guidance approach called Success by Design. The team is an organization of Solution Architects spread across the world that engage both directly with customers, and indirectly through qualified partners, to share recommended practices and identify deployment blockers in order to drive successful implementations.

This chapter will help you better understand what FastTrack for Dynamics 365 offers and how you can engage with the program to accelerate your implementation.

Success by Design

To understand the FastTrack for Dynamics 365 program, you need to understand Success by Design, which is the basis for how FastTrack engages with customers and partners. Success by Design is the collection of prescriptive guidance, approaches, and recommended practices, for designing, building, and deploying Dynamics 365 solutions.

There are three core principles in Success by Design:

1. **Early detection.** Issues and risks to implementation success should be found as early in the process as possible so that any potential negative impact can be avoided or greatly reduced. Success by Design relies on planned reviews, occurring throughout the implementation, that provide the opportunity to pause and reflect at key points in the implementation. In these reviews, issues and risks can be captured and mitigated in a timely fashion.

2. **Proactive guidance.** Recommended patterns and practices should be identified and used to ensure future success. By gathering and disseminating patterns and practices that have been observed to be successful, Microsoft provides guidance that can be used to drive successful solution design and implementation approaches. FastTrack aggregates these patterns and practices through thousands of engagements with customers and partners. These patterns are both incorporated in the Dynamics 365 product as well as broadcast through FastTrack engagements and various educational channels such as the Dynamics 365 Community, FastTrack Bootcamps, Microsoft Learn, and Microsoft Docs.

3. **Predictable success.** The combination of the first two principles, early detection and proactive guidance, provide a basis for predictable, successful outcomes in customer implementations. This success is monitored and measured to continually refine and optimize the program along with solution guidance.

In many cases, a customer project will be delivered in waves. Waves beyond the initial deployment might have the same or even more scope than the first phase; for example, expanding to cover additional facilities, countries, or functional areas. It is important to apply the same Success by Design principles and practices to these subsequent waves.

Success by Design Phases

The FastTrack for Dynamics 365 engagement is organized in a series of phases that relate to the types of activities that occur throughout the implementation. It is important to understand that FastTrack and the Success by Design approach does not dictate an implementation methodology or style. While the following phases may seem sequential in nature, the activities within the Implement phase can be conducted in a variety of implementation models, including waterfall, iterative, and other hybrid approaches.

- **Initiate.** This phase includes all the activities required to start up the implementation. In this phase, the FastTrack team will conduct kick-off activities with the customer and partner. The solution blueprint review process starts in the initiate phase and validates the plan and conceptual design going into the Implement phase.
- **Implement.** This phase includes most of the implementation activities. The order of these activities is dependent on the implementation methodology being employed by the customer and partner. FastTrack activities in this phase will be executed based on the customer's specific needs. These activities, known as "Implementation Workshops," are deep dives into specific aspects of the solution design and implementation approach.
- **Prepare.** This phase includes the activities following the conclusion of the primary system testing. It begins with a go-live readiness assessment that recaps the implementation activities and validates the path to a successful go-live. FastTrack will stay particularly close in this phase to ensure that any go-live blocking issues that arise can be quickly resolved.
- **Operate.** The operate phase signals the end of the FastTrack engagement. In this phase, following the stabilization of the go-live, the FastTrack team will perform the post go-live assessment workshop to ensure that the customer team is ready to own and operate the solution successfully in the future.

Success by Design Workshops

Success by Design workshops are used within the FastTrack for the Dynamics 365 program as an opportunity to review the details of the implementation at various points throughout the phases described above. The number of workshops conducted for each implementation will vary depending on the circumstances of the solution being implemented. Each implementation will begin with a solution blueprint review and will include some combination of implementation workshops. Each implementation will also have a go-live readiness workshop prior to deploying the production environment. Figure B.1 illustrates the overall program and the various types of workshops.

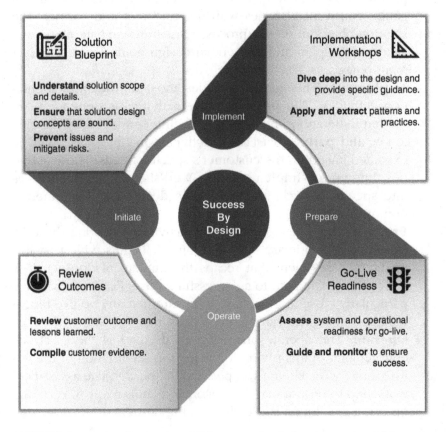

FIGURE B.1 Success by Design Within FastTrack for Dynamics 365
Source: © Microsoft. Used with permission from Microsoft Corporation.

Solution Blueprint Review Workshop

The solution blueprint for any implementation should lay out the overall scope, approach, and conceptual design of the solution. It is reasonable to expect that any implementation that has defined a budget and timeline would have an underlying solution blueprint upon which those things are based. That blueprint may take a variety of different forms. It could be one cohesive document or a collection of documents. The blueprint may be more or less detailed depending on the where the solution is in its lifecycle, but it must exist, regardless of the form it takes. Without a solution blueprint, the solution may be lacking the basic foundation to make it successful.

The solution blueprint review is the first major workshop conducted through the FastTrack program. The solution blueprint review should be conducted as the implementation is starting up. This workshop is both critical to the success of the implementation and foundational to the overall FastTrack engagement. The intention of the review is as follows:

- **To understand and to validate the scope of the solution.** There is a common set of things that make up any Dynamics 365 implementation, which include business requirements, functional designs, technical designs, and an implementation approach. The solution blueprint review is used to ensure that these aspects are accounted for in a meaningful way.
- **To understand and to validate the conceptual design and approach of the solution.** Regardless of the details of how a solution will be implemented, there must be a concept for how the various technical components will come together to form a solution and how the various activities within the implementation will be conducted. The solution blueprint review is used to ensure that those concepts are based on recommended patterns and practices.
- **To drive communication and understanding.** Business application implementations are often complex. They may involve many business areas, processes, applications, datasets, integrations, migrations, cutovers, etc. The process of initiating these implementations typically involves a customer organization

working together with one or more partner organizations to agree on scope, approach, budgets, and timelines. The opportunity for omission and miscommunication is significant, especially as the implementation transitions from the group of people involved in pre-sale activities to what is typically a larger group of people who will ultimately be responsible for delivering the solution. The solution blueprint review provides an opportunity to review the approach and conceptual solution at a broad level to ensure a common understanding.

■ **To identify issues and risks at an early stage.** One of the foundational principles of Success by Design is early detection. Conducting a solution blueprint review in the initiation phase of the project provides the opportunity to optimize designs and approaches before time and valuable resources have been invested in downstream activities that may produce suboptimal results.

■ **To scope and plan the FastTrack engagement.** The insights gained by the Solution Architects who conduct the solution blueprint review not only allow them to provide findings and recommendations that will immediately impact the implementation, but they also provide a basis for determining the implementation workshops that will be needed throughout the remainder of the program.

The solution blueprint review looks at the solution from a breadth perspective and includes the functional, technical, and implementation strategies for the implementation. The typical agenda of a solution blueprint review is as follows:

■ Program Strategy
■ Testing Strategy
■ Application Strategy
■ Business Process Strategy
■ Application Lifecycle Management Strategy
■ Data Strategy
■ Integration Strategy
■ Intelligence Strategy
■ Security Strategy
■ Environment and Capacity Strategy

Prior to the workshop, the solution architect who is conducting the review will request that existing artifacts that can provide insight into the solution be submitted for review. Since this workshop is conducted as the project is just starting up, it is typical that many detailed artifacts will not yet have been created. In some cases, the necessary information will come from pre-sales designs and statements of work. The architect will provide a template as a guidance to help gather the necessary information, but the implementation team will have similar documents, and it is fine for them to use those documents too as long as they cover all aspects of the necessary information to be gathered.

The time to conduct the solution blueprint review will vary based on the scope and complexity of the implementation, but in general the intent is to try to cover the material in no more than 8 hours. This does not seem like a lot of time to cover this much material but it is important to keep in mind that the solution blueprint review is intended to review the high-level conceptual designs and approaches. Digging into the details is reserved for the implementation workshops that will follow.

The solution blueprint review workshop must be attended by project leadership from both the customer and the partner organizations. Project managers and architects are essential to driving the conversation. These team members should be prepared to present their plans and conceptual designs for the solution during the workshop. They will benefit most from the opportunity to ensure they understand the entire solution. The broader team can be included in the entire review or in individual sections when needed to provide subject matter expertise.

The output of the Solution Blueprint Review workshop is a Fast-Track Findings and Recommendation Document.

Implementation Workshops

Implementation workshops make up the bulk of the FastTrack engagement and include all the workshops that are executed between the Solution Blueprint Review and the Go-Live Readiness Assessment Workshop. There is a standard set of workshops defined in the Fast-Track program, which are described below. The FastTrack Solution

Architect may also define non-standard workshops to address implementation specific needs. Following the execution of the Solution Blueprint review, the FastTrack solution architect will determine which workshops will benefit from a specific implementation.

The following describes the standard set of implementation workshops most commonly executed by FastTrack:

- **Data Migration Strategy and Design.** This workshop is designed to review the data migration strategy and technical design. This would normally be executed once the data migration requirements have been gathered and the design for data migration has been drafted. The intention is to ensure that the planned approach considers the broad set of requirements including extraction, cleansing, transformation, mapping, security, and performance, and that the related designs conform to recommended practices.
- **Security Model Design.** This workshop is designed to review solution security including the internal structures within Dynamics 365 and those external factors that may impact the solution. This would normally be executed once the requirements have been gathered and the security design has been drafted. The intention is to ensure that the security design is comprehensive in addressing the solution's security needs while not having a negative impact on usability, operability, and performance.
- **Solution Performance Workshop.** This workshop is designed to ensure that the solution design and implementation approach have adequately understood and addressed the performance needs of the solution. This includes verifying non-functional requirements in terms of overall system throughput as well as understanding user experiences that are sensitive to response times. This workshop will typically be executed once the requirements have been gathered. It can be executed multiple times or in parts if it is necessary to review early system designs to ensure performance. This workshop will also review the plans to validate the performance of the solution, including a review of the design for a "Day in the Life" performance test.
- **Integration Design.** This workshop is designed to review each of the interfaces included in the solution to ensure that

the proper considerations have been made when selecting integration models, interface technologies, and middleware designs. This workshop will typically be executed following the gathering of requirements and the drafting of the initial designs. The intention is to ensure that each interface supports the functional needs of the business while providing performance, scalability, resilience, operability, and the right integration pattern.

- **Test Strategy.** This workshop is designed to review the test strategy and to understand how that strategy is laid out in the overall project schedule. This workshop can be executed any time after the solution blueprint and generally should be executed early in the implementation to ensure that opportunities for early testing are not missed. The intention is to ensure that the design for testing the solution is comprehensive, that the plan allows for adequate execution time, and that the responsible parties are capable and prepared.

- **Application Lifecycle Management Strategy.** This workshop is designed to ensure that the application lifecycle management (ALM) strategy is optimized to allow the implementation to develop and promote code and configuration through the pre-production environments and into production in a safe and efficient manner. This includes ensuring that considerations have been made for how these processes will work post go-live as part of a continuous update process. This workshop can be executed any time after the solution blueprint and should be executed as soon as possible, as many implementations will need to ensure that a smooth ALM process is in place early in the plan.

- **Gap Solution Design.** This workshop is designed to take a deep dive look at key gap solutions. It is not intended to be a review of requirement fit gap analysis but rather a review of draft gap solution designs. This workshop will be executed after requirements are gathered and key gap solutions have been drafted. Not all gap solutions will be reviewed; just those that represent the most significant opportunity for risk and impact. This determination will be made by the FastTrack architect. For each gap solution, the implementation team should be prepared to discuss what the business requirements are, the standard solutions that have been considered, the specific gaps that prevent the use of standard capabilities, and any proposed extensions. The intention of the review is to ensure that standard capabilities and viable workarounds have been considered and that any proposed extension is in line with current recommended practices and future product strategy.

- **Cutover Strategy.** This workshop is designed to review the cutover strategy, plans, and execution scripts that are being prepared for the go-live event. The cutover strategy framework should be in place from the early stages of the project and should be built up with details as the implementation progresses. The workshop should be executed once there are initial drafts of artifacts like the cutover script to review. The workshop will review the depth of the cutover plan detail to ensure that it is sufficient to guide the cutover process. The intention is to ensure that the cutover strategy has a broad enough view to ensure that the overall go-live event is smooth. The go-live event is considered to include the periods leading up to the cutover window, the plan to execute mock go-live in production if time permits, and the period after go-live where hyper-care will be executed.
- **Business Intelligence and Analytics Design.** This workshop is designed to understand the planned implementation of business intelligence and analytics technologies that will address the solutions to the business intelligence requirements. The workshop should be executed once the requirements for business intelligence and analytics have been gathered and a design has been drafted. The intention is to ensure that the design is using current recommended practices for facilitating business requirements as well as ensuring any data aggregation is done using an optimal approach.

The output of each Implementation workshop is a FastTrack Findings and Recommendation Document.

Go-Live Readiness Assessment

The go-live readiness assessment workshop is the final gate in Success by Design that an implementation goes through to get the green light to proceed with the go-live. In this workshop, you review the key aspects of the implementation to ensure that all required activities have been completed, validated, and signed off. Specifically, the go-live readiness will focus on:

- **Testing and Acceptance.** Ensure that proper testing has been completed and key stakeholders have signed off that the solution is ready to support the business in production.
- **Data Migration.** Ensure that data migration has been tested in total and that the proper planning and testing has been completed to ensure that final migration can be completed successfully during the cutover window.
- **Change Management.** Ensure that the proper actions have been taken throughout the implementation to facilitate the smooth adoption of the solution. This includes ensuring the proper proactive communications and readiness activities have been conducted and there is a viable plan to provide various reactive means of enabling users post go-live.
- **Cutover Planning.** Ensure that the detailed plans are in place to orchestrate the cutover activities and that these activities have been tested to ensure they can be executed with a predictable outcome in the timeframe available for cutover.
- **Mock Cutover.** Ensure that the cutover plan is ready and has been tested in the target production environment that happens in cutover and just after the go-live readiness assessment. For secondary deployments, where testing in production is typically not possible, the aim is to ensure that the mock cutover has been performed with simulated production conditions.
- **Supportability.** Ensure that the plans and processes are in place to provide supportability during the hyper-care period, where there is a reasonable expectation of elevated volumes of issues related to systems stabilization as well as gaps in end user training. This will also review the readiness of the organization to manage and operate the solution in the mid to long term.

The outcome of the go-live readiness assessment will include a findings and recommendations document. This workshop may also result in the identification of critical blocking issues that need to be mitigated prior to the production deployment.

Findings and Recommendations

Within each workshop, the FastTrack solution architect will gather findings that are categorized as one of three types:

- **Assertions.** Assertions are findings that generally follow recommended patterns and practices but may have significant importance to the architecture and, as such, are important to call out. However, despite following recommended practices, there may be some opportunity to optimize the approach further.
- **Risks.** Risks are findings that indicate there is a potential for negative impact and these need to be listed and identified throughout and also need to be mitigated throughout the project lifecycle. These might be areas where the design or approach are not based on recommended practices or in some cases where they are based on known anti-patterns. This could also include risks related to timing, organizational issues, external factors, or any other observation that could negatively impact the outcome.
- **Issues.** Issues are findings where there is either a certainty of impact or where the implementation is currently being negatively impacted. Issues need to be addressed prior to go-live.

FastTrack provides written documentation of each finding along with a set of recommended actions. These recommendations will range from specific actions, to recommended resources that can be reviewed, to follow-up workshops that will further explore the finding.

Project Closure

The FastTrack service is not a long-term support offering. The goal of the FastTrack service and Success by Design is to establish an implementation based on a solid and repeatable pattern as a framework and practices for the next phases. In using these patterns and practices to get to the initial go-live, it is expected that the customer and their implementing partner can continue to use them for subsequent phases and rollouts. Following the initial go-live, approximately 30 days after, FastTrack will look to disengage. For most customers this means that they have got through hyper-care and have closed the books on their first financial period following the go-live. For future phases, the solution blueprint needs to be revisited and might need different quality gates, but at least the whole framework and pattern is known to the entire team.

Project closure includes the final workshop in the program. In this workshop the team will review the operational readiness of the organization and will provide final recommendations and insights on support channels and a solution roadmap.

Getting Started with FastTrack

All customers of Dynamics 365 Finance and Operations can benefit from the FastTrack program in some way. The type of FastTrack services a customer is eligible for is driven by their annual contract spend. Every customer who invests up to $100,000 will benefit from self-service resources, such as TechTalks and automated go-live readiness assessments for Unified Operations applications. Customers who invest between $100,000 and $300,000, who are working with a gold or silver certified partner in the Cloud Business Applications Competency, who has been trained in Success by Design, can benefit from the broader FastTrack program led by their partner. In this model the partner is the primary driver of Success by Design and is supported by Microsoft FastTrack solution architects. Customers investing $300,000 or more are eligible to engage in the FastTrack program, which is led by Microsoft FastTrack solution architects. For these customers, even though the program is delivered by Microsoft FastTrack, it is essential that the customer has a qualified partner engaged. Projects on the top two levels need to go through a nomination process where FastTrack will confirm the participation. FastTrack will not be offered to customers who are implementing Dynamics 365 without the assistance of a qualified partner.

Figure B.2 shows how these services map to the various tiers.

Customers who are eligible for engagements based on investment of over $100,000 must be nominated for the program. Nominations are processed and accepted based on assessment of which customers can benefit most from the program and the overall program capacity.

Dynamics 365 Annual Spend ◆	Gold/Silver Partner Trained on Success by Design	Customer Nomination	FastTrack Project Onboarding & Updates	Success by Design Execution	Milestone Reviews	FastTrack Solution Architect Support
$300K above	REQUIRED	REQUIRED	FASTTRACK-LED	FASTTRACK-LED, PARTNER - SUPPORTED	BLUEPRINT IMPLEMENTATION, GO-LIVE	DESIGNATED ARCHITECT
New! $100K - $300K	REQUIRED	REQUIRED	PARTNER-LED	PARTNER-LED, FASTTRACK - SUPPORTED	BLUEPRINT, GO-LIVE	AS NEEDED
$100K and below	RECOMMENDED	NOT REQUIRED	NONE	SELF-SERVE	GO-LIVE*	NONE

◆ Based on total billed spend over the contract coverage period

* Only for Dynamics 365 Unified Operations products

GCC customers are currently served only in the $300K and above threshold

FIGURE B.2 Service Maps per Tier

Source: © Microsoft. Used with permission from Microsoft Corporation.

Paul Langowski,
Dynamics 365 for
Finance and Opera-
tions, Global Fast
Track Program Lead,
Microsoft

"The FastTrack team is intended to provide guidance and to help customers get maximum benefits from Dynamics 365. In some cases that means making sure that critical issues in solution design and implementation are addressed before going live. FastTrack is not intended to implement the solution for our customers. Customers that are engaged with FastTrack are still responsible, along with their implementation partner, for all aspects of their implementation. FastTrack's role is to provide guidance, share recommended practices, offer recommendations, and ultimately enhance the success of the implementation."

Customer Story

MICHAEL HILL ENHANCES INVENTORY AND INCREASES SALES WITH MICROSOFT DYNAMICS 365

Challenge

Founded in 1979, Michael Hill is a global retailer in the mid-market jewellery sector known for high-quality, exceptional service, and long-term customer loyalty. It operates in 286 stores in Australia, New Zealand, and Canada and is publicly traded on the ASX and NSX.

Michael Hill has been running a transformation journey to completely change their operating paradigm and put the customer first at the very beginning, from production to fulfilment. The company had 500,000 customers in their loyalty program database; they wanted to be customer centric, and have a better way to manage and keep customers happy. The company wanted to increase visibility across its supply chain and availability of inventory, and increase efficiency in its shipping and warehousing processes to architect the retail experiences it envisaged.

Solution

The company started their journey in 2016, embarked upon multiple digital and physical initiatives to meet the demands of a modern-day customer. Michael Hill chose Microsoft Dynamics 365 Commerce as a solution and worked with DXC Technology and Microsoft to build a digital retail operations platform with end-to-end, multichannel capabilities and connected processes. The solution was implemented in 2017–2018 across all three countries using Modern POS for front end and Dynamics 365 Finance and Operations for back end, using the Microsoft FastTrack program that has allowed the company to implement with agility to deliver solutions. Through the Fast Track program they were able to access expert setup advice, detailed metrics, and agile assistance with issues that arise. For project governance, Michael Hill utilized Azure DevOps for documentation, user stories, and test cases. DevOps allowed them to keep on task and provide clear reporting and escalation to senior management. Test cases and plans within the DevOps tool benefited in preparing for the initial and continuous release cycles. Releases and environments were executed through LCS.

Michael Hill began by launching an internal initiative to optimize in-store retail operations, customer service, warehousing, inventory, stock movement, and other retail processes by using Dynamics 365 Finance and Dynamics 365 Supply Chain Management to expand its retail operations platform.

With COVID-19, the company had to accelerate their plan to sustain their business brand and increase their efficiency and visibility of valuable stocks across stores, temporary closures, and shipping and distribution complications. They also went live during the COVID lockdown period and faced challenges implementing with most of the team being remote.

Michael Hill also uses Microsoft Power Apps, Power Automate, and Power BI to extend its Dynamics 365 platform and accomplish day-to-day tasks in its retail stores. The native look and feel and UX of Power Apps for certain business processes in stores have made it a really good choice for Michael Hill.

Michael Hill has been able to improve customer experience, drive efficiencies across stores, and accelerate business performance by capturing important operational data aligned with business improvement strategies.

Outcome and Benefits

"Taking advantage of the capabilities of Dynamics 365 and working seamlessly with some of the best-of-breed retail management platforms has put us in a much, much stronger position. We are seeing economies of scale with the use of skills and talent across our singular platform on Dynamics 365, providing greater confidence that these digital assets are being put to work for our business strategies. Visual merchandising is very important to us, and consistency in visual merchandising is the key business goal. We can now stitch together the views of all the stores and allow our experts to review and critique and identify training opportunities for various stores."

Matt Keays, Chief Information Officer, Michael Hill

"Dynamics 365 has given the business extraordinary opportunities to rapidly change the system to fit to the extremely volatile requirements of a COVID world. The multitude of configurations and power platforms has allowed us to meet business requirements and release changes that bring increased governance and efficiency without the need for a scheduled code release."

Joseph Colvile, Dynamics 365 Lead for Warehouse and Supply Implementation and Continuous Improvement, Michael Hill

"With Dynamics 365 we can map great technology to outstanding business processes that will help us continue to expand our markets and adopt new business models. Everyone benefits from that. The company benefits, the customer benefits—it's win–win for all."

Matt Keays, Chief Information Officer, Michael Hill

Michael Hill has achieved:

- For the period ended 20 December 2020, online sales increased by 102% when compared with the same period in FY19–20. Digital purchases make up 5.8% of total sales.
- Solid growth in the same store sales in all markets and channels.
- Retail managers and sales staff can deliver best customer experience with all information on a single platform.
- Offering customers a contactless option for picking up their orders.
- Optimized demand fulfilment by reducing the human interaction on stock transfer.
- Large multitude of configurability of the D365 system has allowed the company to rapidly change business functions.
- Continuous Microsoft releases brings new functionality and has allowed the company to vastly improve customer order processing via the cross-docking functionality.
- Azure DevOps wiki became the go-to source for all information regarding the upgrade and user documentation.

Index

A

Abacus Medicine (rapid growth), Microsoft Dynamics/Power Platform usage (customer story), 254–256
Acceptance Test Library (ATL) resources, 269
Action (AI component), 10
Agile, 146–147, 156–160
  decision-making, adoption, 158
  team, hierarchy organization (hybrid approach), 128
Agile project management, 156–158
Algorithm, selection, 53f
Alignment/autonomy, balance, 158
Ambition (leadership team risk factor), 106
Analysis (AI component), 10
Analytics design, 284
Apollo DX Eco-System, 126–128
Apollo DX Eco-System DX Cycle, 127
Apollo DX Teams, 126
Apollo Teams, high-level DX cycle, 127f
Application lifecycle management (ALM) strategy, 283
Applications
  interaction, process, 215–216
  team, process flow (simplification), 236f

Applications Support team, composition, 204–205
Application Support Team, example, 231f
Approval gates, decisions (logging), 93
Artificial intelligence (AI), 9–10, 55
  AI Builder, 271
  application, 14
  scenarios, usage, 29
Assistance, documentation, 188
ATL. *See* Acceptance Test Library
Attendees (design authority reference term), 242
Azure Boards, support team collaboration, 266
Azure DevOps, 263–267
  environments, operation, 265–266
  Lifecycle, 264f
  services, 267
  usage, benefits, 272f
Azure DevOps applications, 265–266
  complements, 272–273
Azure innovation, 213
Azure IoT capability/functionality, 57–59
Azure Pipelines, 267
Azure Repos, 267
Azure Test Plans, 266